MODERNIZATION IN CHINA
THE CASE OF THE SHENZHEN
SPECIAL ECONOMIC ZONE

Modernization in China

The Case of the Shenzhen Special Economic Zone

EDITORS

Kwan-yiu Wong   David K.Y. Chu

CONTRIBUTORS

David K.Y. Chu   Mo-kwan Lee Fong   Steve S.I. Hsu
Kin-che Lam   Yen-tak Ng   Qingquan Wei
Kwan-yiu Wong   Anthony G.O. Yeh   Tianxiang Zheng

OXFORD NEW YORK HONG KONG
OXFORD UNIVERSITY PRESS
1985

Oxford University Press

Oxford   New York   Toronto
Kuala Lumpur   Singapore   Hong Kong   Tokyo
Delhi   Bombay   Calcutta   Madras   Karachi
Nairobi   Dar es Salaam   Cape Town
Melbourne   Auckland

and associated companies in
Beirut   Berlin   Ibadan   Mexico City   Nicosia

© Oxford University Press 1985

First published 1985

ISBN 0 19 583864 5

OXFORD is a trade mark of Oxford University Press

Printed in Hong Kong by Liang Yu Printing Factory Ltd.
Published by Oxford University Press, Warwick House, Hong Kong

Preface

SINCE the end of the Second World War, developing nations in the Asian region have employed various strategies to speed up their industrialization and modernization process. One move which has found favour among Asian governments and which has achieved varying degrees of success is the establishment of export processing zones (EPZs). By offering a suitable package of investment incentives to both foreign and domestic entrepreneurs for the setting up of modern manufacturing plants within certain defined areas, it is hoped that overseas capital and technology can be attracted to accelerate economic growth and to promote exports. China's special economic zones (SEZs) are also being developed with similar objectives in mind and are basically modelled after the EPZ system. They are set up as experimental laboratories to test new concepts and policies of development and to expedite the process of modernization in China. Although China is a relative late-comer in this field of development, the SEZs have attracted a great deal of attention from all over the world; partly because EPZs are typically found in countries with market economies, whereas SEZs are the product of an open economic policy in a socialist country. Much interest has been focused on the feasibility and implications of adopting such a model of development in a socialist setting.

As the export processing system is completely foreign to China, there is little material available with which to provide a clear picture of how the system will function. The demand for a greater understanding of the implementation of SEZs in China and for more basic information on these zones has prompted scholars to engage in research studies in these areas. A team of researchers from the Department of Geography at the Chinese University of Hong Kong started a research project on the Shenzhen SEZ in 1980, shortly after China's first SEZ was established. Through extensive fieldwork and interviews with top government officials in Shenzhen, the first book in the English language that provides a comprehensive treatment of China's largest SEZ was published in early 1982 (entitled *Shenzhen Special Economic Zone: China's Experiment in Modernization*). Subsequently, another book on the subject (*The Largest Special Economic Zone of China — Shenzhen*, written in Chinese) appeared in 1983. The present volume is written by six members of the original research team together with contributions from research workers at the University of Hong Kong and at Zhongshan University, Guangzhou. It aims to provide up-to-date information on the progress of the SEZs in China as well as in-depth analysis of the background, economic potential and planning implications of SEZ development.

The book is divided into four parts. Part I deals with the background of the establishment of SEZs in China and includes an analysis of (a) China's

SEZs in the setting of the export processing system in Asia; (b) the political and economic factors leading to the establishment of SEZs; and (c) the geographical endowment of the four SEZs in China. Part II looks at the progress made in the development of manufacturing, tourism and agriculture in the Shenzhen SEZ and surveys the future potential for these activities. Part III discusses various planning issues including the drawing up of a master plan, the land development process, population growth and related issues, and transportation demands. The environmental implications of economic development in Shenzhen are also discussed together with an overall evaluation of the investment environment in terms of its administrative structure; legal, financial and tax systems; incentives offered; land use and infrastructure provision; and labour supply and labour productivity. Part IV reviews the concept of modernization in both the Western and the Chinese context, and discusses the lessons of the SEZs.

The editors wish to express their sincere appreciation to all those who have assisted in establishing contacts with government officials and production unit heads in the SEZs. Thanks are also due to Mr Frank Leeming at Leeds University and Dr Leslie Sklair of the London School of Economics for reading part of the manuscript and providing helpful comments. Clerical and technical assistance given by Mrs Jane Wan, Mr Frankie Tsang, Mr S. L. Too and Mr Philip Yeung is also gratefully acknowledged.

KWAN-YIU WONG AND DAVID K. Y. CHU
Department of Geography,
The Chinese University of Hong Kong.

Contents

Preface   v
Tables   ix
Figures   x
Contributors   xii

PART I: THE SPECIAL ECONOMIC ZONE — ECONOMIC,
          POLITICAL AND GEOGRAPHICAL FACTORS

1. Export Processing Zones and Special Economic Zones as
   Locomotives of Export-led Economic Growth
        KWAN-YIU WONG AND DAVID K.Y. CHU   1
2. The Politico-economic Background to the Development of the
   Special Economic Zones   DAVID K.Y. CHU   25
3. The Geographical Endowment of China's Special Economic
   Zones   YEN-TAK NG AND DAVID K.Y. CHU   40

PART II: THE ECONOMIC POTENTIAL OF SHENZHEN —
          INDUSTRY, TOURISM AND AGRICULTURE

4. Trends and Strategies of Industrial Development
        KWAN-YIU WONG   57
5. Tourism: A Critical Review   MO-KWAN LEE FONG   79
6. Agricultural Land-use Patterns and Export Potential
        TIANXIANG ZHENG, QINGQUAN WEI AND
        DAVID K.Y. CHU   89

PART III: PLANNING — INFRASTRUCTURE, LABOUR AND
          THE ENVIRONMENT IN SHENZHEN

7. Physical Planning   ANTHONY G.O. YEH   108
8. Population Growth and Related Issues
        DAVID K.Y. CHU   131
9. Forecasting Future Transportation Demand and the Planned
   Road Network   DAVID K.Y. CHU   140
10. Environmental Considerations
        KIN-CHE LAM AND STEVE S.I. HSU   159
11. The Investment Environment
        KWAN-YIU WONG AND DAVID K.Y. CHU   176

PART IV: CONCLUSION

12. Modernization and the Lessons of the Special Economic
    Zones   DAVID K.Y. CHU AND KWAN-YIU WONG   208

Bibliography   218
Index   225

Tables

3.1 The Economic Status of the Coastal Provinces   41
4.1 Changes in the Industrial Structure of Shenzhen, 1978–81   60
4.2 Planned Industrial Districts in the Shenzhen SEZ   65
4.3 Targets for Industrial Development   75
4.4 Targets for Industrial Production   75
5.1 The Relative Significance of Tourism in Attracting Foreign
    Investment   81
5.2 A Proposed Scheme of Diversity for Tourism in Shenzhen   84
6.1 A Summary of the Distribution of Existing and
    Recommended Vegetable Fields   105
7.1 Planned Land-use Distribution   113
7.2 Major Functions and the Target Population of Planning
    Districts   115
7.3 Lease Periods and Land-use Fees   119
8.1 Population Targets in Various Districts of the Shenzhen
    SEZ by the Year 2000   134
9.1 The Number of Journeys Generated by Activities and
    Purposes   144
9.2 The Number of Journeys Absorbed by Area   147
9.3 Resultant Optimal Flows of Passengers as Estimated by the
    Linear Programming Model ('000)   148
9.4 The Volume of Freight Traffic Generated or Absorbed by
    District   152
9.5 The Projected Utilization of Road Sections   156
10.1 The Number of Days with Inversions Below 600 m,
     1950–68   168
10.2 A Comparison of Water Quality Control in China, Hong
     Kong and the United States   173
10.3 A Comparison of Air Quality Control in China, Hong Kong
     and the United States   173
11.1 A Comparison of Investment Conditions in Industry in the
     Shenzhen SEZ, Hong Kong, Taiwan, South Korea and
     Singapore   193
11.2 The Size of the SEZs and Selected EPZs   198
11.3 The Classification of Land in the Shenzhen SEZ   198
11.4 Population and Labour Statistics of the Shenzhen SEZ   205

Figures

1.1 The Location of Asian EPZs and SEZs   4
1.2 The Concept of Free Zones   23
2.1 The Location of the Fourteen City-ports with Economic
     Development Zones and the Four Special Economic
     Zones   38
3.1 The Shenzhen SEZ   44
3.2 The Zhuhai SEZ   46
3.3 The Shantou SEZ   48
3.4 The Xiamen SEZ   52
4.1 Industrial Districts in Shenzhen Municipality   62
4.2 The Location of Planned Industrial Districts in the
     Shenzhen SEZ   64
4.3 The Revised Land-use Zoning Plan of Shekou   66
5.1 Existing and Proposed Tourist Resorts in Shenzhen   85
6.1 Von Thünen's Theory of Agricultural Land Uses   91
6.2 The Four Concentric Rings of Peri-urban Agricultural Land
     Uses in China   92
6.3 The Theoretical Agricultural Land-use Pattern of Shenzhen
     in the Year 2000   97
6.4 Existing Land Uses in Shenzhen and the Theoretical Land-
     use Belts with Futian as the Town Centre   98
6.5 The Topography of Shenzhen and Hong Kong   100
6.6 The Distribution of Existing (1980) and Recommended
     Vegetable Fields in Shenzhen   104
7.1 The Organization of the People's Government of Shenzhen
     Municipality and the Departments Responsible for
     Planning and Land Development Control   110
7.2 Proposed Planning Districts of the Shenzhen SEZ   114
7.3 The Land Development Procedure in the Shenzhen SEZ   121
9.1 The Distribution of Population in the Shenzhen SEZ in the
     Year 2000   142
9.2 The Provisional Plan of Land Uses in the Shenzhen SEZ   145
9.3 Aggregate Passenger Flows Among the Functional Districts
     of the Shenzhen SEZ   150
9.4 Projected Freight Flows Among the Functional Districts of
     the Shenzhen SEZ   154
9.5 The Provisional Plan for the Transport Network of the
     Shenzhen SEZ   155
10.1 The Structure and Linkages of Industries in the Shenzhen
      SEZ   162

10.2 Population Distribution and Industrial Allocation in the
      Shenzhen SEZ   163
10.3 Location of the Daya Bay Nuclear Plant and the Shajiao
      Coal-fired Power-plant   166
10.4 Schematic Potential Polluted Areas in the Shenzhen SEZ   169
11.1 Administrative Domains in Shenzhen Municipality   178
11.2 The Administrative Hierarchy of Shenzhen Municipality
      before 1981   179
11.3 The Structure of the Shenzhen Municipal Government
      before Reorganization   181
11.4 The Administrative System of Shenzhen Municipality after
      Reorganization in 1982–3   183
11.5 The Present Investment Flow Chart   185
11.6 Land Types in the Shenzhen SEZ   199

Contributors

Dr Kwan-yiu Wong
Senior Lecturer, Department of Geography, The Chinese University of Hong Kong.

Dr David K.Y. Chu
Lecturer, Department of Geography, The Chinese University of Hong Kong.

Mrs Mo-kwan Lee Fong
Lecturer, Department of Geography, The Chinese University of Hong Kong.

Dr Steve S.I. Hsu
Lecturer, Department of Geography, The Chinese University of Hong Kong.

Dr Kin-che Lam
Lecturer, Department of Geography, The Chinese University of Hong Kong.

Mr Yen-tak Ng
Lecturer, Department of Geography, The Chinese University of Hong Kong.

Mr Qingquan Wei
Lecturer, Department of Geography, Zhongshan University, Guangzhou, People's Republic of China.

Dr Anthony G.O. Yeh
Lecturer, Centre of Urban Studies and Urban Planning, University of Hong Kong.

Mr Tianxiang Zheng
Lecturer, Department of Geography, Zhongshan University, Guangzhou, People's Republic of China.

PART I: THE SPECIAL ECONOMIC ZONE — ECONOMIC, POLITICAL AND GEOGRAPHICAL FACTORS

1. Export Processing Zones and Special Economic Zones as Locomotives of Export-led Economic Growth[*]

KWAN-YIU WONG AND DAVID K.Y. CHU

AN export processing zone is generally considered to be an adaptation of the free trade zone system (Currie, 1979, p. 1), which is itself a familiar phenomenon. Indeed some scholars have argued that the existence of such a system could be dated back as far as Roman times (Kreida, 1975, pp. 43–4). From the eighteenth century onwards, these commercial free trade zones have been established on the world's major trade routes with the functions of trans-shipment, storage and then the re-export of goods without customs formalities. They are normally located in a defined geographical area such as a port. More recently, the free trade zone concept has been adapted and modified as a means of initiating export-oriented industrial development in Third World countries and the zones so designated have been given a new name — the export processing zone (EPZ). Unlike its predecessors, an EPZ need not necessarily be located adjacent to a port. According to the United Nations Industrial Development Organization, EPZs are defined as areas involved in the 'establishment of modern manufacturing plants inside an industrial estate, by offering a suitable package of investment incentives to both foreign and domestic entrepreneurs' (Vittal,

---

[*] This chapter is an updated version of an article published in *Geografiska Annaler*, Vol. 66B, No. 1, 1984, pp. 1–16.

1977, p. 1). It should be noted, however, that today many free trade zones (such as those in Malaysia) are also involved in export-oriented industrial production and are in fact EPZs by nature. Some free trade zones, particularly those located in a free port, have developed a diversified economy with entrepôt functions, manufacturing, commerce and finance as their mainstays. Hong Kong and Singapore are the best-known examples (Pollock, 1981, pp. 37–45). One should, therefore, be very cautious in classifying free trade zones because the original concept has evolved with time and has acquired different meanings in different contexts.

The first successful implementation of an EPZ occurred in 1956 in Ireland at the Shannon International Airport. It provided the impetus for other countries to pursue similar lines of development. Puerto Rico (in 1962) and India (in 1965) were the first two countries in the developing world to experiment with the EPZ concept. They were soon followed by Taiwan, the Philippines, the Dominican Republic, Mexico, Panama and Brazil between 1966 and 1970. The great expansion in the number of EPZs came after 1970. A further 23 were established between 1971 and 1975 (Currie, 1979) and another 24 between 1976 and 1980. By the end of 1981, there were 24 EPZs in East and South Asia (see Fig. 1.1), 10 in the Middle East and the Mediterranean, 4 in Africa, 6 in the Caribbean, 15 in Latin America and 1 in the Pacific Islands. More EPZs are now being planned, but most of them are to be outside Asia.

The latest development of the concepts of free trade zone and EPZ has been the creation of four special economic zones (SEZs) in the People's Republic of China. Although the package of investment incentives offered to foreign investors is very similar to that offered by the EPZs, economic activities in the SEZs are much more comprehensive, embracing not only manufacturing but also agriculture, tourism, commerce and real estate development. However, in comparison with the free port cities, such as Hong Kong and Singapore, the scope of operation in the SEZs is very limited. In the following sections, emphasis will be placed on Asian EPZs and SEZs, and the free ports will be discussed only when appropriate.

The Characteristics and Objectives of EPZ and SEZ Development in Asia

The development of EPZs is the outcome of pressure for industrialization in Asian countries since the end of the Second World War. Various strategies have been employed in order to speed up the pace of economic growth. In the 1950s and 1960s, the desire for import substitution was one of the most important factors in directing the pattern of industrialization in Asian nations. However, in order to reduce or eliminate the importation of foreign industrial goods through domestic production, manufacturing in Asian countries was set up behind protective tariffs, resulting in high production costs and a waste of capital resources. Governments in Asian countries soon realized that development by way of import substitution was counter-productive. Many of them, therefore, decided instead to direct their production towards export markets. However, lack of capital, low levels of technology and limited access to international markets have meant that dependence on foreign assistance is inevitable. The relatively cheap and abundant labour supply in Asian nations has attracted transnational corporations who have taken advantage of this new international division of labour (Frobel, Heinrichs and Kreye, 1980) in their production process. To the host country, the import of foreign capital and technology is seen as a way to accelerate economic growth and improve the utilization of local resources. However, if foreign participation in the industrialization programme is applied to the whole country, conflicts with existing political, economic and social systems may emerge. Furthermore, problems of administration and resource allocation may also arise. Therefore, in order to control the new economic system, export-oriented production is confined to certain zones only, and investors are provided with incentives to persuade them to participate in the industrialization programme. Concentrated efforts in developing selected zones also allow the host country to channel local resources to build up the infrastructure needed for development.

The selection of sites for EPZs depends primarily on accessibility, with access to water and air transport being important considerations. Thus, EPZs in Asia are located (a) where port facilities are readily available; (b) near international airports; or (c) where both sea and air freight are possible. Examples of the first category are the Bataan EPZ in the Philippines, the Masan Free Export Zone and the Iri Free Export Zone in the Republic of Korea, and the majority of free trade zones in Malaysia. Zones which depend mainly on air transport include the Santa Cruz Electronics EPZ in India and the Baguio EPZ in the Philippines. Examples of EPZs where both sea and air transport are available include the Kaohsiung and Nantze EPZs in Taiwan, the Kandla Free Trade Zone in India and the Krebang EPZ in Thailand.

As important as the question of access to transport is the issue as to whether EPZs should be located near existing growth centres or in less developed frontier areas. The main argument in favour of the former option is the ready provision of infrastructure and other supporting services that are available in existing centres of population. Reasons for choosing underdeveloped areas derive from the desire to stimulate economic development in the more backward regions of the country as part of a policy of reducing the wide economic gap between urban and rural areas. This is exemplified by Malaysia's Second Plan (1971–5) which stipulated the 'provision of locational incentives to firms, domestic or foreign, establishing their plants in the less developed parts of the Federation, including Sarawak

Fig. 1.1 The Location of Asian EPZs and SEZs

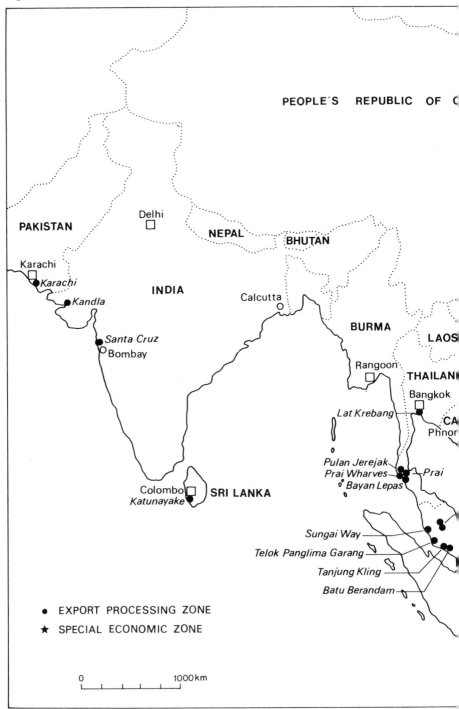

and Sabah' (Ople, 1974, p. 52). The Philippines' five-year plans also aimed
to 'disperse new industries to various regions in order to achieve a better
balance of economic opportunities and more equitable income distribution'
(Gonzaga, 1977, p. 39). The establishment of the Bataan EPZ at Mariveles
Bay, 170 km from Manila, was inspired by this policy. However, judging
by the location of those EPZs that now exist in Asia, it appears that dispersal
plans for industrial and economic growth have not yet been fully realized,
because most investors still prefer the well-established areas and also because
infrastructural provision in many of the new EPZs is still inadequate. The
more successful EPZs are now located near major urban centres: for example,
in Taiwan, the Kaohsiung and Nantze EPZs are sited in Kaohsiung City
and the Taichung EPZ is only 9 km from the city of Taichung. Thus the
question of the location of EPZs in Asia is worthy of further consideration
by Asian governments.

Another important characteristic of EPZs in Asia is that they are normally
relatively small in scale, mostly under 100 ha in area. The larger EPZs are
Bataan in the Philippines (345 ha), Kandla in India (284 ha), Katunayake
in Sri Lanka (202 ha), Bayan Lepas in Malaysia (202 ha) and Masan in the
Republic of Korea (175 ha). However, as the Asian EPZs seek to involve
foreign participation in manufacturing production, these 'industrial estates'
need not be particularly large in area. What is more important is the effect
that EPZs can have in encouraging increased employment opportunities, the
influx of foreign exchange, the transfer of technology and management skills,
an expansion of exports and the establishment of contacts with overseas
markets.

In China, the SEZs bear some similarity to the EPZs inasmuch as
preferential treatment is likewise offered to foreign investors in order to
attract overseas capital and technology. Their establishment, therefore, is
also one element in a policy to expedite the process of modernization or
economic development. However, the Chinese SEZs differ from EPZs in
other Asian nations in several important respects. Firstly, the People's Republic
of China is a socialist country and the SEZ system represents a Western,
capitalist economic concept which is quite contrary to the planned economy
in force elsewhere in the country. By allowing foreign participation, including
foreign sole proprietorship, the SEZs serve as an important laboratory for
experimentation with Western technology and management methods. They
are therefore likely to have far greater implications for the country than
would be the case in other Asian countries. Secondly, the Chinese SEZs are
usually much larger in scale than the Asian EPZs. The Shenzhen SEZ, for
example, has an area of 32,750 ha. The Zhuhai, Xiamen and Shantou SEZs
are 1,516 ha (formerly 680 ha), 250 ha and 160 ha in area respectively.
(According to reports from the China News Agency and other sources, one
of the recommendations made at the Special Economic Zone Conference
held between 26 March and 6 April 1984 was the expansion of the Xiamen
SEZ to 12,550 ha (*Wen Wei Po*, 21 May 1984) and the Shantou SEZ to

5,260 ha (Chu, Wong, and Ng, 1984).) Thirdly, SEZs, unlike EPZs, are usually comprehensively developed units where foreign investments are not only confined to manufacturing, but may also be applied to real estate development, tourism, agriculture and other services. In practice, in the Shenzhen SEZ, most of the investments in the early stages of development have been concentrated in the real estate and construction business and in tourism (together they accounted for about 68 per cent of total investment at the end of 1981) (Wong, 1982, p. 28). Fourthly, the Chinese government has taken a rather flexible position by allowing preferential treatment to be given to investors setting up in areas adjacent to, but outside the boundaries of, the SEZs. This applies, of course, only to undertakings that the Chinese consider to be important and desirable. Finally, in order to facilitate overseas investment in the SEZs, various forms of financial participation have been designed: these include sole proprietorship, joint venture, co-operative production, intermediate processing and compensation trade (Wong, 1982, pp. 25–7). The Chinese government has, therefore, played a variety of roles in negotiating financial agreements with investors.

The Chinese SEZs are all located in the southern provinces of Guangdong and Fujian. They are sited away from the major Chinese urban agglomerations. With the exception of the Xiamen SEZ, port facilities are generally poor. The Shenzhen SEZ, for example, has to depend on Hong Kong for most of its external connections. The choice of such locations is understandable as the SEZs represent a 'foreign' system in China and it is thought to be undesirable to have them located near existing centres of population.

It is obvious, therefore, that the establishment of EPZs and SEZs in Asian countries is intended to foster and stimulate economic development, either at the national or regional level. In the case of China, the SEZ also serves as a platform to test and observe capitalism at work. The more specific objectives of EPZs and SEZs as stated by the countries concerned include: (a) the attraction of foreign investment; (b) the expansion of exports and the promotion of foreign exchange earnings; (c) the provision of employment opportunities; (d) the transfer of technology and management skills; (e) a more efficient use of domestic material resources and the forging of links with the domestic sector; and (f) the stimulation of economic growth in less developed regions of the country. In order to attract potential investors and to achieve the objectives mentioned above, a number of incentives are being offered to foreign entrepreneurs. Even though the details vary greatly from country to country, these incentives can be grouped into four major categories: (a) preferential treatment which includes exemption from customs duties for the import of material and the export of products, reduced profit tax, low land utility costs but long lease periods, accelerated depreciation rates on fixed assets and financial assistance in the form of loans and preferential credit; (b) the freedom granted to investors, such as 100 per cent foreign ownership, the freedom to repatriate and remit profits and the absence of foreign exchange controls; (c) local advantages such as cheap labour costs and the provision of infrastructure, standard factories, housing and various amenities, warehousing and other supporting services; and (d) a centralized administration to simplify and unify administrative procedures regarding investment and operations in the zone.

An Assessment of the Performance of EPZs and SEZs in Asia

EPZs in Asian countries have been developed primarily in order to implement the policy of export-led growth. However, considering the magnitude of the problems involved in the industrialization and economic transformation of these nations, the role played by the EPZs can only be limited. Despite efforts by many governments to increase the number of new zones being established, their contribution to the overall industrial development programme of the country and to the fulfilment of more specific objectives such as the generation of employment, the earning of foreign exchange and export growth, is quite minor, except perhaps in the case of Taiwan. This is due partly to the relatively small scale of development in these zones (compared with the domestic tariff sector) and partly to the conflict of interests between the investor and the host country (for example, with regard to the nature and types of industry and the reinvestment of profits). Furthermore, being export-oriented, EPZs are easily influenced by the international economic situation and are likely to be the first to suffer during periods of recession.

Similar caveats apply to SEZs in China. It is quite clear that, at present, SEZs can at most serve as laboratories to test the usefulness of Western economic concepts in the process of modernization in China. The model is completely foreign to a socialist country: because China has just started to pursue a more pragmatic and open economic policy, the SEZs are essentially experimental stations. Even if they prove to be a success, the direct benefit to China will still be quite limited compared with the scale of the problems faced in China's recent drive for modernization. On the other hand, the success or failure of the SEZs will have important policy implications for the Chinese government and their performance will certainly be viewed with great interest by China's trading partners.

It is now almost two decades since the first EPZ was established in Asia. But the experiences of individual countries vary because of differences in their historical and political backgrounds, in objectives, policies and methods of implementation. Perhaps one of the best ways of assessing the progress of EPZ and SEZ development in Asia is by comparing the actual performance of these zones with the objectives originally laid down by policy-makers. Such a comparison may be conveniently discussed under several headings.

The Attraction of Foreign Investment

In general, Asian governments have taken quite a liberal attitude towards foreign investment in the EPZs, usually allowing 100 per cent foreign ownership of zone enterprises. Although the attraction of foreign capital seems to be one of the main objectives of most zones, the practice of individual countries varies greatly on this point. India, for example, has adopted a policy of strict control of foreign investment, especially in the early stages of EPZ development, resulting in only limited foreign participation so that much of the capital has to come from the domestic sector. However, the situation has improved slightly with the establishment of the Santa Cruz Electronics EPZ where most of the projects now have foreign collaboration in equity capital with Indian interests. But 100 per cent foreign-owned firms are still extremely rare in Indian EPZs. On the other hand, Taiwan has shown considerable success in attracting foreign capital. In April 1982, wholly foreign-owned enterprises accounted for 66 per cent of the total investment in the three EPZs (Kaohsiung, Nantze and Taichung), with an additional 6 per cent provided by overseas Chinese. Only 11 per cent of the total represented domestic investment, the remaining 17 per cent being joint ventures (EPZ Administration, Taiwan, 1982b, p. 48). Other examples that have demonstrated a fairly high degree of achievement in attracting foreign capital can be found in the Republic of Korea and in Sri Lanka. In the former case, the Masan Free Export Zone has attracted 89 per cent of its total investment from foreign sources. Wholly foreign-owned firms account for 81 per cent of the enterprises in the Masan Free Export Zone, the other 19 per cent being joint ventures (Rabbani, 1980, p. 16). In Sri Lanka, of the 121 projects approved by mid-1980 in the Katunayake Investment Promotion Zone, 104 were joint ventures with foreign capital and 17 were wholly locally owned. In terms of the amount of investment, 73 per cent represented foreign capital (Rabbani, 1980, p. 17). However, 100 per cent foreign ownership, though allowed, is not practised. Wholly foreign-owned concerns are also permitted in other Asian EPZs such as Bataan in the Philippines and the pilot EPZ project in Indonesia.

In China's SEZs, the attraction of foreign and overseas Chinese capital has been accorded high priority. Although useful statistical data is not available for analysis, the significance of outside capital can be inferred by the fact that the Chinese have devised various forms of foreign financial participation in projects in the SEZs. Besides sole foreign ownership, four other means of investment, generally known as joint venture, co-operative production, intermediate processing and compensation trade, are being practised. These represent different forms of joint development between the Chinese and foreign investors. Figures available for the Shenzhen SEZ indicate that by November 1981 56.8 per cent of total investment derived from co-operative production; 33 per cent from sole foreign ownership; 5.6 per cent from intermediate processing; 2.8 per cent from joint ventures and 1.8 per cent from compensation trade (Wong, 1982, p. 27). By the end of 1983, total intended investment in the Shenzhen SEZ reached HK$132 billion (on 3 January 1984 HK$7.82 = US$1), with over 80 per cent of this coming from neighbouring Hong Kong (*People's Daily*, 29 March 1984).

As a whole, the incentives and other advantages offered by EPZs in Asia have been quite successful in attracting foreign capital to participate in the zones' development programmes. In some cases, such as in Taiwan, the amount of foreign investment is several times greater than the original target set and therefore has contributed much in enhancing capital formation. On the other hand, there are also instances, such as in India, where government policy has prevented a free and unlimited flow of foreign capital. But the performance of EPZs in countries which have regarded the attraction of foreign investment as a major development objective has generally been satisfactory. In the case of China's SEZs, most of the outside capital today comes from Hong Kong and from overseas Chinese. The amount of 'foreign' participation is still relatively small. Despite the fact that the preferential terms and resources available in the SEZs are very attractive, many potential foreign investors still see a cloud of uncertainty over the security of their investment in a socialist country. The lack of efficient administrative, legal and financial systems has also caused many potential investors to bide their time before making any commitment. As laws and regulations governing the SEZs are gradually implemented, the investment environment will improve and the amount of foreign investment will certainly increase (see Chapter 11).

Foreign Exchange Earnings and Export Growth

Figures are not available to give a clear picture of the net benefits derived from the establishment of EPZs. In terms of export performance, there are great variations between countries. Generally speaking, exports from EPZs contribute only a very small proportion of the country's total export volume. An exception has been Taiwan where figures for 1981 showed that exports from the three EPZs accounted for 7 per cent of the total export volume for the whole island (this already represented a reduction from the peak figure of 9 per cent in 1973 and 1974). Furthermore, in Taiwan, the aggregate trade balance of the EPZs up until 1981 amounted to US$3,733 million — nearly 70 per cent of the total trade surplus of the country — thus greatly enhancing its international payments position (EPZ Administration, Taiwan, 1982a; 1982b). Apart from Taiwan, the Republic of Korea seems to be the only country in which exports from EPZs play an important part in the sum total of the nation's exports. Figures available show that between 1974 and 1979, exports from the Masan Free Export Zone represented 4 per cent of Korea's total exports (Rabbani, 1980, p. 20). In both of these cases, it has been reported that the amount of foreign exchange earned is far in excess of the amount of money invested by the governments concerned in the provision of infrastructure and other construction in the EPZs, so they have produced handsome profits.

Export performance and earnings in other Asian EPZs have been less impressive, as in the case of Kandla in India or the pilot EPZ in Indonesia. This raises the question of whether the present organization of EPZs can actually result in great foreign exchange earnings. Certain features of the incentive system offered to investors and the huge capital outlay required for the construction of the zones are probably the major obstacles to a truly profitable endeavour. The repatriation of profits in full, long tax holidays, exemption from duties, licences and fees, low wages and low land utility charges or rents all threaten to defeat the purpose of accumulating foreign exchange. In some instances, the provision of financial assistance to zone enterprises actually results in firms borrowing more capital than they have brought in from abroad. Under such circumstances, the contribution of EPZs to foreign exchange earnings or to the balance of payments can only be limited.

Although some of the Asian EPZs have experienced such setbacks, the contribution of EPZs in terms of export growth and foreign exchange earnings seems to be more impressive when viewed from a different angle. In many Asian countries, the export of manufacturing products constitutes a small or even negligible part of total exports. EPZs, being confined primarily to industrial production, make important contributions to manufacturing exports, if not to the total exports of the countries concerned. This has the catalytic effect of helping these countries to export new products and find new markets, and to promote the image of their products. India's Santa Cruz Electronics EPZ, for example, which is a single-product zone, contributes 25 per cent of the country's total electronics exports (Rabbani, 1980, p. 19).

Another contribution made by EPZs can be expressed in terms of the domestic value-added content of exports. Significant amounts of foreign exchange can be generated through the purchase of local raw materials, payment for utilities and services, wages, rents and local expenditure on items such as food and housing by foreign firms and their staff. The domestic value-added content of exports from EPZs has been quite impressive: for example, nearly 55 per cent for India's Santa Cruz Electronics EPZ (higher than the minimum 30 per cent required by the Indian government); 52.5 per cent for Korea's Masan Free Export Zone; 32 per cent for Taiwan's three EPZs (the original target set by the government was 25 per cent); and 26 per cent for Sri Lanka's Katunayake Investment Promotion Zone (Rabbani, 1980, pp. 19–21).

It is anticipated that with the gradual evolution of EPZs in Asia, their contribution to foreign exchange earnings will improve. Those EPZs with a relatively longer history of development, in Taiwan and the Republic of Korea, have all recorded favourable balances of payments and substantial earnings in foreign exchange. Despite heavy capital outlays, they have netted handsome profits. It is hoped that their experience can be shared by other 'younger' EPZs in the region.

The lack of data and the short history of development make it impossible to assess the achievements of China's SEZs in terms of foreign exchange earnings. According to the latest figure available, between 1979 and 1983 Shenzhen earned a total of US$970 million in foreign exchange (*Wen Wei Po*, 28 June 1984). Export value from the SEZs is negligible in comparison with the nation's total, but there has been a gradual diversification of export items. Furthermore, foreign exchange earnings from tourism and real estate development are believed to be quite substantial.

Employment Generation

In the early stages of the development of EPZs and SEZs in Asia, labour-intensive industries such as garments and electronics assembly predominated, thereby generating more employment than would have been the case with technology-intensive industries. An adequate supply of semi-skilled and unskilled labour together with generally lower wage levels in Asian countries have prompted foreign entrepreneurs to invest in production with a high labour content. The Asian EPZs and SEZs have undoubtedly been able to create job opportunities for local people; but employment figures have to be seen in context and compared with original targets or expectations before any assessment can be made. Again, variations among the Asian nations are great and it is generally true that zones with a longer history of development seem to be more successful than the newer zones. In Taiwan, for example, the planned employment for the three EPZs was 65,000 persons (EPZ Administration, Taiwan, 1981). By the end of 1979, however, the employment figure had reached a peak of over 80,000 although it then gradually declined to about 77,800 at the end of 1981 (EPZ Administration, Taiwan, 1982a). On the other hand, the Philippines' EPZ Administration predicted that the Bataan EPZ would generate the direct employment of 40,000 persons by 1978; but this expectation has not been realized and by 1981 direct employment had not reached 25,000 (Angangco and Jurado, 1982, p. 20). Even more disappointing has been the performance of the Kandla EPZ in India which was established in 1965 but had generated only 1,400 jobs by 1978 (Currie, 1979, p. 46).

An assessment solely in terms of the number of jobs created is not enough, for there are certain characteristics of the employment situation that should be taken into consideration. Firstly, labour requirements for industries are heavily weighted in favour of young, single, female workers, so that a high percentage of the employment generated has been of female workers: 85 per cent in Taiwan's EPZs (1981), 75 per cent in the Masan Free Export Zone (1979; but as high as 90 per cent in 1971); 85 per cent in the

Katunayake Investment Promotion Zone (1980) and 80 per cent in Bataan EPZ (1981) (EPZ Administration, Taiwan, 1982a; Rabbani, 1980, pp. 21–2; and Angangco and Jurado, 1982, p. 20). The mobility of these young female workers is great, thus leading to a high turnover of labour. Secondly, employment originating in EPZs is unstable and sensitive to changing conditions in the local and world economies. Increased unemployment often follows an international recession, as in the 1970s. It has been observed that assembly plants in the EPZs are frequently the first to face production cutbacks when a transnational corporation adjusts its overall output to reduced world demand. Production patterns in the zones are, therefore, highly volatile, so that lay-offs and rehiring are frequent and unpredictable. Likewise, a lack of orders or an interruption in the supply of raw materials have often caused temporary suspension in employment. Finally, after periods of development in the EPZs when wages begin to rise or when labour is in short supply, foreign enterprises usually take one of two steps: either they simply move out and relocate in other places where cheap female labour is available; or they switch to automation and the use of more sophisticated technology, thus reducing the demand for labour (especially female labour). In either case, a reduction in jobs is the result. Such a phenomenon has already occurred in Taiwan and the Republic of Korea.

It can be concluded that EPZs and SEZs in Asia have been successful in generating employment in their initial or formative stages when investment is mainly in labour-intensive industries. Even then, the number of jobs created is still insignificant in the context of the country's total labour force. An unstable employment structure due to the high percentage of female labour and vulnerability to world market forces is always a problem. As the zones reach a more mature stage of development, employment generation becomes a less important objective and employment may in fact shrink.

The Transfer of Technology

The introduction of technology-intensive production units is being encouraged under a deliberate policy in most zones, but has received special emphasis in, for example, the Santa Cruz Electronics EPZ in India and the Shenzhen SEZ in China. The aim is, of course, to upgrade the skills of local workers and to create greater or more lasting links with the rest of the economy of the host country. This may take the form of either technological co-operation with zone enterprises, in which the foreign investor provides the modern equipment and components, or training local people in zone enterprises. But the transfer of technology is a slow process and the achievements of the Asian EPZs and SEZs in this respect have been limited. The very structure of production in most zones militates against a rapid transformation. A great majority of zone enterprises depend mainly on cheap labour to manufacture their products, with operations generally confined to technically simple assembly or packaging work. Such industries (for instance, garments, electronics and textiles) account for a high percentage of the total investment, employment, number of firms or value of production in practically all EPZs and SEZs. For instance, they account for over 95 per cent of the total investment in Indonesia's pilot zone and in the Katunayake Investment Promotion Zone; 75 per cent in Taiwan's EPZs; and 63.7 per cent in the Masan Free Export Zone (Rabbani, 1980, pp. 18–20). In China's Shenzhen SEZ, 93 per cent of the revenue from industrial production in 1981 came from such sources (Wong, 1982, p. 47). It is perhaps disappointing to note that there are reports of foreign participating firms importing outdated machinery for production in the zones, often with the argument that local staff do not yet have the expertise to operate more modern equipment. In order to accelerate the pace of economic growth, the introduction of more sophisticated production technology and scientific management methods, as well as the training of local personnel, are essential. Zone authorities should, therefore, define their objectives clearly and formulate policies and incentive packages to channel foreign investment into such priority areas. The situation, as in China's Shenzhen SEZ, where technology-intensive industries have been given priority but most of the investment projects are in fact labour-intensive, is all too common.

Some of the better and older Asian EPZs have achieved a gradual shift to technology-intensive production. A fairly high degree of technological sophistication has been obtained in Korea's Masan Free Export Zone and Taiwan's three zones. In the Masan zone, more than a third (36.3 per cent) of the investment has already been channelled into technology-intensive industries such as precision instruments, machinery and metal products. About 4,000 local staff have received technical training and between 700 and 800 of these have qualified as engineers or technicians (Van, 1980, pp. 68–73). In Taiwan, many foreign enterprises have gradually replaced expatriate technicians with locals, and in many cases both production and management are now entirely in the hands of local personnel. About 25 per cent of the total investment in Taiwan's EPZs is now in technology-intensive industries (EPZ Administration, Taiwan, 1981 and 1982b). In order to move further in this direction and to import even more sophisticated technology, the concept of science-based industrial parks has been promoted in Taiwan since May 1980 (Wang, 1980).

A truly effective transfer of technology requires time and patience. It involves the training of local personnel, both on the job and abroad, and technical co-operation between foreign zone enterprises and domestic firms. One problem is that well-trained and competent technicians are highly mobile and often leave zone enterprises for better jobs elsewhere. In Korea about half of the trained technicians and engineers have left the Masan zone to join other firms (Van, 1980). However, if they are still contributing their services to other production units within the country, then the nation will continue to benefit from their experience and a further transfer of technical skills may even be achieved.

Domestic Links

One of the objectives of establishing EPZs is to provide possible backward and forward links between zone enterprises and local firms. It is believed that EPZs can stimulate the inflow of local raw materials, equipment, components and packaging materials from the domestic sector, and can also provide an impetus to subcontracting, thus encouraging the growth of supporting industries and ancillary services. However, it appears that such links are by no means immediate or extensive, at least in the initial stages of the development of EPZs. With regard to materials, for example, firms use few locally available sources and depend heavily on imports. There are good reasons for such action. Firstly, preferential treatment given to firms in EPZs includes exemption from import duties on imported raw materials, so that the latter remain competitive *vis-à-vis* local supplies. Secondly, as most of the enterprises are engaged in assembly-type work, it is normal for all components to be sent over directly from the parent company, assembled in the zone and then shipped out again.

Despite these problems, many zone authorities have made conscientious efforts to enforce greater utilization of local resources and more effective links with the domestic sector. This has been the deliberate policy of the Indian and Sri Lankan governments. An example of progress being made in this respect can be found in Taiwan. In the initial stages of development of its three EPZs, foreign firms used only very limited local supplies of materials and parts. In 1969, local supplies accounted for only 8 per cent of total imports to the zones; but this figure had increased to 46 per cent by 1979 (Rabbani, 1980, p. 25). In other words, local raw materials and equipment now supply almost half of the needs of industries in the Taiwanese EPZs. In Korea's Masan Free Export Zone, about 35 per cent of all production materials are being supplied by local firms (Rabbani, 1980, p. 24). However, figures are less impressive for the other more recently established zones.

There is no doubt that, with the gradual shift towards more technologically oriented production in the EPZs, domestic links will increase. This will normally be achieved by subcontracting the production of parts and components out to local firms, leaving the integration of the more advanced production lines to zone enterprises. Such a practice is now going on, for example, in Korea's Masan zone, where the zone enterprises actually provide technical assistance to local subcontracting firms. In Taiwan, it has been reported that a great number of factories around the cities of Kaohsiung and Taichung are exclusively satellite plants of zone enterprises. Such links should be further encouraged and promoted.

In China's Shenzhen SEZ, there has been much serious discussion since May 1983 concerning the promotion of domestic links in the development of the zone. But the approach will probably be rather different from that adopted in Asia's EPZs. Here, the idea is to provide preferential treatment to encourage Chinese enterprises from other parts of China, especially those with advanced technology, good management and competitive products, to set up production units in the Shenzhen SEZ. Through their interaction with foreign enterprises they should be able to digest modern advanced technology and scientific management methods. These may then be applied in other parts of China thereby expediting the realization of the Four Modernizations. These local firms will most likely use more local materials than do foreign enterprises; but if they require essential raw materials, modern equipment and parts from Hong Kong or anywhere else in the world, such goods can be imported duty-free. Products for consumption within the Shenzhen SEZ or for export are exempted from duties; but measures will be taken to reduce the amount of domestic sales (that is, sales to other parts of China). If more than 70 per cent of the total amount of raw materials used comes from local sources, the firm can negotiate with the government for a certain percentage of its products to be sold within China (*Shenzhen Special Zone Daily*, 16 May 1983). At present, domestic sales by foreign enterprises in the SEZs are normally discouraged, exceptions being high technology products or those products that are in short supply in China.

This problem of local sales is, in fact, an important aspect of domestic linkage. It is most unlikely that zone products will be supplied to local industries, both because these products are intended primarily for export, and because the products do not normally need further processing by local firms. In terms of the supply of goods produced in the EPZs for the local consumer market, most zones restrict or even prohibit domestic sales of zone products. However, there are great variations among Asian EPZs, and in zones where access to the local market is possible, it will normally be restricted to surplus products, seconds and rejects. Malaysia has been rather liberal in this respect, allowing local sales of up to 20 per cent of total production. In Sri Lanka, up to 10 per cent may be sold on the local market. Taiwan originally banned all local sales but now allows 2 per cent of annual production into the domestic market (Rabbani, 1980).

Although zone enterprises may be able to initiate the necessary domestic links, they may thereby come into competition with production from the domestic tariff sector. In order to avoid this, certain industries which are likely to compete with home products may not be permitted to operate in some zones. In Taiwan, for instance, no new clothing firms have been allowed in the zones since 1974, and in Sri Lanka no further investment in the garment industry is permitted.

Regional Development

Some Asian governments regard the development of EPZs as a way of developing the more backward sections of their countries. This was a major consideration for zones like Bataan in the Philippines and Kandla in India.

However, in both these cases, and in other areas, the benefits to regional development have been limited. There are a number of inherent drawbacks to the location of EPZs in more remote areas. Infrastructure and supporting facilities, a skilled workforce, and access to international ports and airports, which are the ingredients that foreign investors look for, are usually lacking or inadequate in these locations. Such facilities are more readily available in developed centres of population. As a result, many governments favour the establishment of EPZs near existing metropolitan areas to avoid heavy expenditure on the construction of roads, ports, airports and various other facilities in more remote locations.

China's SEZs are nevertheless all located in peripheral regions. Even the largest SEZ, Shenzhen, evolved from a small border town. The reason, however, is not so much a desire for regional development as the wish to isolate the SEZ experiment from the economic system that prevails in other parts of China. Until the results of this experiment become more apparent, it is considered undesirable to locate such zones near major population centres. The authorities can thus better control movement in and out of the zones and minimize the spillover effect of zone development on the social and economic life of neighbouring regions.

Difficulties in Development

It is evident that the performance of EPZs and SEZs in Asia has been rather varied. Some, like Kandla in India, are complete failures. Others, such as Taiwan's three EPZs or Korea's Masan Free Export Zone, have enjoyed considerable success. It might, therefore, be useful to give a brief review of the major problems encountered in the development of EPZs and SEZs in Asia. These problems can be divided into two broad categories: (a) those relating to the host countries and the zones themselves; and (b) those resulting from international economic fluctuations and competition.

The Provision of Infrastructure

The first and most pronounced problem encountered by the less successful EPZs in Asia has been the lack of provision for infrastructure. This is especially true for EPZs whose locations were decided on the basis of political considerations such as regional development. Away from major cities and sited in remote areas, these EPZs required considerable expenditure on infrastructure before they became viable. Experience has shown that unreliable supplies of electricity and water and a lack of housing and communication links have deterrent effects on investment which in turn prevent the achievement of set goals. However, because of the heavy capital outlay involved, funds are not always available to maintain adequate provision of these facilities. This has happened, for example, in the early stages of the development of the Bataan EPZ which was established in 1969. Owing to the lack of funds for infrastructural improvement, the zone did not come into operation until considerable expenditure had been incurred (about US$30 million by the Philippines' government and US$24 million borrowed from Japan) on the provision of facilities in the early 1970s (Rabbani, 1980, p. 12; and Zheng, 1983). When the Kaohsiung EPZ in Taiwan was first established in 1966, the roads, sewage system and other essential facilities were inadequate; residential accommodation was lacking and there were no hotels to accommodate expatriates. It was only after the expansion of the port and the airport, the establishment of a dry dock and a shipyard, and the erection of high-rise office buildings, department stores and international hotels that the Kaohsiung EPZ became a successful venture. The Nantze EPZ was later located in the vicinity so that infrastructural costs would be reduced by taking advantage of the facilities and services available at the Kaohsiung EPZ. It was estimated that by mid-1974, the Taiwan government had invested over US$30 million (of which 34 per cent represented loans from the United States government) in the provision of infrastructure for its EPZs (Rabbani, 1980; and Zheng, 1983).

Being much larger in area, China's SEZs will undoubtedly require more investment in the provision of infrastructure. It was reported that up to August 1982 over US$265 million had been spent for such purposes in the Shenzhen SEZ, with overseas investors contributing about one-third of this figure (*Shenzhen Special Zone Daily*, 24 December 1982). But the infrastructure of Shenzhen is still far from satisfactory. This problem has been recognized by the Shenzhen SEZ authority and massive investments have been made in the construction of infrastructure as may be seen in the rapid increase in the cumulative sum spent in this area. By the end of 1983, total investment in the provision of infrastructure had reached Rmb 1,963.7 million or US$785 million (*People's Daily*, 29 March 1984). Because of the vast size of China's SEZs, this problem of infrastructural provision will exist for a considerable time to come.

Social Problems

Although few Asian governments have explicitly stated that the social development of zone workers and residents was one of their objectives, the EPZs and the export system which they typify have had a considerable effect on the lives and social values of the local people and have at the same time created new social problems.

Amongst these problems is the increase in the number of unmarried females. Owing to the nature of the work and the wage levels, most of the workers in zone enterprises are young girls from rural areas or from low-income urban families. Their new circumstances soon expose them to the hazards of city life. Low wages, a poor working environment, long working hours and overcrowded living conditions in dormitories affect their health and their chances of getting married. Although many of these female workers will leave their jobs after six or seven years to marry or to pursue other careers, quite a number of them will stay on for a longer period of time. In Asian countries, these unmarried females are members of societies that traditionally define the role of women in terms of marriage and child-bearing — but they are denied that role by the social environment of the EPZ factories in which they work (Rabbani, 1980, p. 29; and Fitting, 1982).

Another problem is the phenomenal rise in the price of land and rents in the EPZs and their environs. In towns and cities where EPZs are located, the immigration of workers, management staff and expatriates creates severe pressure on food, housing and other supplies which then triggers off an inflationary spiral. Although some, such as landowners, benefit from this price increase, most people suffer from declining standards of living and the difficulties of making ends meet. Consequently, social problems and crime rates have increased. Few EPZ workers are able to save enough to remit money back to their relatives in the rural provinces (see, for example, Angangco and Jurado, 1982).

The power of workers in the Asian EPZs to improve their position is minimal. Reliance on foreign investment gives all governments a vested interest in ensuring that the demand for cheap labour is met and that industrial peace is maintained. Strikes are banned and labour union movements are kept under strict control. Exploitation and job insecurity are tolerated. In cases where occupant firms decide to close down or move to another location (as may happen after the lapse of the tax holiday period), the inevitable result is unemployment with little compensation (Rabbani, 1980; Fitting, 1982; and Angangco and Jurado, 1982).

These problems are not unique to the EPZs of the capitalist countries of Asia. In China's Shenzhen SEZ, the cost of living rose by 66.6 per cent between 1979 and 1982, seriously affecting the livelihood of local residents who were not employed in joint-venture enterprises and who were, therefore, not receiving higher wages (*Shenzhen Special Zone Daily*, 19 July 1982). The exploitation of workers in China's SEZs is tolerated. Sun Ru, Director of the Guangdong Bureau of Trade, said in 1980 that 'Investors [from] abroad will aim at profits. Whatever form of economic co-operation [is practised], there exists exploitation. This is not new to us [Chinese]. In order to realize the Four Modernizations and develop the socialist economy, we will allow exploitation to a certain degree' (Sun, 1980, p.46). Thus, the Chinese government, despite its socialist ideology, has a strong incentive to ignore the interests of its labour force for the sake of attracting foreign investment and enhancing economic growth. This may give rise to a social problem not found in the EPZs of the capitalist economies — an ideological conflict among people who are brought up in a socialist environment with a deep-rooted belief that the exploitation of workers is evil and that their government is an opponent of the capitalistic mode of production.

Administration and Co-ordination

One of the conditions for the successful development of EPZs in Asia is efficient management. Vittal (1977, p. 13) suggested that 'Other things being equal, the extent of ability of various EPZs, both existing and those to be established, to attract foreign investment may largely depend on the degree of efficiency of particular zone administrations. This is because unless zone administrations are efficiently managed, there is a definite possibility that the inducements and benefits offered to foreign investors would remain as offers and never in part or in whole become effective benefits to foreign investors.' Many of the governments responsible for the Asian EPZs are notorious for their inefficiency and inflexibility. On the one hand, the government administration of the departments concerned must be strengthened, but at the same time the flexibility of business enterprises should be maintained lest the strengthening of the administration increase inflexibility rather than operational efficiency. In recognition of the importance· of these factors, the development of EPZs and SEZs in Asia is normally under the direct control of the central government. However, in the course of operation, problems such as the lack of co-ordination between departments, an unclear division of responsibilities, and power struggles among officials and units have arisen. Kandla's failure is largely attributed to poor management and low operational efficiency. Investment procedures have become unnecessarily complicated and too many departments are involved in these procedures. In the early stage of the development of China's Shenzhen SEZ, similar problems emerged; but with a complete reorganization of its administrative structure since early 1982, many improvements have been made and the lines of responsibility, though still complicated in certain cases, have been clarified (see Chapter 11). Thus, for the future growth of EPZs and SEZs, it is pertinent that the administrative machinery should become more efficient. Related to this question is a whole range of issues which includes, for example, the understanding and interpretation of legal provisions, language barriers and translation problems, and financial and banking structures. It normally takes some time before the nature of these provisions is fully understood by potential foreign investors. This is particularly so in host countries where English is not widely understood.

World-wide Recession

It has been observed that EPZs are vulnerable to changing conditions in the world economy, such as recession and inflation, which may bring about extensive closures and lay-offs. In the mid-1970s and the early 1980s, employment in the Asian EPZs shrank as a result of global recession. Should economic fluctuation cause massive unemployment in the home countries of transnational corporations, there is always the danger that those corporations will be forced to close down their foreign branch plants. Coupled with this there is of course the export quota and tariff system instituted by developed countries as part of a protectionist policy which becomes particularly stringent during periods of recession. In the Bataan EPZ, for example, many firms ceased operation in 1979. According to officials of the Philippines EPZ Authority, the main reasons were 'mismanagement, failure to raise working capital and the imposition of quotas in the buyer countries' (Salita and Juanico, 1983, p. 33). Similar experiences were also recorded in other Asian EPZs such as those in Taiwan where many factories have closed down in the last few years due to the economic recession. China's SEZs have also been affected by changing conditions in the world economy particularly in the land and real estate development sectors.

Competition

The proliferation of EPZs and SEZs in Asia has intensified competition among them because their products and their markets are very similar. Increases in the cost of production in some EPZs due to rising labour costs (as in Taiwan and Korea) and the expiry of tax holidays have often resulted in firms leaving such zones for more favourable regions. The administrations of the established zones have not regarded this phenomenon as a serious threat to their existence as it fully accords with their policy to shift gradually to technology-intensive industries. In fact, such moves have been viewed by the Taiwan government as a sign of progress and better utilization of its limited land resources. Indeed, Taiwan considers that its three EPZs contain too many labour-intensive industries and fail to effect the transfer of technology that was expected. The establishment of the Hsinchu Science-Based Industrial Park represents Taiwan's answer to this question. As in the case of its EPZs, investors are offered preferential treatment in the Hsinchu Science-Based Industrial Park, but only those factories involved in high-technology production and with research and development (R & D) units are eligible to operate in the industrial park (Wang, 1980).

Although other newly established EPZs in Asia also prefer factories that use advanced technology, the inadequate supply of local technicians, engineers and other technical back-up is a major impediment to their establishment. In the foreseeable future, the concept of a science-based industrial park seems to be inapplicable to most Asian developing countries, although Taiwan, Korea and India are notable exceptions.

China's SEZs offer two new attractions in answer to the problem of competition with long-established zones in other Asian countries. One is to offer more generous preferential terms such as reduced land utility costs and longer tax holidays. The other is to allow some of the products manufactured in the SEZs to enter the domestic market (*Shenzhen Special Zone Daily*, 24 January 1983). In the face of such keen competition, one wonders if other Asian EPZs will adopt similar measures — although these will diminish their possible gains and may make them the victims of their own competition.

Conclusion

The setting up of an EPZ is only a first step: its efficient operation is a far more complex task. When EPZs were first established, they were usually not integrated with the domestic economy. In the long run, however, they should be an integral part of national development and should complement the growth of the domestic tariff sector. There will undoubtedly be conflicts of interest between the foreign investor and the host country, as is already reflected in the arguments over who actually benefits most from the investment projects in the EPZ. However, although EPZs are only one of the means of promoting economic development and encouraging industrial exports, they seem to have found favour among the governments of developing countries. This does not necessarily mean that they are the only or the most appropriate method of effecting export-led growth. Much depends on the geographic, economic, social and political background of the countries concerned. A further review of the concept of free zones in the Asian setting may cast some light on their advantages and disadvantages.

According to the spatial coverage and economic sectors involved, the general concept of free zones can be viewed as made up of five levels of development (Fig. 1.2), although these levels do not necessarily form a natural sequence or continuum. Customs-bonded warehouses (CBWs) are the simplest manifestation of the free zone concept and involve only the trans-shipment, storage and re-export of goods without customs formalities. Customs-bonded factories (CBFs), sometimes called 'export processing factories', represent the addition of a manufacturing function to the CBW system. They are to be found in a number of Asian countries and usually operate when the country is not yet ready to adopt the more organized enclave-type export processing zone system (owing, for example, to inadequate provision of infrastructure and public utilities, lack of overall economic planning or the absence of managerial or planning staff). CBFs are engaged in export processing, but they need not be established in an enclosed area of the country. Any factory producing for foreign markets, irrespective of location, will be provided with the same package of preferential treatment that is usually offered to enterprises in EPZs. These bonded factories must satisfy certain basic requirements: (a) they must be exclusively engaged in the processing or assembly of products for export; (b) they must have the

Fig. 1.2 The Concept of Free Zones

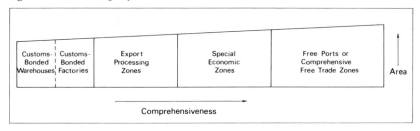

proper equipment for such production; and (c) they must have warehouses certified by the customs authorities concerned as appropriate for the storage of raw materials and finished or semi-finished products. The advantage of such a system is that production in CBFs can be started immediately without the huge amount of effort, in terms of both time and cost, that is required for the planning and construction of EPZs. Furthermore, CBFs can be set up anywhere in the country, particularly in areas rich in raw materials and/or having a large unemployed work-force at hand, thus reducing the need for the migration of people within the country. The flexibility of the CBF system allows the less developed countries to pursue a course of export-oriented economic development before they have sufficient resources to undertake the establishment of a full-scale EPZ. But CBFs should not be considered only as a feature of a transitional phase because even in countries like Taiwan, where the EPZ system has been successfully implemented, more than 300 bonded factories are still in full operation (Wang, 1980). However, the CBF system is not without its limitations because it requires an efficient government machinery to facilitate and supervise the operation of these production units, and this is absent in many Asian countries.

EPZs need not necessarily evolve from the CBF system. Typically, EPZs are specified areas within a country, often located near a port or airport, which have been designated as industrial zones and supplied with the basic infrastructural facilities. They are normally clearly demarcated from the domestic tariff sector. Although the incentives offered by these zones differ among Asian countries, their essential characteristic is that raw materials and parts can be imported and processed within the zone and then exported elsewhere free of duty and with minimal customs regulations. EPZs represent a planned and organized approach to export-oriented industrial production in developing countries. But as may be seen from the experiences of Asian nations, they may not be the most appropriate strategy of development for all countries. The success of EPZs depends on a number of physical and non-physical factors. These include, for example, the geographical location of the area concerned, the availability of port and/or airport facilities, the supply of land and labour, and the provision of infrastructure and supporting services. Of equal importance is a secure investment environment which offers political and economic stability, as well as an efficient government, so that the EPZ can operate with a minimum of bureaucratic interference.

Although SEZs are basically modelled on the EPZ system, they display significant differences in terms of physical size and comprehensiveness of economic activities. But perhaps of even greater importance is the fact that EPZs or similar developments are typically found in countries with a market economy whereas SEZs are the product of an open economic policy in a socialist country. By allowing foreign profit-seeking enterprises to operate within its territory, China seems to have taken a major initiative towards the expansion of the free zone system.

EPZs and SEZs will undergo a gradual transformation as they evolve. The number of simple processing industries will diminish, to be replaced by industries requiring more sophisticated technology. The idea of a science-based industrial park (such as the one established in Taiwan) is a move in this direction and will further reinforce the inherent strength and dynamism of the EPZ concept. Therefore, although simple processing industries in Asian countries may decline to the extent that the term 'export *processing* zone' becomes quite obsolete, the guiding principle and spirit of the EPZ system will remain alive and may even be extended further. Ultimately, it may be possible to apply the concept of the EPZ or SEZ to an even more extensive area such as a whole city or port, culminating in the development of free ports (such as Hong Kong) or comprehensive free trade zones.

With the evolution of an international division of labour and the strengthening of economic relationships between all countries of the world, a whole range of free zone establishments are to be found in the developing countries of Asia. They multiplied rapidly in the 1960s and 1970s, and continue to gain new ground in the 1980s. Despite differences in their characteristics, they have evolved from the same central concept. The continuing growth in the number of such zones indicates an increasing interest on the part of Asian governments in the adoption of the EPZ and similar systems as locomotives of export-led economic growth. However, statistics are usually not available to provide a detailed evaluation of the contributions of these zones to the national economy. Perhaps there is a need for more research on the role of such zones as stimulants of economic development and, indeed, on the feasibility and efficiency of alternative methods of achieving such development.

2. The Politico-economic Background to the Development of the Special Economic Zones

DAVID K. Y. CHU

TOGETHER with the adoption of flexible practices in export trade and the careful utilization of foreign capital, the development of special economic zones is regarded as one of the three major instruments in the expansion of China's foreign economic relations since 1977 (Wang and Chen, 1982). Therefore, in spite of their small area and relatively isolated location, the SEZs deserve close attention. They should be evaluated in the light of recent changes in Chinese policy that point towards a new economic development strategy and a much more extensive network of economic links with the capitalist world. This chapter attempts to describe the politico-economic background on which the SEZs are founded.

The Reinterpretation of Self-reliance

In summing up the flaws in the strategy for economic development during the thirty years from 1949 to 1978, Ma (1983a) ranked the narrow interpretation of the theory of self-reliance and the consequent closure of China to international contacts as one of the eight mistakes that pushed the country into its present economic difficulties. Indeed, the three major devices for the expansion of China's foreign economic relations represent the latest attempt to break away from Mao Zedong's interpretation of self-reliance that prevailed until 1976.

Mao stated that each country should be doing 'the utmost for itself as a means toward self-reliance for new growth, working independently to the greatest possible extent, making a principle out of not relying on others, and not doing something only when it really and truly cannot be done . . . Reliance on other countries . . . is most dangerous' (Mao, 1977, p. 103). Although Mao did not rule out exchanges between China and foreign countries, he did recommend the minimization of such co-operation, stressing that goods should only be imported after attempts have been made to produce them locally and that exports should only occur when local needs for a product have been satisfied (Lovbraek, 1976, p. 221). This is what Eckstein called 'a deliberate pursuit of an import substitution and import minimization policy' (Eckstein, 1977, p. 238). In other words, Mao explicitly rejected the argument of the international division of labour and comparative advantage propounded by Western theorists of interdependent development (for instance, Eckstein, 1977, p. 233; and Gourevitch, 1978, p. 891). Furthermore, besides maintaining its own self-reliance and independence, from Mao's point of view a truly socialist state has an additional international obligation. This is to help countries in the developing world 'towards escaping and limiting the consequences of the international capitalist division of labour' (Friedman, 1979, p. 822).

Although there is little doubt that self-reliance as a principle has enjoyed unanimous and consistent support among the ruling élite in China, the same cannot be said of self-reliance as a practical policy of development pursued by the People's Republic since its establishment. The policy of self-reliance has been debated, sometimes exalted, and at other times played down and weakened, by the presence of countervailing forces within China and abroad. When the People's Republic was founded in 1949, it inherited a war-torn economy. The stubborn pursuit of a development strategy of self-reliance would have been self-defeating at such a time. As Mao realized, '[China] must compromise'. In the early years of the People's Republic, the hostility of the United States towards Communism left the regime with no viable option but to rely on the Soviet Union. But the period of dependence proved to be short-lived and it came to an end with the abrupt and total withdrawal of Soviet economic and military aid in 1960. As Mao later recalled, 'In those days [1949–57] . . . we copied almost everything from the Soviet Union, and we had very little creativity of our own. At that time it was absolutely necessary to act thus, but at the same time it was also a weakness — a lack of creativity to stand on our own feet. Naturally this could not be our long-term strategy. From 1958 we decided to make self-reliance our major policy and striving for foreign aid a secondary aim' (Mao, 1962, p. 178).

The Great Leap Forward (1958–60) was the first test of Mao's self-reliance strategy on a national scale: it stressed mass mobilization, decentralization, local self-sufficiency and the development of comprehensive, cellular economic units known as communes. However, a combination of unrealistic expectations, inadequate planning, mismanagement and poor harvests turned Mao's experiment into an economic disaster and the nation suffered from widespread famine. By withdrawing to the second line of decision-making in the government, Mao by implication took the blame for the Great Leap Forward. Liu Shaoqi and Deng Xiaoping now came forward to restore order to the chaotic economy. Domestically, the extremes of Mao's doctrine of local self-sufficiency were modified. Externally, attempts were made to alleviate China's agricultural problems by huge imports of grain and chemical fertilizer. An attempt was made to fill technological lacunae by purchasing complete plants from industrialized countries such as Germany and Japan. Some of these purchases were financed by medium-term credits and included the services of foreign technicians stationed in China. Hence, although the slogan of self-reliance was to be championed throughout the 1960s, the economic practices introduced under the leadership of Liu and Deng began to change the substance of the original policy.

In 1966, the Great Proletarian Cultural Revolution, inspired by Mao, was once again to restore his policy of self-reliance. As Dernberger has observed, the period between 1967 and 1969 was a time 'when emphasis on self-reliance as an operational policy was at its *greatest* level of any period in the preceding 25 years' (Dernberger, 1977, p. 245). This was reflected particularly in China's foreign relations where self-reliance was manifested in the form of xenophobia. During the Cultural Revolution, China broke diplomatic relations with three countries, strained its relations with over half a dozen more, recalled all but one of its ambassadors, and cut down substantially on its import of industrial plant and equipment from foreign countries. Thus, during this period, self-reliance was pursued to the extreme of autarkical self-isolation.

These practices, however, proved to be short-lived. By 1969, the 'moderates' gathered around Zhou Enlai were able to convince Mao that the almost total isolation of China from the rest of the world had driven the country into a very precarious and vulnerable position *vis-à-vis* the Soviet Union. A series of policy modifications in the 1970s led to China's rapprochement with the United States, Japan and many other countries, with the exception of the Soviet Union and the East European bloc. A major consequence of this policy change was a dramatic expansion of economic transactions between China and the capitalist countries. Trade with non-Communist countries increased from US$3.5 billion in 1970 to US$12.2 billion in 1975 (Batsavage and Davie, 1978).

This policy shift, however, encountered persistent resistance from the ideological Left led by the 'Gang of Four'. Beginning in 1974, Zhou Enlai and later Deng Xiaoping, who had been rehabilitated from political disgrace in 1973, became the targets for heated political criticism from this left-wing faction. Zhou was accused of being 'an expert in fawning on foreigners' who had consistently 'begged for foreign capital economically' (*Hongqi*, August 1974). Deng was charged with 'lust for foreign technology and equipment, blatantly opposing the principles of independence and self-reliance' (*People's Daily*, 29 February 1974). Deng was consequently dismissed immediately after the death of Zhou.

The death of Mao in 1976 and the subsequent downfall of the 'Gang of Four' paved the way for the return to power of the twice-purged Deng Xiaoping and the official launching of the Four Modernizations in 1977. A more relaxed and flexible approach to self-reliance and interdependence soon evolved: self-reliance is now regarded as a long-term goal rather than as something to be put rigidly into immediate practice. Establishing contacts in all spheres with foreign countries means 'absorbing the good experience and techniques from abroad for our own use so as to enhance our self-reliance capabilities and build China into a powerful, modern socialist country before the end of this century' (*Beijing Review*, 8 July 1977).

Apart from stating that self-reliance is to be a long-term goal rather than an immediate necessity, the Chinese media has carried out a major ideological campaign to reinterpret Mao's principle of self-reliance. The hope is that this principle may be harmonized with the new economic programmes which seek to resolve the practical needs of contemporary China. The reinterpretation of Mao's principle of self-reliance in China after 1976 emphasizes four major points: (a) the 'Gang of Four' is alleged to have distorted the principle and exploited it for their own political gains; (b) the study of foreign ideas and the import of foreign technology do not contradict the basic tenets of the principle; (c) the change in economic and political conditions both within China and abroad makes it favourable today to adopt a more flexible approach to the issue of self-reliance; and (d) a discriminating and planned absorption of foreign ideas and technology will further strengthen China's national self-reliance in the long run (Wu, 1981, p. 164).

In short, China has now recognized that self-reliance can only be a long-term goal and can only be realized through the short-term importation of factors of production such as technology, capital and management expertise from the developed countries. These imports are meant to tackle the current problems of China's economy which are to be discussed in the next section. Participation in the international division of labour, borrowing from foreign banks and governments and the setting up of SEZs are conceived as means to finance these imports and are thus given much weight in the current drive towards the modernization of China.

Practical Considerations and the Role Played by the SEZs

The three major instruments in the expansion of China's foreign economic relations since 1977 are in fact not merely the outcome of the new interpretation of self-reliance. As illustrated in the case of the development of SEZs, these instruments are sometimes designed and implemented ahead of ideological justification. As described by Ma Hong, after the downfall of the 'Gang of Four' the Chinese economy deteriorated to such an extent that it fell into 'an unsound economic cycle of high speed, high accumulation, low efficiency and low consumption' (Ma, 1983a, p. 26). Measures to break the cycle are thus urgently required and a great strategic shift in China's socialist economic development is necessary. As far as external economic relations are concerned, the three instruments represent part of the Chinese answer to their economic problems. These problems are discussed below.

Declining Economic Results and Living Standards

The growth rates of China's industrial and agricultural production have on the whole been fairly high. Between 1958 and 1978, the average annual growth rate of the gross value of industrial and agricultural output was 7.6 per cent, with industry growing by 9.7 per cent. However, compared to 1957, the total output value produced per hundred Rmb of industrial fixed assets had declined by 256.4 per cent by 1978, while the profits and taxes turned over per hundred Rmb of funds fell by 30.3 per cent (Ma, 1983a). With more capital input and less output of profits and taxes, the economic results clearly declined. During the First Five Year Plan (1953–7), the amount of investment needed to increase national income by one Rmb was Rmb 1.68 (on 3 January 1984 Rmb 2.524 = US$1), but by the Fourth Five Year Plan (1971–5), the amount had risen to Rmb 3.76, an increase of more than 100 per cent (Ma, 1983a). Consequently, the high average annual growth rates of China's economy could only be sustained by very high accumulation at the expense of the people's everyday needs. The accumulation rate exceeded 30 per cent during the period from 1958 to 1960, as well as during the 1970s, while during the First Five Year Plan period it was only slightly over 20 per cent. It was due to the excessively high rate of accumulation that the people's livelihood in China did not improve at the same pace as the growth rate in production and that at times there was no improvement at all. The average monetary wage for workers and staff members of state-owned enterprises rose from Rmb 637 in 1957 to Rmb 644 in 1978, an increase of only 1.1 per cent over a period of 21 years. Since the cost of living index for workers and staff members of state-owned enterprises rose by 14.3 per cent during the same period, real wages actually declined. The average real wage of workers and staff members of state-owned enterprises dropped from Rmb 581 in 1957 to Rmb 514 in 1978, a decline of 11.5 per cent (Ma, 1983a). The livelihood of the peasants was also difficult. The converted average money wage of per capita income (for some of the peasants' income was in kind) in 1957 was Rmb 40.5, whilst in 1978 it was Rmb 133.57 (*Wen Wei Po*, 3 March 1983). At constant prices (the base year being 1957) the annual per capita income in the rural sector in 1978 was about Rmb 94.23, approximately one-fifth of that of workers and staff members of state-owned enterprises which are mainly located in the cities.

In other words, if the trend of declining economic results cannot be reversed by some drastic changes in the economic development strategy, the targets set for the Four Modernizations by the turn of the century are unlikely to be met. Declining economic results and living standards are partly, if not largely, the result of past mistakes committed during the era of the autarkic economic development policy. To reverse the trend, more open foreign trade policies are required.

The contribution of the SEZs to reversing the national trend of declining economic results and living standards should be assessed with care. With a total area of 346.8 sq km of which the Shenzhen SEZ represents 327.5 sq km, the Zhuhai SEZ 15.16 sq km, the Shantou SEZ 1.6 sq km and the Xiamen SEZ 2.5 sq km, and with a population of less than a million, the direct contribution of the SEZs to China's economic growth in general should not be overstated, but the indirect impact of their success could be profound. Subject to revision, it has been proposed that the Shantou SEZ will be enlarged to 52.6 sq km (Chu, Wong and Ng, 1984, p. 27) and the Xiamen SEZ to 125.5 sq km (*Wen Wei Po*, 21 May 1984). An impressive improvement in the output-input ratios has been recorded in many joint-venture enterprises in the SEZs, such as the Friendship Restaurant, the Garlock Furniture Factories and the Guangming Overseas Chinese Husbandry Farm in Shenzhen (*Gangao Jingji*, 1982, No. 5, pp. 43 and 45; and No. 6, p. 61). These enterprises have now become models for production units in other parts of China. With the rapid rise in its living standards, the Shenzhen SEZ has outranked any other city in China. The average monetary wage for workers and staff members of state-owned enterprises in the Shenzhen SEZ jumped from Rmb 571 in 1978 to Rmb 1,359 in 1982, an increase of 138 per cent (*Shenzhen Special Zone Daily*, 10 March 1983). Farmers in the Shenzhen SEZ are receiving an annual average income of Rmb 685, an increase of 320 per cent over 1978 (*Shenzhen Special Zone Daily*, 10 March 1983). This amount is almost two and a half times that of the national average which also recorded a sharp increase from Rmb 133.57 in 1978 to Rmb 270.11 in 1982 (*Wen Wei Po*, 3 March 1983).

Because of their late start, the performance of the other three SEZs has not been as impressive as that of the Shenzhen SEZ. However, the increase in the number of overseas investors indicating their intention to invest in these zones suggests that they will soon see a period of rapid economic growth.

To sum up, the improved economic results and living standards in the SEZs indicate that poor industrial performance and low living standards in the past have partly been the result of self-isolation, although other factors may have been equally important. The open policies adopted in the SEZs can at least offer a possible solution to these problems.

The Foreign Trade Bottle-neck

Up until 1978, Chinese foreign trade displayed five major characteristics, as summarized by Teng (1982, pp. 168–73).

The Small Volume of Trade

In terms of gross value (measured in Rmb), China's foreign trade in 1977 was merely 6.6 times that of the low level of 1950. Consequently, in spite of its vast size and huge population, and a modest rise in its total trade value, China's proportion of the total value of world trade dropped from 1.4 per cent in the 1950s to 1.1 per cent in the 1960s and to only 0.8 per cent in the 1970s, signifying that China's external economic links were shrinking during this period or at least were not expanding as rapidly as were those in other countries.

Fluctuations in the Rate of Growth

The growth rate of foreign trade has not been stable. In nine of the thirty years from 1949 to 1979, the gross value of foreign trade was lower than that of the previous year. Three major periods of fluctuation have occurred: a big drop in the three years after 1960, and two drops during the Cultural Revolution, which was a period of political interference from 'leftists' who interpreted self-reliance narrowly.

Changes in Trading Patterns

In the 1950s, some 65 per cent of the gross value of China's foreign trade was with the Soviet Union and East European countries. After the rupture in Sino-Soviet relations at the end of the decade, trade began to shift towards the capitalist market. This process accelerated during the 1970s with the improvement of China's relations with Japan, the European Economic Community (EEC) and the United States. However, China's trade with these capitalist countries was and still is in deficit. They are the major sources of expensive producer goods and grains whilst Chinese export commodities have difficulty in penetrating their markets. Hong Kong and Macau, China's major export partners, supply few goods on China's shopping list and have become the chief sources of foreign currency to help China cover its trading deficit with the advanced capitalist countries. The gross value of trade with the Soviet Union has declined to only 2 per cent of its 1959 peak and now accounts for a mere 1 per cent of the total of China's foreign trade.

Changes in the Structure of Foreign Trade

The fastest growth in export trade was recorded in light industrial products and textiles, and petroleum and chemical products which took over the place traditionally occupied by agricultural and mineral products. During the twenty-five years from 1955 to 1979, the proportion of agricultural and agriculture-related products dropped from 55.7 per cent to 22.2 per cent of the gross value of total exports, while that of light industrial products and textiles grew from 26.9 per cent to 42.7 per cent and heavy industrial products (including petroleum) from 17.4 per cent to 32.1 per cent. In the import trade, producer goods dominated the scene, except in the period between 1960 and 1965 when economic difficulties, a readjustment of the economy and large increases in grain purchases boosted the import of consumer goods to 40 per cent of the total. In the 1970s, imports of consumer goods declined and settled at about 19 per cent. Nevertheless, it is now recognized by the Chinese government that in the present structure, exports of high-quality products with well-known brand names are lacking, and the import of complete sets of equipment is considered to be an inefficient method of technological upgrading.

Unified State Control

Throughout the period from 1949 to 1979, foreign trade was conducted under strict, unified state control. On the one hand, this is recognized to have had the merit of helping China to maintain its balance of international payments, but on the other hand, it has discouraged the initiative of the provinces and other local units to promote exports.

To sum up, the trading pattern of China before 1978 restricted the role of foreign trade in promoting China's economic development and raising living standards. It has been pointed out that 'insufficient attention has been paid to achieve the most economically effective form of trade, and the structure of exports still does not match our requirements . . . For a long time, we have neglected the importance of foreign trade and placed one-sided emphasis on the policy of independence and self-reliance. We have regarded foreign trade merely as a supplement to make up for the gaps in our economy and we have failed to use it to its fullest extent as a means of maximizing our comparative economic advantages and our best interest' (Teng, 1982, p. 172).

More important than the volume of foreign trade are the qualitative issues of how trade is conducted and financed. Before 1978, the Chinese eschewed the notion of indebtedness and the government was proud of having no internal or external debts (*Beijing Review*, September 1977). Most of China's import trade was financed by cash, and export credits were seldom used, whilst there was even less borrowing from foreign banks, governments or international organizations. Foreign capital investment and other means of trading (for instance, compensation trading) were considered as anti-socialist and were not permitted.

However, since 1978 recognition of the inefficiency of the trading system has stimulated new and more innovative ways of trading. The adoption of less rigid trading policies and trade financing represent a new attempt to give the necessary flexibility to China's trading system and to its rapidly increasing import trade. The SEZs, on the other hand, could be regarded as areas which specialize in export trade and which are designated for the utilization of foreign capital. Indeed, in terms of export trade, the future role of the SEZs should not be underestimated. The projected export trade target for China in the year 2000 represents a fourfold increase over the 1980 figure, that is from US$20 billion to US$80 billion. By that time, the four SEZs will have been completely developed and their estimated exporting capacity will be around US$5.2 billion (Chu, 1982), that is 6.5 per cent of the country's total.

Much more important is the zones' current contribution to the utilization of foreign capital and technology. Between 1979 and 1982, 84 joint-venture projects were finalized between China and overseas firms and 35 of these (42 per cent) were located in the Shenzhen SEZ (*Wen Wei Po*, 1 May 1983). In terms of foreign capital actually invested, China attracted US$1.7 billion during that period (*Wen Wei Po*, 7 September 1983) of which US$0.3 billion was invested in the Shenzhen SEZ (*Wen Wei Po*, 10 September 1983) and US$50 million in the Zhuhai SEZ (*Wen Wei Po*, 12 September 1983). In other words, two of the SEZs alone accounted for as much as one-fifth of direct foreign investment in China in the period between 1979 and 1982. Progress made in 1983 was even more remarkable: the Shenzhen SEZ alone received another HK$1.1 billion (on 3 January 1984 HK$7.82 = US$1) in direct foreign investments (*People's Daily*, 29 March 1984). From these figures, one can measure the relative importance of the SEZs in the non-commodity trade between China and the outside world.

Perhaps an even more important implication of these direct investments lies not in the actual amount of overseas capital inflow, but in the technology and management techniques involved in joint-venture direct investments. This is exemplified by the rapid growth of the electronics industry in the Shenzhen SEZ. In 1979, this industry did not exist in the zone. Now Shenzhen is one of the most important centres for the manufacture of electronics in China and the industry accounts for 35 per cent of the total industrial output of the SEZ (*Wen Wei Po*, 10 September 1983). The trend towards an inflow of more advanced technology seems likely to continue for some time and it is expected that the contribution of the SEZs in this respect will be even greater than their share in export trade and in the utilization of foreign capital.

Economic Management Deadlocks

In the early 1950s, China established an economic planning system modelled quite closely on Soviet practices in which the state level of the management system is the highest in the planning hierarchy and the most powerful. Immediately below the state level come the provinces. The units directly engaged in production form the lowest level of the management hierarchy. Like other socialist countries, China has formulated a series of Five Year Plans to set the tempo of its economic growth. However, these long-term plans have never been properly co-ordinated and seem to have comprised little more than a collection of branch proposals brought together in one set of documents (Hare, 1983, p. 193). What really matters in practice is the annual plan. Most types of plan information are passed from enterprises to state-level authorities via the standard territorial administrative bodies and via the various levels of branch ministries. Based on this information, the State Planning Commission works out guidelines for the plan year. These guidelines are then sent to all the branch ministries and the provincial planning commissions for their consideration. In consultation with the provincial bureaux, companies and enterprises under their supervision, the branch ministries and the provincial planning commissions formulate draft plans for the plan year, and these are then submitted to the State Planning Commission. Since these initial drafts almost certainly fail to balance when combined at the national level, the State Planning Commission, the Bureau for Material Allocation and other central agencies have to propose adjustments, cuts and revised targets in order to achieve a balance. The vastness of the country, the shortage of trained personnel, poor communications and a paucity of data-processing devices mean that the task of balancing is extraordinarily complex: no centrally planned economy has ever solved this difficulty to its satisfaction. After balancing, the plan is approved by the State Council and then returned to the branch ministries and provinces for implementation.

When a province receives its plan, it may add further tasks before directives are issued to regional commissions, bureaux, prefectures and municipalities which in turn hand down directives to the enterprises under their control. The assigning bodies are responsible for the supply of raw materials necessary to the production laid down in the plan and for the marketing of the finished products. The enterprises are responsible for fulfilling the tasks assigned. As the system frequently fails to reward excellence and ignores the principle of payment 'to each according to his work', the enterprises have neither the incentive nor the ability to fulfil more than their assigned targets: output which exceeds the plan normally requires extra materials for which the central plan does not provide. Those enterprises that do have some surplus materials with which to produce more goods do not know to whom they can sell those goods. Any profits or excess materials must be handed over to the authorities to which the enterprises belong. As a result waste is incurred in the production section and little initiative or incentive is possible among the workers and managerial staff (Hare, 1983).

The resolution of this dilemma of economic management is thus an essential prerequisite to the reactivation of the economic system of China. More flexibility and the reintroduction of monetary or material incentives, shop-floor management techniques and the market system are regarded as possible remedies. Many practices of market economies outside China offer models from which China could learn. Before an overall adoption or adaptation, these models and techniques will need to be studied intensively and be tested in a Chinese context. Many factories and some small cities or counties have been allotted a role in this experiment, whilst SEZs are obviously designed as a laboratory for studying the mechanism of market systems in a Chinese (socialist) context. The objectives of the SEZs, as stated by Wu Nansheng, are (1) to observe and to understand capitalism at work and to follow the trend of modern economic development in the capitalist world; (2) to test different policies, especially those connected with various economic systems, by using the special zones as laboratories, and (3) to acquire modern technology and management methods (*Wen Wei Po*, 6 March 1981).

The Chinese system of economic management will probably benefit most from the SEZs through their experience of 'the leading role of market regulation under the direction of the State Plan'. Because of the uncertainties of the international market, the heavy involvement of overseas capital and the desire to experiment with the market system, the municipal governments of the SEZs have much greater autonomy than is the case anywhere else in China in decision-making and in the use of foreign currency to purchase the necessary commodities for the construction of infrastructure and for local consumption. Apart from a few items, such as rice and fuel, the prices of commodities are regulated by the market mechanism. The meaning of 'the direction of the State Plan' is limited to the demand that those who formulate the medium- to long-term economic and social plans of the SEZs should seek approval from the central government so that the direction of economic development, its scale, composition and targets are in line with the principles of the Chinese drive towards modernization (Zhang, 1983). A portion of the materials needed in the SEZs is allocated by the Bureau for Material Allocation at fixed accounting prices as in other parts of China. However, the SEZs are free to purchase whatever they want in the trade fairs hosted by the Foreign Trade Ministry in Guangzhou just like overseas traders. Moreover, if the trade fairs cannot supply what is required, the SEZs can shop in foreign markets.

Since the successful implementation of market regulation in the SEZs, similar practices are now to be promoted in other parts of China. For example, it is now planned to develop Hainan Island and fourteen city-ports along the lines of the SEZs although they will not be so called.

The Ideological Justification of the SEZs: A Review

In 1978, the two southern coastal provinces of China, Guangdong and Fujian, were granted special status in the development of foreign trade with considerable autonomy. Subsequently, the concept of SEZs was discussed and ideas were formulated. The first initiative to be taken was the announcement of the setting up of an industrial zone on the Shekou peninsula opposite the New Territories of Hong Kong to be managed and planned by a Hong Kong-based company sponsored by the Chinese government, the China Merchants' Steam Navigation Co. Ltd. The official status of Shekou as a special economic zone was granted on 1 January 1979. The idea of setting up the Shenzhen, Zhuhai and Shantou SEZs was first discussed in July 1979 but a final decision was not reached until the end of 1979 and their legal status was not granted until 26 August 1980 (*Wen Wei Po*, 12 September 1983). The Xiamen SEZ was designated in October 1980, two months after the Guangdong SEZs (Zou and Jiang, 1983).

The SEZs bear some similarities to the export processing or free trade zones of other developing countries, although they also differ in many respects (see Chapter 1). The concept of the SEZ is a rather sensitive one since it is reminiscent of the foreign concessions in the treaty ports which were one of the major targets of the anti-colonial campaigns in China before 1949. Many left-wing newspapers and scholars outside China regard the SEZs and joint ventures as 'political retreats' (see, for instance, Cannon, 1983).

In order to justify the establishment of SEZs, many Chinese scholars and officials have tried to affirm the socialist nature of these zones. They have attempted to find ideological support in the works of Marx and Lenin. Whilst they do not have much success with Marx, they have found some statements of Lenin useful and relevant to their *ex post facto* justification. The most frequently quoted statements from Lenin include his elaboration on concessions and state capitalism. The following is an example:

Within the limits indicated, however, this is not at all dangerous for socialism as long as transport and large-scale industry remain in the hands of the proletariat. On the contrary, the development of *capitalism*, controlled and regulated by the proletarian *state* (i.e., 'state' capitalism in this sense of the term), is advantageous and necessary in an extremely devastated and backward small peasant country (within certain limits, of course), inasmuch as it is capable of hastening the immediate revival of peasant farming. This applies still more to *concessions*: without denationalizing anything the workers' state *leases* certain mines, forest tracts, oilfields, and so forth, to foreign capitalists in order to obtain from them extra equipment and machinery that will enable us to accelerate the restoration of Soviet large-scale industry . . .

The payment made to the concessionaires in the form of a share of the highly valuable products obtained is undoubtedly a tribute which the workers' state pays to the world bourgeoisie; without in any way glossing over this, we must clearly realize that we stand to gain by paying this tribute, so long as it accelerates the restoration of our large-scale industry and substantially improves the condition of the workers and peasants (1964 edition, p. 626).

It is argued that the foreign-owned enterprises in the SEZs are comparable to Lenin's idea of concessions with factory sites, tourist resorts and mines leased to foreign capitalists. Joint ventures and other non-socialist trading practices are regarded as state capitalism. Xu Dixin, for example, stated that

Processing, compensatory trade, cooperative enterprises and joint ventures are all state capitalist economic activities. Strictly speaking, the enterprises run by foreign or overseas Chinese capital constitute a kind of capitalist economy but the activities of such enterprises are subject to control and regulation by the governments of the special zones. As a result they are special kinds of capitalist enterprises (Xu, 1981, p. 14).

In other words, the nature of the economic activities in the SEZs of China is a mixture of socialism, state capitalism and foreign capitalism on concessionary terms. Lu Zifen of the Xiamen SEZ, for example, points out that

Thirty years of experience has made us realize that it is difficult for a developing socialist country to base itself solely on the state-owned economy. Various other forms of economy must also be used — among them, imports of foreign capital and joint-venture enterprises (*China Reconstructs*, June 1981).

By accepting foreign capital and technology, China is aware of the price that it must pay.

For foreign private investors to conduct economic co-operation with China, no matter in what form, their purpose is to make profits. This has been clear to us from very early on. To fulfill the Four Modernizations and develop [the] socialist economy, we will allow the investors their share of reasonable profits. Our principle is equal and mutual benefit. Foreign investors are after profits and we are after socialist modernization (Sun Ru, 1980, p. 77).

Consequently, a small element of capitalism in the national economy was said to be incapable of undermining socialism (Li Xiannian, as quoted by Sun Ru) especially if the impact of the SEZs is confined to defined limits. To what extent the Chinese political economy theorists were convinced by this justification is unknown. However, little opposition was spelt out in public. It later became evident that the SEZ policy was initiated and supported by Deng Xiaoping. So it is no wonder that criticisms were only aired in private — with the exception of a few strictures on poor industrial management and acts of ideological contamination in the Shenzhen SEZ (personal communication).

Conclusion

The latest visits by Deng Xiaoping to the Shenzhen, Zhuhai, and Xiamen SEZs in February 1984 and by Hu Yaobang to the Shantou SEZ signified their endorsement of the success of China's four SEZs. Their remarks on the SEZ policy subsequently led to a major coastal district conference under the chairmanship of Gu Mu, a prominent economist and State Councillor, in Beijing between 26 March and 6 April 1984. The existing policy on SEZs was reviewed and new proposals were put forward. On 29 March 1984, the success and remarkable progress of the Shenzhen SEZ were praised in the *People's Daily*, the most important newspaper in China. This apparently paved the way for the announcement on 6 April 1984 that, apart from the four SEZs, fourteen city-ports along the Chinese coast will have their own economic development zone or zones (Fig. 2.1) (*China News Agency*, 6 April

*Fig. 2.1 The Location of the Fourteen City-ports with
         Economic Development Zones and the Four Special Economic Zones*

1984). The economic development zones will bear many of the characteristics
of the SEZs. They will be delimited, fenced and governed by special
committees for the introduction of foreign capital, technology and economic
management. As for the four SEZs, the Xiamen SEZ will be enlarged to
cover the whole of Xiamen Island (about 123.8 sq km) and the Shantou
SEZ will incorporate the adjacent port zone and an extensive area of
agricultural land (*South China Morning Post*, 21 March 1984).

   The aim of the new proposal is to develop the coastal provinces more
rapidly than other provinces in the country with the help of the SEZs and
economic development zones. The hope is that the development of the

coastal provinces will eventually lead to the quickening of the rate of economic growth of the inland provinces. However, in the short term, the addition of as many as fourteen city-ports with economic development zones will surely lead to severe competition, and perhaps rivalry, among the zones themselves and perhaps among the provinces. But together, they will reinforce the Chinese open-door policy in general and special zone policy in particular.

3. The Geographical Endowment of China's Special Economic Zones

YEN-TAK NG AND DAVID K. Y. CHU

THE geographical endowment of a place may be defined in terms of proximity or accessibility to other factors of economic development. In simple language, Wilbanks explains that, 'proximity has utility because it reduces the effort involved in doing desirable things' (Wilbanks, 1980, p. 74). In this chapter, the authors attempt to examine the geographical endowment of the four Chinese special economic zones, firstly from the point of view of the relative positions of the provinces of Guangdong and Fujian in which the four SEZs are sited, and secondly from a narrower point of view, that is the proximity of the four SEZs to the factors of development in their environs. The resultant findings will then be used to evaluate the recent performance of the zones. The final section of this chapter includes a discussion on the possible impact on the four original SEZs of the creation of fourteen more economic development zones or regions, plans for which were announced in 1984.

The Peripheral Location of Guangdong and Fujian and their Special Attractions

The establishment of the four SEZs is an offshoot of the policy, initiated in 1979, of granting special authority in economic affairs to Guangdong and Fujian. The selection of Guangdong and Fujian rather than other provinces and autonomous regions is interesting, for besides Guangdong and Fujian there are a further six coastal provinces. In terms of economic strength, as well as industrial and commercial power, Guangdong and Fujian lag far behind both the provinces of Liaoning, Jiangsu and Zhejiang and the cities of Shanghai and Tianjin (Table 3.1). Indeed neither Guangdong nor Fujian has very much heavy industry. They are only a little better off than the least developed coastal province of Guangxi. Owing to its peripheral location relative to the major industrial hubs and political centres, Fujian has received scant attention in terms of investment funding from the central government. Guangdong is in a slightly better position for it is located at the southern end of the north-south railway and acts as a gateway to the outside world.

Table 3.1 The Economic Status of the Coastal Provinces

Coastal Province/ City	Per Capita Output of Light Industry (in Rmb)	Per Capita Output of Heavy Industry (in Rmb)	Per Capita Agricultural Output (in Rmb)	Investment in Fixed Assets (in Rmb billion)	
				Total	Amount from Central Government
Liaoning	472.5	860.8	252.9	5.44	1.21
Hebei	206.4	227.4	255.3	3.93	1.41
Shandong	276.9	217.0	303.6	4.31	0.99
Jiangsu	493.1	338.4	386.7	3.48	0.70
Zhejiang	279.0	214.3	353.9	2.07	0.56
Fujian	214.0	126.7	241.0	1.51	0.33
Guangdong	296.6	162.3	240.8	5.63	1.03
Guangxi	155.7	88.0	233.6	1.35	0.28
Tianjin	1,571.7	1,157.0	271.8	3.00	1.29
Shanghai	3,025.8	2,342.8	326.0	6.16	3.41

Source: Chinese Statistical Yearbook, 1983.

Nevertheless, it is clear that economic factors were not the primary consideration in the selection of the two provinces for the establishment of SEZs. Social or ethnic ties were more important: Guangdong and Fujian have a special appeal for a large proportion of overseas Chinese as most of them are natives of these two provinces.

Since the early fifteenth century, there has been substantial emigration from Guangdong and Fujian, mostly to South-east Asia, Hong Kong and Macau. The economic opportunities available in these areas have helped to transform the Chinese immigrants from labourers into middle-class urban entrepreneurs and traders. According to Chang (1968), 98 per cent of overseas Chinese (ethnically defined) are to be found in South-east Asia, Hong Kong and Macau. The latter two places together account for one-fifth of all overseas Chinese. Through hard work, an active exploitation of economic opportunities, a colonial *laissez-faire* policy and a wise use of available resources and management techniques, the Chinese in Hong Kong have transformed what was once a mere entrepôt into a major manufacturing and financial centre. Macau, on the other hand, has developed its economy mainly on tourism, with gambling as its chief attraction. The descendants of those who emigrated to Thailand, Malaysia, Singapore, Indonesia and the Philippines have also achieved remarkable success, especially in the lumbering, mining and trading sectors. Of equal importance have been the wealth and technical and managerial skills and experience accumulated in the Chinese communities in various European countries and in the United States.

The capital and other resources of these overseas Chinese could make a significant contribution to China's current drive for modernization. Many overseas Chinese possess the capital, banking experience, marketing know-how and modern management techniques which are lacking in China. The granting of special authority in economic affairs to Guangdong and Fujian and the establishment of four SEZs within them are part of a policy designed to attract these resources to China. With special authority in economic affairs, the two provincial governments will thus be able to minimize bureaucratic delays and reduce the length of negotiations for joint ventures in which they and overseas Chinese investors participate. Those overseas Chinese who prefer sole ownership to joint ventures can also operate in the SEZs. Although, in theory, joint ventures and even sole-ownership enterprises are not restricted to overseas Chinese or to the provinces of Guangdong and Fujian, in practice most of the investment agreements hitherto concluded have been between the governments of Guangdong and Fujian and overseas Chinese from Hong Kong. This, on the one hand, indicates that without further revision of the existing policy and an improvement in the investment environment, the current open-door policy will appeal mainly to overseas Chinese whose origins are in Guangdong and Fujian. On the other hand, the SEZs of Guangdong and Fujian may act as an arena for the Chinese government to experiment with various strategies of managing overseas capital, thus paving the way for further advances in its open-door policy and the extension of this policy to other provinces.

There is a real possibility of a decline in the importance of the special status of Guangdong and Fujian in general, and the four SEZs in particular, in view of the growing importance to China of foreign (other than overseas Chinese) capital investment. The stiff competition offered by other coastal provinces and municipalities with stronger economic bases and more central locations, and perhaps greater favour with the central government, may outweigh the attractions of Fujian and Guangdong to the investor. This point will be further discussed in the final section. In the following section, the geographical endowment of the individual SEZs will be reviewed in order to obtain a better understanding of the locational advantages and disadvantages which will affect their chances of success.

The Geographical Endowment of Individual SEZs

Shenzhen

The most obvious advantage of the Shenzhen SEZ is its proximity to metropolitan Hong Kong (Fig. 3.1) and its size. An international commercial, industrial and financial centre, Hong Kong has a population of over 5 million with a per capita GNP of over US$4,000 (1980 figure: Hong Kong

Government, Census and Statistics Department, 1982). Hong Kong is a huge consumer market with extensive commercial ties. It is served by excellent port facilities and is the third largest container port in the world. Although few of the Chinese in Hong Kong actually come from Shenzhen, in dialect and culture they do not differ greatly from the inhabitants of Shenzhen. The Shenzhen SEZ is, therefore, in a good position to attract investments from Hong Kong itself and from foreign financial groups through their agents in Hong Kong. More important, Hong Kong, with its shortage of space, high land values, rampant inflation and high labour costs, has begun to lose its competitiveness in labour-intensive types of industry. The Shenzhen SEZ, however, with a total area of 327.5 sq km, has 98 sq km ready for building purposes, and offers low rents and low labour costs. Shenzhen is an ideal site for factories which would yield only marginal profits if operated in Hong Kong. Furthermore this vast area of land can also be used profitably in recreational and residential development for residents of Hong Kong.

Before 1978, Shenzhen was a small town with a population of about 20,000. It had only twenty-six small factories with a total industrial output amounting to less than US$10,000 (Cai, 1981), and urban facilities were far from adequate. The setting up of an SEZ in Shenzhen almost amounted to the building of a new city, requiring an enormous investment of capital and the introduction of large numbers of skilled labourers (Chu, 1982).

The facilities and capacity of Shekou, the port designated to serve the Shenzhen SEZ, are insufficient for its needs. Even after dredging, Shekou will only accommodate ships of under 3,000 d.w.t. The Chiwan deep-water port, on the other hand, has been designed to serve the needs of the South China Sea oilfields. Eventually the majority of goods processed in the Shenzhen SEZ will need to pass through Hong Kong for trans-shipment. Transportation by rail and road between Hong Kong and Guangzhou, however, is convenient. The Shenzhen Reservoir and the Xili Reservoir are able to provide an adequate and stable supply of water to the zone. Once a few technical problems have been resolved, an adequate supply of electrical power will also be assured. The electricity network in Shenzhen has been linked with that of Hong Kong. Telecommunications have also been established with the help of a Hong Kong corporation (Wong, 1982).

It is expected that eventually the population of the Shenzhen SEZ will be made up mainly of people from other parts of China. The question is whether newcomers will adapt to the peculiar institutions and environment of the zone. Social problems arising from maladjustment are unavoidable (Wong, 1982).

Zhuhai

The Zhuhai SEZ has an area of only 15.16 sq km (formerly only 6.8 sq km) (Fig. 3.2), and is thus very much smaller than the Shenzhen SEZ. It

Fig. 3.1 The Shenzhen SEZ

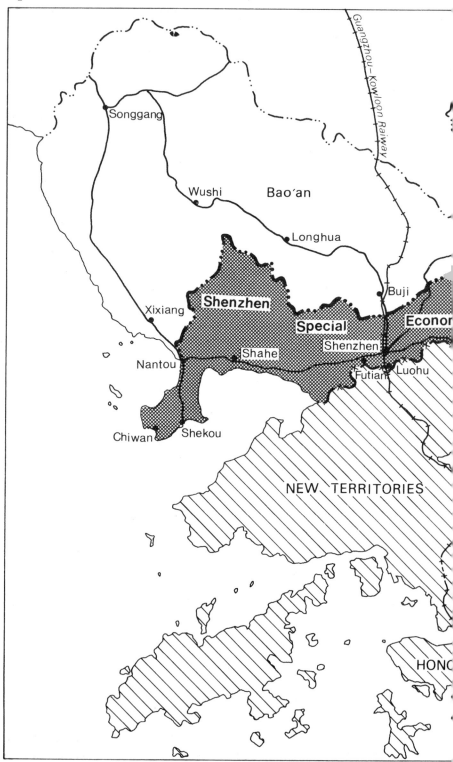

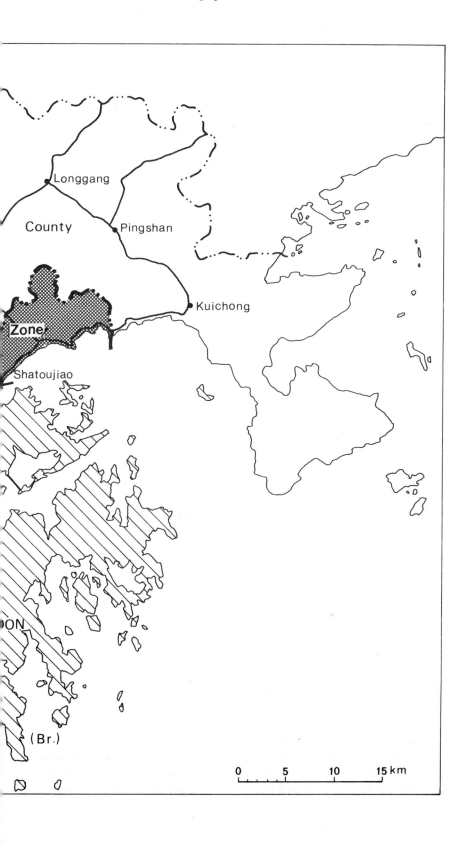

Fig. 3.2 The Zhuhai SEZ

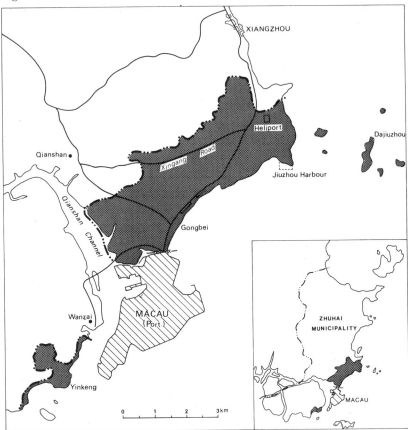

is adjacent to Macau, the Portuguese enclave, and is only 62 km from Hong
Kong by sea. A great proportion of Macau's residents came originally from
the counties of Zhuhai and Zhongshan. It is reasonable to expect that the
Zhuhai SEZ will provide an outlet for investments from Macau and possibly
from nearby Hong Kong. However, Macau has a population of only 360,000
(1979 figure). It lacks a deep-water port and the extent of its industrial
development is limited. Its GNP in 1977 was less than US$208 million
(Cai, 1981). It is very unlikely that the Zhuhai SEZ will benefit from Macau
to the degree that the Shenzhen SEZ benefits from its proximity to Hong
Kong. Furthermore, most factories in Macau are subsidiaries of Hong Kong
enterprises and depend upon Hong Kong for capital, technology, raw materials
and also the distribution and marketing of all processed goods. However,
the development of recreational resources in co-operation with investors from
Macau may be the most profitable venture for the Zhuhai SEZ.

In competing with the Shenzhen SEZ for investment in industry, Zhuhai
faces a number of geographical disadvantages. There is no transport problem
between the Zhuhai SEZ and Macau, but the road link with Guangzhou

is less than satisfactory. At the time of writing, Guangzhou is connected with Zhuhai only by a third-class highway. The route is slow as it involves many ferry-crossings. The port which serves the zone can only give berthing to ships of under 3,000 d.w.t. (Zhang, 1981b), and is thus very similar in capacity to the port at Shekou in Shenzhen. The Zhuhai SEZ is further handicapped by both an inadequate electricity supply and a small work-force. Xiangzhou, the county seat, has a population of only 13,000. Together with other smaller towns like Gongbei, Qianshan and Wanzai, the total urban population of the county including the Zhuhai SEZ is only 25,000. Urban facilities are minimal. The whole county of Zhuhai has only 130 factories, most of which operate on a small scale and involve very simple technology. Total annual industrial output in 1979 did not exceed US$20 million (Xu, 1981). To industrialize this zone, therefore, would entail a tremendous investment in urban facilities and housing developments and the importation of large, numbers of labourers. As in the Shenzhen SEZ, these new immigrants might well suffer from social problems relating to maladjustment to a new social and economic environment.

Shantou

The Shantou SEZ is situated east of the city of Shantou (Fig. 3.3). Quite a number of overseas Chinese now residing in Hong Kong, Macau and particularly Thailand are from this general area (Chen, 1981). With a population of 360,000, the city of Shantou has a ready supply of skilled labour and a good light industrial infrastructure. The industrial processing area is located only 3 km from the city. In this first stage of industrial development, there is no immediate need for the construction of large-scale residential complexes, thus reducing the amount of capital investment that is required.

The port of Shantou can provide berthing for ships of over 10,000 d.w.t. and it possesses a sheltered harbour 8 to 10 m deep. However, an offshore bar at the entrance to the harbour is a hazard to shipping. Because of this, the port can now only admit ships of around 5,000 d.w.t. At present, transportation of raw materials from the interior to the Shantou SEZ is difficult because the area is not served by a railway. Furthermore, the Shantou SEZ lacks an adequate supply of electricity. This is a great hindrance to its industrial development (Cai, 1981).

However, the Shantou zone has a sound fishing and agricultural base, and its potential for tourism is promising. The Chinese government is now concentrating its efforts to develop the zone on the expansion of the Longhu Industrial District from an original 0.8 sq km to 1.6 sq km. In addition, 1.7 sq km of port and warehouse space has been earmarked for port industries and it has been proposed that an area of more than 19.3 sq km for the production of vegetables, flowers, fruit, pork, poultry, fish and shrimps solely

Modernization in China

Fig. 3.3 The Shantou SEZ

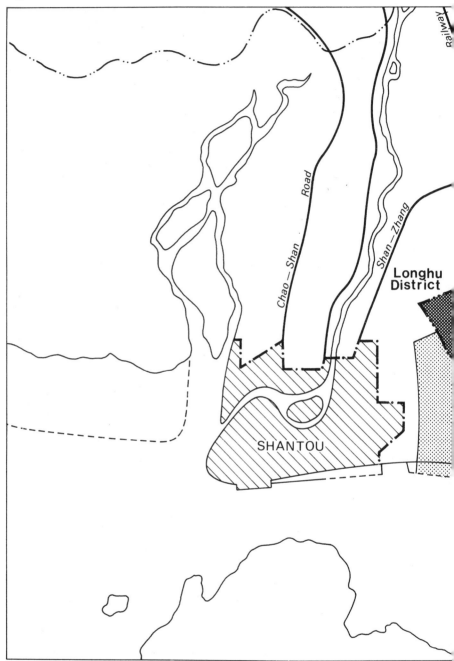

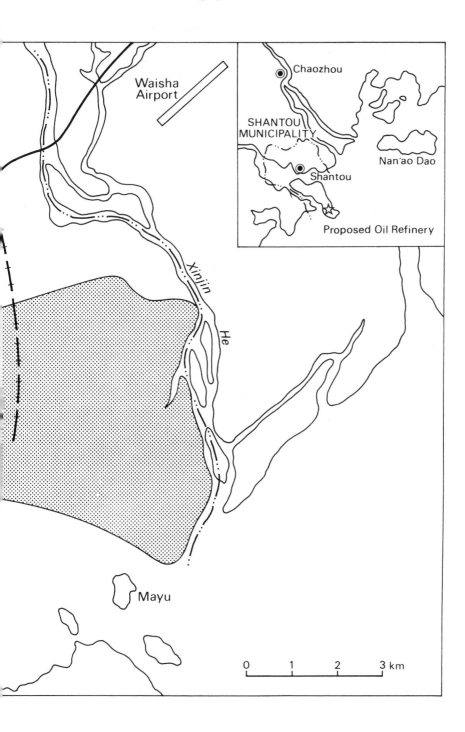

Waisha
Airport

Xinjin He

Chaozhou

SHANTOU
MUNICIPALITY

Nan'ao Dao

Shantou

Proposed Oil Refinery

Mayu

0   1   2   3 km

for export should be included in the Shantou SEZ (*Beijing Review*, 14 December 1981; and *South China Morning Post*, 21 March 1984). In late 1984, a press release from the Shantou SEZ indicated that the area of the planned oil refinery would also be included in the proposed expansion of the zone (Chu, Wong and Ng, 1984).

Xiamen

The Xiamen SEZ is the only SEZ in Fujian. The Huli Industrial District of the Xiamen SEZ, with an area of only 2.5 sq km, is situated on Xiamen Island which is 123 sq km in size (Fig. 3.4). The city of Xiamen is also situated on the island and has a population of 270,000: it will become part of the SEZ when the proposal to extend the Xiamen SEZ to embrace the whole of Xiamen Island is put into practice (*China News Agency*, 7 April 1984). Over 200,000 Chinese residents of Hong Kong and Macau originated from Fujian Province, and there are even more Fujianese in Singapore and Malaysia. Many of them have risen to prominence in the commercial field. It is probable that they will be the first to contribute to the development of the Xiamen SEZ if the investment climate there proves to be attractive.

The educational level of the workers in the Xiamen area is relatively high and the area has a long history of industrial development. There is plenty of labour available, skilled or otherwise. As is the case in Shantou, there should be little immediate need for large-scale urban or residential construction. The Xiamen SEZ has one attribute that sets it apart from the other zones, namely a seaport 10 to 30 m deep. Dongdu New Port is designed to accommodate ships of 50,000 d.w.t. This zone also has railway links with other parts of China and the road network is adequate. However, Xiamen Island lacks a fresh-water supply. Water for the island is supplied from a reservoir 40 km away and the pipeline is not able to cope with the present needs of the city of Xiamen. The inadequate water supply within the Xiamen SEZ could impede the development of water-consuming industries in the zone. Moreover, Xiamen is very near an outpost of Taiwan — the Jinmen Islands — and individuals and corporations tend to be cautious about investing in such a sensitive area (Chen and Chen, 1981).

As we have seen, the Shenzhen SEZ appears to be the most promising of the four zones if only geographical advantages are considered. The Xiamen SEZ ranks second, as it has some definite attractions. Transportation facilities in and to the Shantou SEZ are less than satisfactory and for this reason it is not expected that any sizeable industrial investment will be drawn in from outside at present. The Zhuhai SEZ seems to be the least attractive as far as industrial development is concerned. However, in terms of potential for tourism, Zhuhai is no less attractive than Shenzhen.

Judging from the progress hitherto achieved, the Shenzhen SEZ has had some success in attracting foreign and overseas Chinese investment for industrial development and through joint ventures in tourism, dairy farming, agriculture and real estate development. The Shenzhen SEZ has certainly capitalized on its geographical advantages and has now become a model for the rest of the country to follow. During his visit to the zone, Deng Xiaoping declared that 'the experience and the development of the Shenzhen SEZ proves the correctness of our SEZ policy' (*Wen Wei Po*, 26 January 1984; and *Cheng Ming*, 1 March 1984).

The Zhuhai SEZ has done reasonably well through joint ventures in tourism, real estate development and industry. It has been reported that since its establishment three years ago (in August 1981), it has concluded 37 joint-venture agreements in port construction, vehicle repair, the distribution of petroleum products, tourism and real estate development. Total contracted investment amounts to US$1.2 billion with industry accounting for 69 per cent, tourism 20 per cent, estate development 9 per cent and others 2 per cent (*Chinese SEZ Handbook*, 1984, p. 244). During his visit on 29 January 1984, Deng commented that '[the] Zhuhai SEZ is good' (*Cheng Ming*, 1 March 1984). This was a fair assessment given the fact that the Zhuhai SEZ has so many geographical limitations.

Neither the Xiamen SEZ nor the Shantou SEZ received favourable comments from the Chinese leaders. Although both of them began to set up infrastructure (the so-called 'five connections and one levelling') in 1982, later than in the Shenzhen and Zhuhai SEZs, the work should have been completed by mid-1984. However, only two factories are now in operation in the Xiamen SEZ and it has concluded only seven joint-venture agreements (these ventures are to be located in the Huli Industrial District of the Xiamen SEZ) (*Chinese SEZ Handbook*, 1984, p. 274). In the Shantou SEZ, only one guest-house and two blocks of general-purpose flatted factories have been completed in the Longhu Industrial District. Altogether, eighteen investment contracts have been concluded and six factories are now in production (*Wen Wei Po*, 20 April 1984).

Although their development is quite modest compared with the growth of the Shenzhen and Zhuhai zones, both the Xiamen and the Shantou zones have finally overcome their teething troubles and have started to move forward. However, large-scale joint-venture (or wholly foreign-owned) enterprises with advanced technology and massive capital investments are still beyond their grasp. This is perhaps why Deng Xiaoping, when he visited the Xiamen SEZ on 9 February 1984, commented that 'the special economic zone should be speeded up and improved', thus expressing his dissatisfaction with the progress of the zone (*Ming Pao*, 23 April 1984). The Shantou SEZ is the only SEZ which Deng did not care to visit. Instead, Hu Yaobang went there to urge the officials of the Shantou zone to do a good job in the hope of giving a boost to their morale (*South China Morning Post*, 21 February 1984). To sum up, neither the Xiamen SEZ nor the Shantou SEZ has matched up to the expectations of the Chinese leaders and their geographical potential is as yet unfulfilled.

Fig. 3.4 The Xiamen SEZ

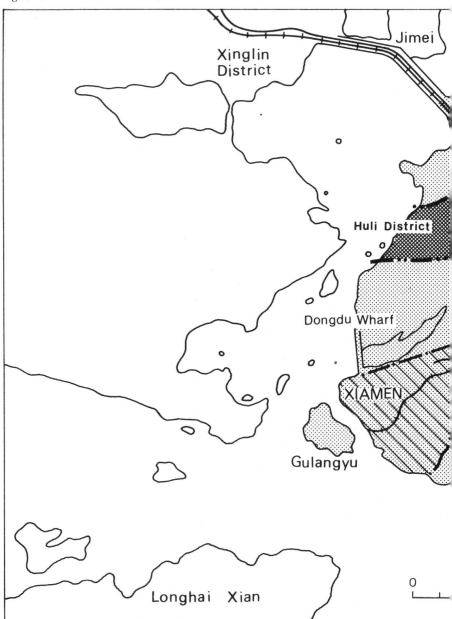

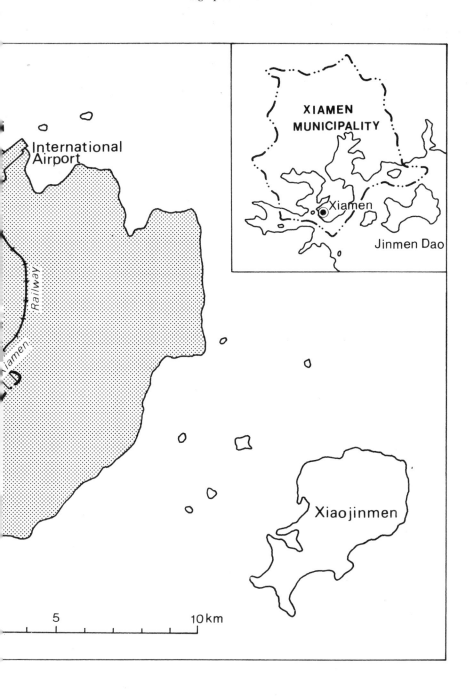

Conclusion

Soon after Deng Xiaoping's visit to the Shenzhen, Zhuhai and Xiamen SEZs and Hu Yaobang's visit to the Shantou SEZ, a major conference was held in Beijing (from 26 March to 6 April 1984) to review policy on the SEZs. However, apart from delegations from the four SEZs, surprisingly representatives from six other districts and cities, namely, Dalian, Qingdao, Ningbo, Wenzhou, Beihai and Hainan Island, were also present (*Wen Wei Po*, 27 March 1984). Perhaps these six had submitted for consideration proposals to launch development programmes similar to those of the SEZs. The first resolution of the conference was even more surprising. Instead of six, altogether fourteen cities and districts are to be awarded the status of 'economic development zone', in addition to Hainan Island which had earlier acquired the status of a 'quasi-special economic zone'. According to the limited information so far released, these economic development zones (EDZs), perhaps with the exception of Hainan Island, will take the form of export processing zones with the emphasis on industrial development. The preferential treatment for industrial investments offered in the SEZs will largely be applicable to these EDZs. The second resolution of the conference was to endorse the enlargement of the Zhuhai SEZ from 6.8 sq km to 15.16 sq km; and to recommend the expansion of the Shantou SEZ from its original size of 1.6 sq km to 52.6 sq km (Chu, Wong and Ng, 1984) and the Xiamen SEZ from 2.5 sq km to the entire Xiamen Island plus an offshore island (125.5 sq km) (*Wen Wei Po*, 21 May 1984). The Shenzhen SEZ, however, will maintain its original size of 327.5 sq km.

The two resolutions made at the conference on the SEZs give much food for thought to 'China-watchers' and raise several questions. First, is it timely to set up so many EDZs which will undoubtedly offer keen competition to the original four SEZs? Second, the original objective in setting up the four SEZs in Guangdong and Fujian, and granting the two provinces special authority in economic affairs, was to take advantage of their special appeal to overseas Chinese capitalists. Does this new development mean that the Chinese government has now shifted its emphasis? Third, does the enlargement of three of the SEZs indicate that the areas originally assigned to them were inadequate thereby hampering their development? If so, what is the optimum size for an SEZ? To answer these questions one has to consider the concept of the export processing zone, the background to China's open-door policy and also the relatively poor geographical endowment of the SEZs (except the Shenzhen SEZ). A further consideration is the possibility of fluctuations in Sino-Japanese and Sino-American relations.

The Chinese open-door policy stemmed initially from China's need to break out of the self-isolation which had been Mao's interpretation of self-reliance. The country's leaders are now anxious to catch up with the West by introducing its capital, technology and management techniques, and thus raise the standard of living. However, the success of the Shenzhen SEZ and to a lesser extent the Zhuhai, Xiamen and Shantou SEZs (and to an even lesser extent the joint-venture projects outside the SEZs), does not dispel the fear in Western countries that China will again close its door sometime in the future. Coincidentally, as of the end of 1983 China has launched a campaign to fight 'spiritual pollution' and 'ideological contamination' and this has aroused much concern in Western nations. With their worries over China's future policy, the Japanese, the Europeans and the Americans are unwilling to run the risk of investing heavily in China. During his visit to China, the Japanese prime minister, Mr Nakasone, explicitly conveyed Japanese concern over the possibility of China reverting to its former path of self-isolation (*South China Morning Post*, 26 March 1984). In order to dispel their doubts and suspicions, China can do no better than to announce further advances in its open-door policy by creating larger SEZs and a further fourteen EDZs. Understandably, this will result in rivalry, albeit very friendly, between the existing SEZs and the newly created EDZs. Given the fact that many EDZs such as Shanghai, Tianjin, Dalian, Qingdao and even Guangzhou, already possess a sound infrastructure dating from before 1949 and far better geographical locations, the Zhuhai, Xiamen and Shantou SEZs will find it difficult to compete with them for foreign industrial investments. Should there be competition for Japanese, European and American investment, these EDZs are undoubtedly better prepared than the SEZs of Guangdong and Fujian, for the geographical endowments of the EDZs are far superior. It is generally conceived that 'these economic development zones will play a major role in modernizing [China] in the final years of the 20th and the first part of the 21st centuries' (*South China Morning Post*, 2 April 1984). The SEZs will at best play a supplementary role.

Because of the limited attraction that the Xiamen and Shantou SEZs have for foreign industrial investment, to develop these areas (for instance, the 2.5 sq km Huli District and 1.6 sq km Longhu District) solely for export processing will severely restrict their potential. A more comprehensive form of development is therefore necessary if these two zones are to survive and grow. The incorporation of adjacent port zones, warehouse areas, tourist resorts and agricultural belts (for producing export-oriented agricultural items) will enable them to maintain a steady flow of foreign exchange earnings on which a modest industrial-agricultural-commercial complex can be built. In fact, the areas which it is proposed to incorporate in the Shantou SEZ have long been prepared for these very purposes (*Beijing Review*, 24 December 1981) although they have not been incorporated into the SEZ and are therefore beyond the jurisdiction of the SEZ authority until the latest proposal is approved. The idea of putting the whole of Xiamen Island under the SEZ authority has been discussed since 1981 (Chen and Chen, 1981, pp. 51–2). Chen and Chen (1981) have argued that it is not only desirable but also necessary from both the developmental and management points of view that the area of the Xiamen SEZ should be extended from the present 2.5 sq km to 125.5 sq km because the original site is just too small for co-ordinated development.

Indeed, given the inefficiency and overlapping of Chinese local governmental structures and the rivalry between various departments (as was to be found in the Shenzhen SEZ before 1982 — see Chapter 11), an under-sized SEZ is hardly able to operate efficiently unless it can gather all necessary resources under its control and within its boundaries. Will the new EDZs in other coastal cities encounter the same difficulties as the Zhuhai, Shantou and Xiamen SEZs have experienced? This question remains open and needs time before it can be answered, but it certainly warrants closer study in the future.

PART II: THE ECONOMIC POTENTIAL OF SHENZHEN — INDUSTRY, TOURISM AND AGRICULTURE

4. Trends and Strategies of Industrial Development

KWAN-YIU WONG

IN contrast to export processing zones elsewhere in Asia, the Shenzhen Special Economic Zone was planned as a comprehensive economic entity, embracing tourism, manufacturing and agricultural production, as well as commercial and real estate development. However, industrial growth has been accorded top priority and industrial production will form the basis of the zone's economy. It has been reiterated by the mayor of Shenzhen Municipality that manufacturing industry is the fundamental production activity on which the generation of economic benefits for the SEZ depends, and that industry should be attracted to the zone by all possible means. However, in the formative period of Shenzhen's development, it has obviously not been possible to fulfil this objective. As figures for November 1981 indicate, more than two-thirds (67.8 per cent) of the foreign capital invested in Shenzhen went to tourism and real estate development and only 16.3 per cent to manufacturing activities (Wong, 1982, p. 28). The main reason is that investment in industry requires a large capital outlay and a long period of return whereas in real estate development, for example, the period of return is short and the profit margin high. Furthermore, the lack of an efficient administrative, legal and financial system has also deterred many potential investors from putting large sums of capital into manufacturing undertakings. They prefer to wait and see how things develop before committing themselves. The inadequate provision of infrastructure also has a negative effect on investment. As a result, overseas participation in the initial period of Shenzhen's industrial development was confined primarily to small enterprises involved in intermediate processing or assembly work.

At the end of 1981 the average investment for each manufacturing project was only about HK$840,000 whereas the averages for other types of economic activities were much higher: HK$47 million for housing projects, HK$439 million for tourism and HK$18 million for commercial development (Wong, 1982, p. 28). Thus, the primary objective of emphasizing industrial production in the hope of importing advanced technology and modern management skills has not been realized in the early stages of Shenzhen's development.

Certain changes since the end of 1981, however, seem to have improved this situation. First, the enactment in November 1981 of four sets of SEZ Provisional Regulations governing labour and wages, entry and exit, business registration, and land administration, represented a change of practice from the traditional reliance on personal contacts to the more impersonal rule of law. Although these Provisional Regulations are only general principles and their scope so far is limited, their enactment was a welcome sign of improvement. Second, a complete reorganization of the administrative structure of Shenzhen was accomplished in early 1982 resulting in a less cumbersome investment procedure, a clearer division of responsibilities, the dismissal of some redundant staff and greater administrative efficiency (see Chapter 11). Consequent upon this streamlining of the administration, the functions and operations of the Shenzhen government were more clearly defined and became more comprehensible to the outside investor, giving him greater confidence to invest in large-scale and long-term projects. Finally, in 1982 there were serious attempts on the part of the Shenzhen government to examine and review the development plan of the SEZ (which had been revised in November 1981). In April 1982, the Social and Economic Development Plan of the Shenzhen SEZ was reviewed by scholars and professionals from China, and later (in September) examined and discussed by experts from Hong Kong. In May 1982, a meeting on 'The Recent Industrial Development of the Shenzhen SEZ' was also held. As a result of this series of seminars and meetings, the objectives and directions of development were more clearly specified. The importance of industrial production was strongly emphasized. (By the end of 1983, for example, of the total amount of investment in economic activities in the Shenzhen SEZ, 43.6 per cent was in manufacturing while real estate and tourism together accounted for 31.6 per cent (*People's Daily*, 29 March 1984).) Although the long-term plan concedes that a large percentage of total investment will finance the provision of public utilities (for example, water, electricity, communications and transportation) and housing (including housing for workers and local staff), industrial development will account for the lion's share of investment among all the economic activities. Furthermore, it is also expected that manufacturing industries will generate a significant proportion of the employment in the Shenzhen SEZ and will absorb at least 40 per cent of the work-force in the zone. As a result of these recent developments, the investment environment in Shenzhen, particularly for industry, has certainly improved.

Characteristics of Industrial Development

Industrial Structure

Despite the fact that tourism and real estate development have initially had greater success than manufacturing in attracting overseas capital to Shenzhen, the number of investment projects in industry far exceeds that of other activities. In August 1981, 66 per cent of the total number of projects in Shenzhen were connected with manufacturing (*Economic Reporter*, 11 November 1981), and by the end of 1983, the figure had increased to 73.7 per cent (*People's Daily*, 29 March 1984). These covered a wide variety of ventures ranging from the basic light industries such as electronics and textiles to more sophisticated industries like motor vehicle assembly, printing and container manufacture. However, the industrial structure of the Shenzhen region has so far been heavily biased towards light industrial production.

A comparison of statistics for 1978 and 1981 (Table 4.1) shows not only the predominance of light industries in the overall industrial structure but also the growing importance of such industries in Shenzhen since the inception of the SEZ. In 1978, light industries accounted for about 83 per cent of the total value of manufacturing production in Shenzhen, then known as Bao'an County (Wu and Yi, 1981). This already represented a very high percentage compared, for example, with the 1978 figure for the whole of China in which the share of light industries in total manufacturing production was only 43.1 per cent (*Xinhua News Agency*, 11 January 1982; also Feuchtwang and Hussain, 1983, Chapter 1). There are two factors largely responsible for the disparity between the national figures and the Shenzhen figures. Firstly, Chinese economic development strategy during the Maoist period and before the downfall of the 'Gang of Four' was influenced by the emphasis placed on heavy industry, with the result that light industrial production was seriously neglected at the national level. Secondly, Shenzhen was originally a small border town and its major activity was agricultural production. Resources for any large-scale industrial development, particularly of heavy industry, were very limited. Statistics for Shenzhen's industrial production revenue in 1978 show that food products accounted for almost two-thirds (63.7 per cent) of the total (Wu and Yi, 1981). It is worth noting, however, that the second major category of industry in Shenzhen

Table 4.1 Changes in the Industrial Structure of Shenzhen, 1978–81

	Light Industries	Heavy Industries
	(percentage of total value of production)	
1978	82.9	17.1
1979	n/a	n/a
1980	85.0	15.0
1981	93.0	7.0

Source: Wong, 1982, p. 47.

was machinery production (about 10 per cent of the total value): this reflects a continuation of the salient features of China's former industrial development policy.

In the wake of the establishment of the SEZ, the share of light industries in the total value of manufacturing production in Shenzhen had increased to 93 per cent by 1981. The share of heavy industries, on the other hand, dropped from 15 per cent to 7 per cent in the space of one year (1980–1). Such growth in the light industrial sector may be attributed to several factors. First, changes in China's economic policy since the death of Mao Zedong, and especially after 1978, have led to a readjustment of the economic development strategy, placing greater emphasis now on light rather than on heavy industrial production. The result is a marked shift in industrial composition from heavy to light industries. Figures for the whole of China show that the share of light industries in total manufacturing production increased from 43.1 per cent in 1978 to 51.3 per cent in 1981 (*Xinhua News Agency*, 11 January 1982). Second, in the formative period of the SEZ when the details of the investment environment were not well known outside China, investors were not prepared to engage in heavy industrial production that required considerable capital expenditure. Rather, manufacturing was confined to small-scale processing or assembly work, taking advantage of the labour resources available in the special zone. Hence, in the early stages of development of the Shenzhen SEZ, labour-intensive light industries such as electronics found favour among overseas investors. Foreign investment in heavy industrial production, on the other hand, has been quite modest. Only the Shekou Industrial Zone has managed to achieve some success in this respect. A third factor, which is very much related to the second one, was the lack of precise development plans when the SEZ was first established and the absence of an efficient administrative and legal structure to channel investment in the proper direction. In order to attract overseas capital and to launch the special zone, the interests of the potential investor were often given greater consideration than the needs or the development goals of the zone. As a result, a large number of small-scale light industrial activities, including some obsolete and polluting ones, were set up, taking advantage of the cheaper production costs in the SEZ to make quick profits from a minimum amount of capital input. As of 1984, the desire of the Shenzhen government for a massive introduction of capital and of technology-intensive industries has yet to be realized.

It is to be expected that in the near future light industries will continue to predominate in the industrial sector in Shenzhen even though the full development of manufacturing projects in the Shekou Industrial Zone will increase the proportion of heavy industrial production. The construction of large numbers of standard factory buildings (multi-storey buildings housing separate production units) in Bagualing, Shangbu and Shekou will further facilitate the setting up of small light manufacturing plants. However, even within the light industrial sector, changes in the main types of manufacturing activities have also been apparent since the establishment of the SEZ. In 1978, production was dominated by the food-processing industry, accounting for more than two-thirds of the total value of light industrial output, followed by building materials, timber, paper and textiles (Wu and Yi, 1981). Production from the electronics industry was negligible. However, in 1982, 35 per cent of the total value of manufacturing production came from the electronics industry (*Wen Wei Po*, 10 September 1983). It has experienced meteoric growth during the last couple of years, with capital and expertise coming largely from neighbouring Hong Kong. The food-processing industry, on the other hand, has dropped to a secondary position and many traditional methods of food-processing are now being replaced by new lines of production. Other light industries of significance today include textiles and clothing, furniture, printing and building materials. Machinery manufacture remains the major activity in the heavy industrial sector. Generally speaking, the establishment of an SEZ initiates a gradual diversification of industry. Electronics, however, will remain the leading industry in the near future, and Shenzhen's land and labour resources will continue to be attractive for this type of industry. But even within the electronics industry, there are great opportunities for product diversification and for the introduction and adoption of sophisticated production techniques.

Industrial Location

Industrial development in Shenzhen Municipality can be classified into three broad regions: (a) the Shenzhen SEZ; (b) the Shekou Industrial Zone; and (c) industrial districts in other parts of the municipality such as Kuichong, Buji, Longgang, Longhua and Songgang (see Fig. 4.1). Some explanation of this classification is necessary because of the complex structure of the Shenzhen SEZ. The Shekou Industrial Zone, although physically part of the SEZ, has gained the status of a separate zone and is managed by the China Merchants' Steam Navigation Co. Ltd. (CMSN) of Hong Kong. Negotiations for development are handled in Hong Kong and the CMSN has the authority to make decisions on overseas investment projects in Shekou (see Chapter

Fig. 4.1 Industrial Districts in Shenzhen Municipality

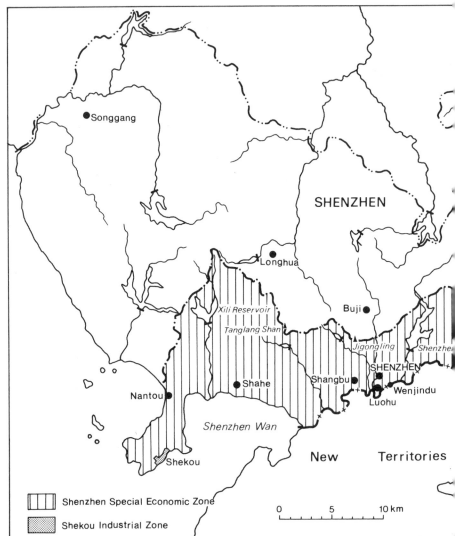

11 on the complex administrative structure of Shenzhen). Although still closely co-ordinated with the Shenzhen SEZ, the Shekou district has obtained a certain degree of autonomy in its operation. With regard to industrial districts in other parts of Shenzhen Municipality, Chapter 1 has already pointed out the flexibility of China's special zone system in offering preferential treatment to firms setting up business in districts adjacent to, but outside the confines of, the SEZs. Applications for projects in these districts are more closely scrutinized and approval will be offered only to enterprises that the Chinese government considers to be desirable, that is to say those employing advanced production techniques or pioneering industries. It is, therefore, expected that industrial development in these outlying districts will be rather

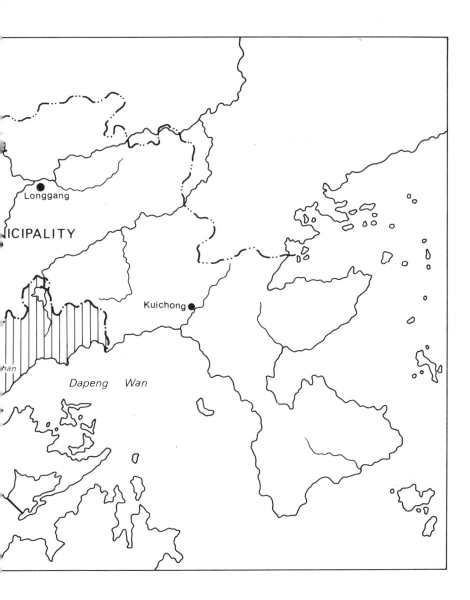

limited as these areas also suffer from an inadequate infrastructure. Thus, only manufacturing districts within the confines of the Shenzhen SEZ (including Shekou) will be considered in this chapter.

With very few exceptions, it is planned to develop industrial districts in the central and western sections of the Shenzen SEZ. Topography, accessibility and infrastructure provision are the main factors accounting for this pattern. A total land area of 15 sq km within the Shenzhen SEZ has been assigned for industrial use and the major industrial districts have already been designated (see Fig. 4.2). Table 4.2 provides some basic information about these industrial districts. However, it must be pointed out that at present only four of these districts are being actively developed: Shekou, Shahe,

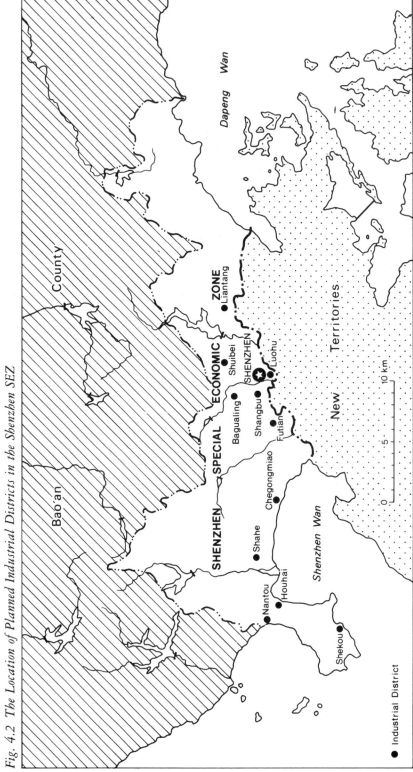

Fig. 4.2 The Location of Planned Industrial Districts in the Shenzhen SEZ

Table 4.2 Planned Industrial Districts in the Shenzhen SEZ

District	Area (sq km)	Major Types of Industries
Liantang	0.8	Light industries/Textiles
Shuibei	0.5	Metal/Machinery
Shangbu	1.4	Electronics
Bagualing	1.0	Comprehensive
Futian	4.8	Comprehensive
Chegongmiao	2.0	Comprehensive
Shahe	1.0	Comprehensive
Houhai	1.0	Comprehensive
Shekou	1.0	Comprehensive
Nantou	1.5	Comprehensive

Source: Personal communication.

Shangbu and Bagualing. The Shekou Industrial Zone, situated at the western end of the Shenzhen SEZ, has a direct hydrofoil connection with Hong Kong and is, as mentioned before, under the management of the CMSN. An industrial land-use plan was first published at the end of 1979, and later revised in 1981 (CMSN, 1981): it provides an idea of the types of industries to be developed in the area (Fig. 4.3). Compared with other industrial districts in Shenzhen, Shekou will concentrate on heavy industrial development which is generally more capital-intensive and requires much space. A number of manufacturing activities which are directly or indirectly related to the main lines of business of the CMSN, that is shipping and navigation, have already been established. These industries have given rise to a certain degree of industrial linkage as they comprise activities such as shipbreaking, steel refining and rolling, the production of oxygen, acetylene, boat paint and fibre glass, the manufacture of containers, shipbuilding and marine engineering. Light industries, too, have been developed in Shekou and include, for example, flour milling and confectionery production. Several standard factories have been constructed: these have enabled smaller firms to engage in light industrial production. Enterprises manufacturing toys and household electrical appliances are amongst the industries being attracted to these standard factories in Shekou.

The Shahe Industrial District is, like Shekou, not under the direct administration of the Shenzhen government. Rather, it is managed by the Overseas Chinese Enterprise Company (which is controlled by the Committee on Overseas Chinese Affairs of Guangdong Province). It is at present producing a variety of electronics products such as radio-cassettes and television sets, but plans have been made for the region to diversify its production into more sophisticated products such as integrated circuits,

Fig. 4.3 The Revised Land-use Zoning Plan of Shekou

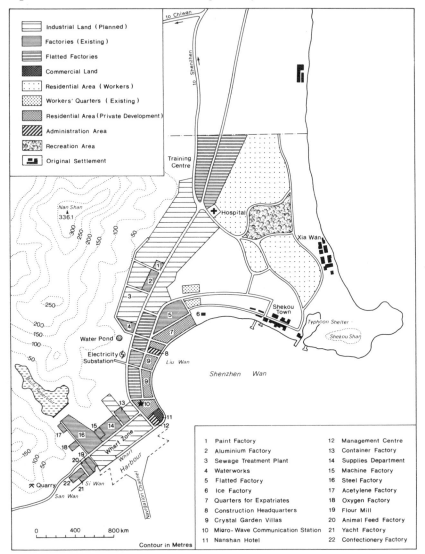

precision meters and computers. Other light industrial activities such as food processing, and furniture and carton paper manufacture are also being undertaken. Shahe, however, is less favourably located than the other three industrial districts. Although it lies along the main Shenzhen-Nantou road, it is much farther away than Shangbu or Bagualing from the major development centres of Luohu and Shenzhen Town, and it does not have direct access to the sea as does Shekou. Furthermore, there is not adequate provision of infrastructure and other basic facilities. It is, therefore, expected that Shahe's development will proceed more slowly than that of the other established industrial districts.

Shangbu is a new urban centre situated just to the west of Shenzhen Town. It is centrally located and has since the very beginning been successful in attracting a number of overseas firms to participate in its industrial development programme. Projects involving foreign investment include a motor vehicle assembly plant and a printing factory. However, Shangbu is planned to be the centre of the electronics industry in the Shenzhen SEZ. Some sizeable electronics firms are already in full operation. Given its favourable location and accessibility, Shangbu is expected to grow into an important centre of concentrated industrial development.

Bagualing is located to the north of Shangbu and has been actively developed only since 1982. In contrast to the other industrial districts, its major development has been in the construction of a number of standard factories supplied with basic utilities. It therefore tends to cater for the needs of smaller enterprises which can commence production there without having to spend huge amounts of capital on plant construction. It will be developed into a comprehensive industrial district. Light manufacturing production, however, will dominate.

Apart from the major districts just mentioned, it is necessary to note that there are also a few old industrial centres in Shenzhen which date from before the designation of the SEZ. They are located in or near the original urban areas of Luohu and Shenzhen Town. Manufacturing development is confined to small-scale light industries such as arts and crafts, textiles, footwear, clothing and building materials. Some of these indigenous industries have benefited from the injection of capital from Hong Kong and overseas since the establishment of the SEZ. Others, however, continue to survive with limited local resources and many remain as collective industrial enterprises.

Finally, it must also be noted that the designation of the ten industrial districts does not rule out the possibility of the establishment of other manufacturing centres within the Shenzhen SEZ as a result of further developments. For example, the likelihood that Chiwan, Mawan and adjacent regions may be developed into a centre for the petrochemical industry is very high following the recent development of Chiwan as a rear service base for the South China Sea oil exploration programme.

Industrial Organization

Industrial production in Shenzhen is being carried out at different levels. Although much attention has been given in recent years to investment projects involving overseas capital, it must be remembered that there is still an indigenous industrial sector which existed before the inception of the

SEZ and which is growing with (rather than being replaced by) the zone. It may be convenient to organize industrial development in Shenzhen into three major categories: state-owned industries, industries involving overseas capital and indigenous industries.

The number of state-owned manufacturing undertakings is small because the main purpose of setting up the SEZ is to attract overseas investment. The government therefore works with private enterprises. Foreign participation in the industrial development programme can take different forms, for example, sole proprietorship, joint ventures, co-operative development, compensation trade and intermediate processing (see Wong, 1982, pp. 25–7), although the last two means are generally not encouraged. By the end of 1983, about 9.6 per cent of all investment items were fully foreign-owned, the rest being mainly joint ventures and co-operative development projects (*People's Daily*, 29 March 1984).

As for indigenous industries, there are now about 200 rural collective units and 16 urban collective enterprises in the Shenzhen SEZ (fieldwork, 1983). The rural collectives are small operations belonging to six former communes and their brigades in Shenzhen. The urban collectives are usually larger in scale and are mainly located around Luohu and Shenzhen Town. These enterprises are mostly engaged in light industrial production (of such goods as plastic flowers, wigs, textiles and clothing). However, with the growth of the SEZ and the adoption of a more open economic policy, the urban collectives have been able to undertake an increasing amount of intermediate processing work for outside firms (particularly those from Hong Kong) which has helped to sustain the growth of these production units. Both the supply of materials and the market have now become more reliable and the technical advice which is always available from the participating firms will, to a greater or lesser extent, upgrade local production techniques. The rural collectives, though many in number, do not contribute significantly to industrial production in Shenzhen. However, they are valuable 'reserves' for an expansion of the local industrial sector which may become necessary as more and more rural land is redeemed by the government for urban development. According to Chinese regulations, the status of residents thus affected will automatically be transferred, or reclassified, from rural to urban, and the rural collectives will also become urban collectives. Such a process is expected to continue in the future. With the growth of the SEZ and with increasing urbanization, the number of urban collective enterprises will also expand. Greater opportunities will then be available for these enterprises to engage in intermediate processing for outside firms. This may help to improve the basic skills of local workers, effect a gradual increase in indigenous entrepreneurship and even achieve the accumulation of some local capital. If properly managed, these urban collective industries may become a useful partner to the larger foreign-funded ventures — for example, in undertaking subcontracting work for modern plants, and thus achieving industrial linkage between large and small, as well as foreign and local, production units.

Suggested Strategies for Manufacturing Development

Development by Stages

Before its establishment as an SEZ, Shenzhen was a settlement of about 20,000 people with a very weak industrial base (in terms of labour supply, technology and infrastructure). In order to develop this area into a modern manufacturing centre, it is necessary to strengthen this base in a systematic fashion. It is envisaged that the industrialization of the Shenzhen SEZ may be divided into three stages.

In the initial stage, because of the zone's weak industrial base, it is perhaps not essential to attract capital-intensive and technology-intensive industries as is advocated by the Shenzhen authorities. Rather the focus should be on small but modern industries which can help to promote exports, accumulate capital and develop the entrepreneurial skills of the local people. Thus, labour-intensive undertakings are acceptable at this stage. Large manufacturing firms employing sophisticated technology and advanced equipment in their production lines are probably not appropriate because of the lack of local technicians and skilled workers. Production should involve only relatively simple processing and assembly work. However, care must be taken not to attract from abroad (for instance from Hong Kong) obsolete and polluting industries which are no longer profitable in their original place of production but which may be able to make some short-term gains in Shenzhen by taking advantage of its cheap labour costs, low rents and other preferential terms.

The choice of industries to be developed in the second stage should be more selective, especially in terms of the level of technology. Rather than confining the range to processing or assembly, greater emphasis should be placed on product diversification within existing industries, especially in the manufacture of more sophisticated goods of a higher value whose production requires greater skill. For example, in the electronics industry, the initial stage would be the assembly of products like radios and cassettes; but the second stage should start with the production of essential components and integrated circuits, gradually proceeding to the manufacture of more advanced products such as precision meters and micro-computers. With product diversification and the accumulation of technology and capital, the industrial structure will likewise change and production will become more technology-intensive. The number of medium- and large-scale firms will also increase to make use of the economies of scale. This has the effect of raising the production and management skills of the local staff and helping to build up local entrepreneurship.

In the final stage of the industrialization process, attention should be given to industrial diversification, particularly into industries with advanced technology and modern scientific methods of management. Emphasis should be placed on the application of sophisticated production techniques, the use of modern equipment, involvement in the design and production of high-quality products and active participation in research and development (R & D). However, in order for these goals to be achieved, it is essential to build up a firm foundation in the previous stages of industrial development and to have a team of trained local staff to support the operation of the system.

Because of the large area of the Shenzhen SEZ, planning for the location of industries is also important. The problems of accessibility and the provision of infrastructure do not allow the simultaneous development of all the industrial districts at present. Besides, it is unwise to spread the limited resources currently available over too large an area. Concentrated development of certain central locations can reap the benefits of external economies of scale. In Shenzhen, therefore, industries should now be attracted to Shangbu, Luohu, Bagualing, Shekou and perhaps Shahe, all of which possess sufficient provision for large-scale urban and industrial development. The construction of standard factories supplied with all the necessary facilities in Shangbu, Bagualing and Shekou is probably appropriate at this stage as it will allow small- to medium-scale undertakings to start production at an earlier date. At a later stage, when massive land development programmes by private developers or by the government are complete, then industries can spread to places like Futian, Chegongmiao and Houhai. But it will still be necessary to co-ordinate development among these districts, for example with regard to the types of industries to be set up or the scale of production. This is not always easy particularly because huge parcels of land in Shenzhen are now being granted to various private developers for land production and the provision of infrastructure. Problems of co-ordination between the developers and the government have already become apparent. Even more serious is the lack of co-ordination between the various private developers. Perhaps a much stronger administrative machinery is required to steer the different phases of industrial development in Shenzhen on to their proper course.

Industrial Allocation

In considering the allocation of industries to an area, it is advisable to maximize the utilization of local resources and advantages. In contrast to areas of industrial development in other parts of China, the Shenzhen SEZ is an export processing establishment whose capital, technology and raw materials are largely imported from outside and whose products are mainly destined for export. Thus, it is not just the needs of China that have to be taken into account but also international economic and market considerations. The geographical proximity of Shenzhen to Hong Kong (one of the major ports and financial centres of the world) means that industrial development in the two places should be quite closely related. It has been shown (Wong,

1982) that most of the capital, technology and material for manufacturing development in Shenzhen comes from Hong Kong and this trend is likely to continue in the foreseeable future. Hong Kong boasts a flourishing industrial sector but room for development is now very limited: thus entrepreneurs in Hong Kong should find Shenzhen a good location for expansion. It is envisaged that industrial development in the SEZ should be able to complement that of Hong Kong. This needs to be taken into consideration in the allocation of industries in Shenzhen.

Shenzhen has an abundant supply of firm land which requires little levelling. This has proved to be particularly attractive to industries that require a lot of space. Although the Shenzhen SEZ has only recently evolved from a small border town, labour can be easily recruited from other parts of China and is never in short supply. Conditions are thus favourable also for the establishment of labour-intensive industries. What seems to be lacking at present is a team of technical and managerial staff; the hope is that this can be built up with training and experience. Although most raw materials have to be imported into the zone, Shenzhen does possess fairly good resources as far as building materials are concerned.

It is thus obvious that the question of industrial allocation in the Shenzhen SEZ should be considered from two angles. First, full use should be made of the advantages offered by the special zone, such as land, labour and its geographical location. Second, it should be remembered that the SEZs are important experimental stations in China's present drive for modernization and that they are, therefore, expected to play a leading role in the import of modern production technology and management skills. Under these guiding principles, the industrial development strategy of Shenzhen should aim, on the one hand, at the integration of labour-intensive and technology-intensive industries, and on the other, at the integration of small, medium-scale and large enterprises. Labour-intensive industries can fully utilize the labour resources of Shenzhen and provide greater opportunities for employment. Technology-intensive industries, on the other hand, can upgrade the standard of production techniques and will have practical significance for China's programme of industrial modernization. The integration of small, medium-scale and large enterprises does not mean the simple co-existence of firms engaged in different scales of production. Rather, it is hoped that through proper planning and co-ordination, it will be possible to establish links in production between the different levels. For instance, smaller enterprises will be doing subcontracting work, such as the manufacture of parts, for larger firms. So the industrial structure is to be composed of manufacturing units whose lines of production should ideally be related to a certain degree. That this interdependence is essential to the successful implementation of industrial programmes in developing countries can be seen in the past performance of Japan. Unfortunately this co-ordination has not been achieved in most South-east Asian countries. Small but modern firms require less capital outlay in their establishment and their production is more flexible in the sense that they can adjust to market needs. These firms can also contribute to the growth of local entrepreneurship. It is envisaged that the skeleton of Shenzhen's industrial development will be these small- to medium-sized enterprises. The construction of large numbers of standard factories will greatly facilitate such development. Large firms, on the other hand, will add much vigour to the system, help to upgrade the levels of production and provide the nuclei for satellite industries and downstream production activities to develop.

Based on the above discussion, the main types of industries that may be allocated to the Shenzhen SEZ can be conveniently grouped into the following categories.

The Electronics Industry

This industry is particularly suited to the Shenzhen SEZ for obvious reasons. Geographical proximity to Hong Kong, which has a flourishing modern sector in the manufacture of electronics products, means that expertise and capital can easily be channelled across the border. As Hong Kong has advanced to the stage of adopting high technology for the manufacture of sophisticated products, much of the production of components and simple assembly work can be undertaken in Shenzhen, taking advantage of its ample supply of labour and lower wage rates. The electronics industry allows production at different levels of sophistication and can thus adapt to the circumstances of the newly established SEZ. As a result, the electronics industry has been given considerable attention since the formative period of industrial development in Shenzhen and has now proceeded from the assembly of parts to the manufacture of electronics components for such products as televisions, radio-cassettes and record-players. However, there are still ample opportunities for expansion to other lines of production, including, for example, electronics instruments and meters, micro-computers and word processors, radio communication and navigation aids, electronic consumer goods such as heaters and microwave ovens, and new electronics products for the television and broadcasting industries. The electronics industry will probably account for a high proportion of the industrial output of Shenzhen in the years to come. According to a report by the mayor of Shenzhen, in 1982 the electronics industry employed more than 5,000 trained workers and over 400 technicians, occupied a total floor space of 110,000 sq m, engaged in more than 40 different lines of assembly and production work, and accounted for 35 per cent of the total value of industrial production (*Wen Wei Po*, 10 September 1983). By the end of 1983, there were more than 60 electronics factories in operation in the Shenzhen SEZ, employing over 13,000 workers and producing more than 100 different products ranging from basic electronics components, household appliances, televisions and broadcasting equipment to computers and precision meters (*People's Daily*, 29 March 1984).

Textiles and Clothing

These industries will be developed to take advantage of the labour resources and traditional skills available, and will be concerned primarily with the production of cotton, wool and synthetic fibre textile products and clothes. However, to modernize the industry, emphasis should be placed not only on improving the equipment used but also on developing high-quality design and tailoring.

Building Materials

This is also one of the traditional industries in Shenzhen which has developed using local resources. Expansion and modernization of the industry will be possible with the injection of overseas capital and technology. The intention is to produce high-quality cement, marble and light synthetic building materials, metallic building materials and building and decoration products.

Food Processing

This used to be the largest industry in Shenzhen, but since the establishment of the SEZ, its development has been greatly overshadowed by other industries. Changes in the nature of production within the food industry are necessary. Attention has now to be diverted from the traditional processing of agricultural produce to other lines of production such as beer and other beverages, confectionery, nutritional food, dairy products and coffee.

The Light Industrial Sector

This is to include a whole range of consumer goods. The sector will evolve towards a diversification of products and the modernization of the production process. Apart from maintaining some traditional arts and crafts, the light industrial sector should diversify into the manufacture of furniture, stationery, plastic products, electrical appliances such as fans, heaters and light fittings, cosmetics and chemical products and printing. This group of industries will feature significantly in the urban collective industrial sector.

Metal and Machinery

This set of industries has been given considerable attention in the past and will continue to expand and modernize with the continued growth of the SEZ. Future development should be centred on the production of advanced electrical appliances and equipment for household use (for example, air-conditioners), refrigerating equipment, elevators and various kinds of machine tools.

The Petrochemical Industry

Consequent upon the development of Chiwan as the rear service base for the South China Sea oil exploration, it is hoped that the Shenzhen SEZ will play an important role in developing the petrochemical industry to make use of the resources available. It is anticipated that some large oil refineries will be constructed together with acetylene plants for the production of synthetic fibres, synthetic resin and synthetic rubber.

The Feedstuffs Industry

Given that China is still predominantly an agricultural country, the development of modern agriculture-related industries is always welcome. The Shenzhen authorities would do well to build feedstuff processing plants in Shenzhen that will produce scientific mixed feeds for livestock farming, arable farming and the stock-breeding industry.

The above eight categories of industry summarize the main directions of manufacturing development to be followed in the Shenzhen SEZ in the years to come. The scale and speed in the growth of individual industries depend not only on China's plans and needs but also on the interest of foreign entrepreneurs and the investment environment of the SEZ. It is now apparent that the electronics industry has gathered the greatest momentum — this is characteristic of industrial development in EPZs in other parts of Asia. Other groups of industries that are expected to expand quite rapidly in the near future will be those that existed in Shenzhen prior to the establishment of the SEZ, for instance, the building materials industry, the manufacture of textiles and clothing, some light industries producing consumer goods and food processing. Production skills in these industries have accumulated over many years to form a good base for modern firms to build on. Growth in other industries will probably depend on the outcome of new developments. For example, the petro-chemical industry will have to wait upon the outcome of the oil exploration programme.

The Targets of Industrial Development

Recent developments have indicated that manufacturing will ultimately become the predominant economic activity in the Shenzhen SEZ. It is expected that industries will grow at a fairly rapid rate, both in terms of the number of factories and the number of persons employed. At the same time, there will be a gradual shift from labour-intensive to capital-intensive and technology-intensive industries. Concurrently, the number of large production firms operating in the SEZ is also expected to increase over the years. Some of the basic targets for industrial development in the Shenzhen SEZ are shown in Table 4.3. A rapid rate of industrial growth is predicted, with manufacturing employment planned to increase fourfold between 1985 and the year 2000. It is also clear from the table that the average number of workers per factory will decrease with time, from about 250 in 1985 to 144 in the year 2000, meaning that the production units will, on average,

Table 4.3 Targets for Industrial Development

Year	No. of Factories	No. Employed in Manufacturing	Total Area of Industrial Land
1985	200	50,000	2.0 sq km
1990	470	80,000	4.7 sq km
2000	1,500	200,000	15.0 sq km

Source: Personal communication; and *Chinese SEZ Handbook*, 1984, p. 26.

become less labour-intensive. This is of course in accordance with the Shenzhen government's intention of placing greater emphasis on capital-intensive and technology-intensive industries.

It is also necessary to view the development targets of manufacturing activities in the Shenzhen SEZ in terms of monetary value. Table 4.4 summarizes the main predictions for production, investment and productivity. The value of industrial production is expected to increase eight times between 1985 and the year 2000. Using 1980 as the base year when the total value of industrial production was Rmb 51 million, the projected value of Rmb 96 billion by the year 2000 gives an average annual growth rate of 29.9 per cent. The maintenance of such a growth rate over a twenty-year period will be a tremendous task. Labour productivity is also expected to increase substantially during that period. In 1980, industrial productivity was Rmb 5,600 per worker per annum: this figure is projected to grow to Rmb 60,000 by the year 2000, giving an average annual growth rate of 12.6 per cent. The total amount of investment in manufacturing, too, is predicted to increase by 640 per cent, or more than seven times, between 1985 and the year 2000. However, it is important to note that the very nature of the SEZ means that, in the process of development and growth, dependence on foreign investment will be paramount. These target figures may be quite meaningless as the Chinese government itself is unable to determine whether or not they can be achieved. What the Shenzhen authorities can do is to improve the investment climate of the SEZ by making it attractive to foreign investors, so that the targets may be attained. Despite such limitations, the

Table 4.4 Targets for Industrial Production

Year	Value of Production (Rmb million)	Amount of Investment (Rmb million)	Annual Productivity (Rmb/worker)
1985	1,200	500	24,000
1990	3,600	1,200	45,000
2000	9,600	3,700	60,000

Source: Personal communication; *Chinese SEZ Handbook*, 1984; and *Wen Wei Po*, 11 November 1983.

target figures do provide a working objective for the Chinese and at the same time reveal the dimension of industrial development that China expects to achieve in the Shenzhen SEZ. However, the task ahead will be a difficult one.

Conclusion

The Shenzhen SEZ has undoubtedly made some remarkable progress since its inception in 1980. According to a report by the mayor of Shenzhen (*People's Daily*, 29 March 1984), up to the end of 1983, the total value of foreign investment agreements in the zone amounted to HK$132.2 billion (about Rmb 33 billion) of which HK$29.8 billion (Rmb 7.4 billion) had already been spent in the SEZ. Of this total investment of HK$29.8 billion, manufacturing industry accounts for 43.6 per cent (or HK$13.0 billion). The report also specifically mentions cases of the successful introduction of capital- and technology-intensive industries to the area. The report also provides figures for the rates of economic growth during the past few years. The value of industrial production increased almost elevenfold between 1979 (prior to the establishment of the SEZ) and 1983, from Rmb 60.6 million to Rmb 720.4 million. During the same period, financial income grew by 1,090 per cent and foreign exchange earnings rose by 200 per cent. By the end of 1983, there were a total of more than 150 new industrial enterprises in operation in the Shenzhen SEZ (*Chinese SEZ Handbook*, 1984). These are certainly encouraging figures, but the percentages are often inflated because the original base was small, and the continuation of growth will depend on the ability of the Shenzhen government to clear certain bottlenecks and solve a number of problems. Among these problems, the inadequate provision of infrastructure, the lack of a sound legal system and the complicated administrative structure are the most pressing concerns. Despite the fact that up to the end of 1983, a total of Rmb 19.6 billion had been invested in the provision of infrastructure (*People's Daily*, 29 March 1984), many areas still suffer the drawbacks of a poor road system and an inadequate supply of water and electricity. Centrally located districts like Luohu and Shangbu are better provided for, but in many of the eighteen functional areas or districts delineated in the Shenzhen SEZ Master Plan, basic facilities for any large-scale urban and industrial development are still inadequate.

In terms of legal framework, although a number of provisional regulations concerning the SEZs were enacted in September 1981 and January 1984 (see Chapter 11 for details), many of the laws that are of direct concern to overseas investors still require immediate legislative action — for instance, those relating to foreign exchange, taxation and customs.

A determined effort towards the reform of the governmental structure since October 1981 has resulted in more efficient management, and the system is now generally more comprehensible to outside investors. However, certain districts within the Shenzhen SEZ are still being administered by units other than the Shenzhen municipal government, namely the Shekou Industrial Zone which is run by the CMSN and the Shahe Industrial District which is run by the Overseas Chinese Enterprise Company. This arrangement has resulted in the existence of different channels of negotiation which have confused and inconvenienced many potential investors. Furthermore, it is open to debate whether the present practice adopted by the Shenzhen government of granting large pieces of land to overseas private developers for massive land production, infrastructure provision and development is very sensible. The result has been the creation of administrative difficulties in co-ordinating and phasing the various development programmes within Shenzhen. Much conflict, for example, has arisen between the developer and the government in the Futian new town project in terms of the general land-use plan, the transportation system, the intended population and other issues. Any delay in the negotiations over land, transportation or other matters will greatly retard the pace of development in the SEZ.

The Shenzhen government should also place greater emphasis on labour and staff training. The technical skills of workers and labour productivity need to be upgraded. The lack of efficient management personnel and local entrepreneurship must be rectified without delay.

At the beginning of this chapter, it was suggested that, in the formative years of the Shenzhen SEZ, it was worrying to see that much more overseas investment had been channelled towards tourism and real estate development than towards manufacturing industry. However, within the last year or so, the Shenzhen government has repeatedly confirmed that economic development in the zone should be based on industry and considerable efforts have been made to point investment in this direction. It is, therefore, encouraging to find that industrial production revenue in 1983 recorded an almost 100 per cent increase over that of 1982 (*People's Daily*, 29 March 1984). Although the shortcomings of the present legal, financial and administrative systems in Shenzhen still provoke doubts in the minds of some potential investors as to the security and the possible gains of engaging in industrial production in the area, it is quite clear that in the long run manufacturing industry must become the backbone of the special zone economy. Through the introduction of advanced production and management techniques, industries can increase the productivity of the community, bring about the development of ancillary and supporting services and obtain the greatest economic benefits. Moreover, compared with real estate and financial development, investment in manufacturing is less speculative because of the greater capital outlay and the longer period of return. It can thus have more positive effects in stabilizing the economy, as is suggested in the objectives of the social and economic development plan. By the year 2000, manufacturing industry will account for almost 18 per cent of the total investment in the Shenzhen SEZ, far above that of commercial activities, tourism or agriculture. In terms of employment, it is expected that by then, industrial workers will represent 40 per cent of the total labour force and will form the largest employment sector in Shenzhen. If these targets can be achieved, manufacturing will be able to contribute significantly to the economic prosperity of the Shenzhen SEZ, not only in terms of employment generation and attraction of foreign investment, but also in the transfer of technology and management skills, in boosting foreign exchange earnings, and in providing the necessary domestic links and encouraging the development of supporting and related economic activities.

There is undoubtedly great potential for manufacturing growth in the Shenzhen SEZ. It has the locational advantage of being close to Hong Kong which can supply the necessary capital, technology and management skills. Shenzhen also has excellent sites for development and a plentiful supply of labour, together with favourable tax rates, land rents and wage rates. What is needed now is the confidence of investors in participating in this industrialization programme. Such measures as autonomy in the management of businesses, efficiency in Chinese administration and the reduction of unnecessary bureaucracy, ease of movement across the border between Hong Kong and Shenzhen, improvements in labour productivity and working attitudes and the more fundamental factors of provision of infrastructure and the implementation of a sound legal and financial system would all help to build this confidence.

5. Tourism: A Critical Review

MO-KWAN LEE FONG

THE Shenzhen SEZ has endeavoured to promote tourism as a major factor in its development. Tourism is labour-intensive, gives a high profit margin, and its period of return is relatively short.* This is especially important in the initial phase of the development of the Shenzhen SEZ which has to be self-financed and has to break new ground without an enormous injection of funds from the central government in Beijing or from the provincial government of Guangdong (Ceng, 1984). In view of the high return per unit of capital investment and the anticipated demand for recreational facilities from the people of Hong Kong, it is understandable that the Shenzhen SEZ authority should put the tourist industry in the forefront of its ambitious development programme. Foreign investors, mainly from Hong Kong, would like to initiate tourist schemes as a means of testing the Shenzhen SEZ investment climate. The initial capital outlay required for the construction of rudimentary tourist facilities is small and the risk involved is relatively minor. This explains, in fact, why so many tourist resorts in the Shenzhen SEZ have been launched with very little forethought or co-ordination, leading to monotony and to the duplication of recreational facilities (such as shooting, archery, fireworks, horse-riding, swimming, camping and boating) in almost every tourist resort completed before 1981 (Fong, 1982). For the same reason, many tourism projects concluded in the early stages were impractical and over-ambitious and these projects had eventually to be

---

* Complete statistics are not available, but the holiday resort at Xili Reservoir could serve as an example. The resort has borrowed HK$1,500,000 from a Hong Kong investor in the form of compensation trade, Rmb 2,000,000 from Chinese banks, and Rmb 20,000 from the local government. Its revenue over the first two years was as follows:

	Turnover (in Rmb)	Profit (in Rmb)	Foreign Exchange Earned (in HK$)
September 1979 to December 1980	248,415	170,000	372,000
January to October 1981	1,081,000	757,000	2,536,000

Within two years it had repaid all the money borrowed from the Hong Kong investor, and it is expected to recover the entire investment in less than five years.
Source: Yearbook of China's Special Economic Zones, 1983, pp. 198–9.

abandoned. This can be illustrated by the divergence between the significant proportion of total investment committed to the tourist industry in 1980–1 and the much reduced amount of capital actually invested by the end of 1983 (Table 5.1). Of the total amount of investment pledged to the Shenzhen SEZ authority from foreign investors in 1980, a third involved the tourist industry. In 1980 it drew up a list of seven sectors inviting foreign investment in the Shenzhen SEZ. In spite of the rapid increase in the number of real estate projects agreed in 1981, the tourist industry still held second place and accounted for a quarter of the total committed foreign investment. However, the *People's Daily* (29 March 1984) reported that by 1983 manufacturing had at last become the leading sector; the relative importance of other sectors, including the tourist industry, is now rapidly declining.

Apart from the decreasing importance of tourism relative to other areas of development, Table 5.1 also reveals that this industry is one of the three sectors (the others are real estate and agriculture) in which the actual investment at the end of 1983 was lower than the amount of investment committed in mid-1981. Evidently, there was excessive enthusiasm among investors, and within the government, with regard to the development of the tourist industry.

Fortunately, there have been signs since the beginning of 1982 that a more cautious approach has been adopted by the Shenzhen SEZ authority in order to rectify these deficiencies in planning and co-ordination. This chapter seeks to assess the potential of tourism in the Shenzhen SEZ and to review some operational aspects of the industry, including the development plan for the tourist industry up to the year 2000. Finally, the issue of diversification will be discussed and suggestions will be made for improving Shenzhen's surroundings with a view to the tourist industry.

The Latent Demand for Tourist Facilities

It is very difficult to define who would be likely to use tourist facilities in the Shenzhen SEZ. As it is a gateway to the south, all passengers entering China by land from Hong Kong, except for those travelling by the direct train to Guangzhou, have to stop at the border. In 1980, over 5.4 million visitors (most of them Hong Kong Chinese) entered China via Shenzhen (Ceng and Luo, 1983) and the figure has been increasing rapidly since then. Although these transit tourists may not stop at Luohu-Shenzhen for more than a couple of hours, there is scope for Luohu and Shenzhen Town to profit from their presence by offering them food, services and goods, including duty-free goods, thus inducing them to become patrons of Shenzhen's tourist industry.

With the growing reputation of Shenzhen as the most successful Chinese SEZ and with the relaxation of its customs procedures at the 'first line' —

Table 5.1 The Relative Significance of Tourism in Attracting Foreign Investment

	1980[1]			Mid-1981[2]			End of 1983[3]		
	No. of Items	Committed Investment (HK$ million)	Per Cent	No. of Items	Committed Investment (HK$ million)	Per Cent	No. of Items	Actual Investment (HK$ million)	Per Cent
Manufacturing	395	160	10	474	375	15.27	1,847	1,299	43.58
Commerce	14	190	12	12	218	8.87	132	225	7.55
Transport	n/a	n/a	n/a	7	9	0.40	28	37	1.24
Real estate	7	530	30	23	1,090	44.35	59	789	26.47
Tourism	15	540	33	19	562	22.86	16	151	5.06
Agriculture	n/a	n/a	n/a	182	103	4.19	423	45	1.51
Miscellaneous	10	0.6	5	3	101	4.06	n/a	435	14.59
Total	581	1,600	100	720	2,458	100	n/a	2,981	100

Note: n/a = not available.

Sources: 1. Kang Ye (1981).

2. Lu Liao (1981).

3. *People's Daily*, 29 March 1984.

the one separating Hong Kong from Shenzhen — most, if not all, of the tourists visiting Hong Kong, who now number over two and a half million each year, may well spend some time in Shenzhen as part of their Hong Kong programme. The merging of the tourist space (Miossec, 1976) of Hong Kong and Shenzhen into the network of international tourism could enhance the tourist potential of both areas.

As most of the residents of Shenzhen are workers and cadres recruited from various parts of China, there would be a regular flow of people from other parts of the country coming to visit their relatives settled in the Shenzhen SEZ if permission could be obtained for such trips. Similarly, the possibility that overseas buyers of the new housing units in Shenzhen may be able to bring their relatives from Guangdong and other parts of China to reside in the SEZ, would serve as a magnet to draw visitors from Hong Kong and China alike. Most recently, Shenzhen has attracted a great number of tourists from other parts of China who come to Shenzhen for shopping and sightseeing. It is surprising to learn that about forty per cent of purchases in shops in Shenzhen are now made by these tourists (*Wen Wei Po*, 13 August 1984). Surveys of shops in Shatoujiao also indicate the significant contribution of these tourists to the local economy. The reasons for their shopping trips are: (a) that the prices of commodities, notably of clothing and electrical goods, are at least ten per cent lower in Shenzhen than in Guangzhou; (b) that there is a better choice of goods in Shenzhen than in other Chinese cities inland; and (c) the goods available in Shenzhen are more modern (fieldwork, 1983). For how long and to what extent the Shenzhen SEZ can maintain this function as a 'shopping paradise' for tourists from the Chinese hinterland will depend on the permeability of the 'second line', the line separating Shenzhen from the rest of China. It has been reported that, from 1985, the 'second line' will be fully implemented; its possible effect on the movement of goods and people between the Shenzhen SEZ and the rest of China is still uncertain. Judging from the growing prosperity of inland China and the freer movement of people all over China, the potential contribution of inland tourists to the economy of Shenzhen should not be overlooked — unless, of course, the 'second line' becomes entirely impermeable, which is unlikely to happen (fieldwork, 1984).

Local Chinese residents are also potential patrons of the tourist resort facilities. Statistics on their relative importance are not available, since inland Chinese and local Chinese clients are grouped together. In the case of the holiday resort at Xili Reservoir about forty-five per cent of clients belonged to this category (Shenzhen Department of Tourism, 1982). Other sources suggested an even higher percentage of patronage of tourist facilities in Shenzhen by local and inland Chinese clients. For example, the Shenzhen Municipality Tourism Company (formerly the Department of Tourism of the Shenzhen Government, and the largest enterprise in the industry) received about 300,000 tourists in 1983, of whom 100,000 were from Hong Kong and overseas countries (*Chinese SEZ Handbook*, 1984, p. 92). In other words, two-thirds of its clients were local and inland Chinese. Finally, the expatriate staff in the foreign and joint-venture enterprises should not be overlooked for their purchasing power is much higher than that of local Chinese residents.

The Operation and Planning of Tourist Facilities

There are now nineteen major operators in the tourist industry in the Shenzhen SEZ (*Shenzhen Special Zone Daily*, 3 August 1984). All of them, whether state-owned or collective-owned, are organized as commercial entities with the right to develop individual projects with foreign investors. Competition among these operators has become the accepted practice. They must strive for economic efficiency and external links in order to survive. They own and manage hotels, shopping arcades, holiday resorts and recreational complexes, restaurants and fleets of tourist coaches and taxis. This trend of vertical integration seems necessary to the viability of these enterprises, because the demand for services is very seasonal. During weekends and public holidays, the demand for facilities of all kinds in the Shenzhen SEZ is so intense that it would not be possible for an enterprise to assure its clients (especially group travellers) basic services such as lodging, transport and recreation if it did not operate all these services itself. Only on weekdays when demand is low can a better choice of facilities be made available to the public and to individual travellers. In order to stimulate demand and bring about a higher rate of utilization of their facilities, most of these enterprises offer discounts during off-peak periods and on weekdays. This manipulation of demand is common practice for hotel management in capitalist countries, but in China it was first adopted in the Shenzhen SEZ and it is still unusual in other parts of China.

As the first joint-venture enterprises to come into full operation in the formative years of the Shenzhen SEZ, tourist facilities were also pioneers in implementing those reforms which have now become standard for business and personnel management in the SEZs. The Friendship Restaurant and the Bamboo Garden Hotel are two of the projects that have been asked to test the new wage system. From March and April 1982 respectively, the conventional wage system of China in these two enterprises was abolished. Instead, all employees are given higher salaries but fewer subsidies. Their salaries are rated according to the nature of their jobs, their qualifications, performance and the turnover of the firm. Although a basic minimum wage has been guaranteed, the total salary received varies in relation to the worker's performance and the profit of the enterprise in the period of evaluation. A worker who fails to carry out his allotted task receives a reduced salary. Similarly, if the number of rooms occupied (in the case of the Bamboo Garden Hotel) falls below sixty per cent, the 'floating' portion of the wages of all employees will be reduced by one-tenth. Supervisors may keep their position only if they carry out their responsibilities — otherwise they will be relegated to the status of worker and will be replaced by one of their subordinates. The successful implementation of the new wage system and the breaking of the 'iron rice-bowl' in the tourist industry serve as examples to other enterprises in the Shenzhen SEZ (*Yearbook of China's Special Economic Zones*, 1983, pp. 179–84).

Although partly dependent on operational improvements, the viability and profitability of all these enterprises and joint ventures of the Shenzhen tourist industry rely more heavily on the co-ordinated and planned development of the zone's tourist resorts. Since 1982, when the master plan on Shenzhen's land use was formulated, the development of tourist resorts has had to comply with the guidelines of this plan. Out of 98 sq km planned as a built-up area, 4 sq km were allocated exclusively for the development of tourist facilities. However, the area now devoted to tourism is actually much more than the 4 sq km of built-up area, for the reservoirs, beaches and hills are all potentially attractive to tourists. Specifically, it is planned that five reservoirs or lakes (the Shenzhen Reservoir, the Xili Reservoir, the Silver Lake, the Xiangmihu and the Shiyanhu) and four beaches (at Xichong, Dameisha-Xiaomeisha, Shenzhen Bay and Shekou) together with the town centre should be the major centres of tourism in the future and the focal points of tourist development (*Economic Daily*, 26 March 1984). Specific sites have also been designated for present and future expansion and construction up to the year 2000. Each site is assigned to attract different types of tourists in order to ward off the standardization and monotony of tourist facilities characteristic of the earlier resorts. Table 5.2 summarizes the different emphases of the nine tourist resorts that are being planned: this framework will provide a far greater diversity of facilities.

Table 5.2 A Proposed Scheme of Diversity for Tourism in Shenzhen

Sites	Emphases
Shenzhen Reservoir*	Sightseeing
Xili Holiday Resort*	Various activities for youths and teenagers
Xili Asian Sport and Recreation Centre	Car-racing and horse-riding
Bijia Shan Silver Lake*	Quiet retreat and camping
Dameisha-Xiaomeisha*	Seaside activities
Xiangmihu*	Comprehensive
Shiyanhu-Yulu Hot Spring*	Hot-spring convalescent resort with golf course
Xichong	Sailing
Wutongshan	Hiking and convalescent uses

Note: *already in use.
Source: *Chinese SEZ Handbook*, 1983, p. 153.

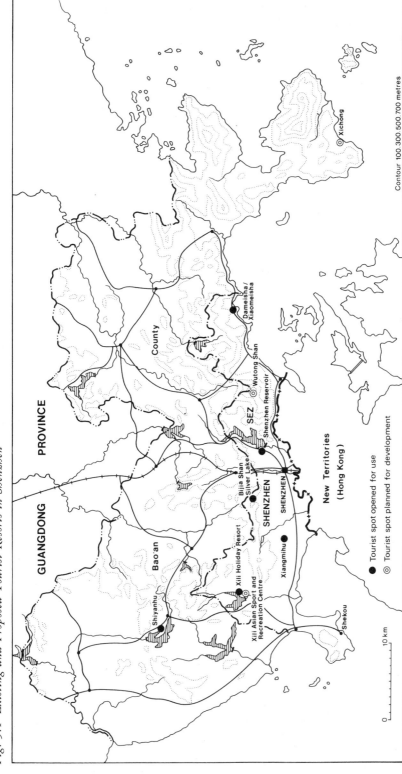

Fig. 5.1 Existing and Proposed Tourist Resorts in Shenzhen

In order to provide enough accommodation, it is planned that by the year 1985 there should be 10 to 15 hotels with 3,000 rooms to accommodate 500,000 tourists annually. And by 1990, there should be 20 to 25 hotels with 5,000 to 6,000 rooms which will cater for 800,000 to 1,000,000 tourists. The targets for the year 2000 are 30 to 50 hotels with 8,000 to 10,000 rooms for 1.3 to 1.5 million tourists.

Recent Performances and Evaluation of the Planning Targets

According to the *Economic Daily* (26 March 1984), the total number of tourists (including foreign and domestic, but probably not transit passengers) patronizing the tourist facilities of the Shenzhen SEZ amounted to 600,000 in 1983. Altogether the tourist operators collected HK$80 million in the form of foreign exchange. In 1984, the prosperity of the tourist industry continued. By the middle of the year, it had entertained over 1 million tourists and collected HK$50 million in foreign exchange (*Shenzhen Special Economic Zone Daily*, 3 August 1984). By the end of 1984, the total number of tourists should exceed 2 million and the amount of foreign exchange earned should be more than HK$100 million. Given that the visible export trade of the Shenzhen SEZ amounted to HK$404.9 million in 1983 (*Economic Daily*, 26 March 1984), the foreign exchange earnings from tourism in the form of invisible exports was almost a fifth of the size of visible exports. This confirms that tourism is an industry that offers high margins of profit which can assist in the accumulation of capital and foreign exchange for the development of other sectors of the economy. The Shenzhen SEZ authority has been wise to emphasize tourism in its formative period. The lessons learnt in these early years will be useful and lead to an awareness of the need for better planning. Fortunately, most of the mistakes that were made are not too costly and have largely been corrected with greater prudence and better planning. Only some cases of incompatibility of land uses still remain — for example, the proximity of the Bizijiao cemetery to the Xiaomeisha seaside resort, which will perhaps be permanent. The proposal to develop the beaches at Shekou is probably misguided. Although the recreational waters may not suffer directly from the pollution emitted from the industrial area nearby, the location is nonetheless unattractive. All in all, the present planning of the nine tourist resorts outside the Shenzhen urban core represents an attempt to create a diversity of tourist attractions out of an area of mediocre natural endowment by maximizing on its proximity to Hong Kong and the distinctive characteristics of the locality. Judging from current trends and potential demand, tourist facilities sufficient to entertain a million and a half tourists annually by the year 2000 may be economically viable and financially desirable. However, it must be remembered that certain parts of the countryside should be kept as far as possible intact and protected to provide a sanctuary for wildlife, and to promote nature conservation and tourist appreciation. The opening up of the countryside for recreational use may disrupt the natural environment. Large numbers of visitors roaming and picnicking in the many scenic areas, especially during the weekends, may effect damage to surfaces and the destruction of vegetation. Such weekend tourism may also bring about unsightly environmental pollution as the visitors leave their rubbish behind them. Careless smokers, neglected barbecues and the lighting of fireworks can all increase the risk of forest fires. Such mishaps are commonplace in Hong Kong and are likely, therefore, to occur in Shenzhen since it will be frequented by the same groups of holiday-makers. Preventive measures must thus be part and parcel of the planning of tourist facilities in the Shenzhen SEZ.

Conclusion

In other export processing zones, the provision of a high standard of apartments, hotels, office buildings and recreational facilities for expatriate employees has been essential to the success of the zones (Rabbani, 1980, p. 12). The size of these export processing zones is generally small. Accommodation and recreational facilities are, therefore, built outside the zone and, if possible, near the existing urban area. In the case of Shenzhen, however, the reverse is true. With an area of 327.5 sq km and a small urban core with minimal urban facilities, the hotels and other tourist facilities of the Shenzhen SEZ have had to shoulder the additional responsibility of providing first-class accommodation and other supporting facilities to the expatriates involved in industrial and other activities within the special zone boundaries. In the case of the Pepsi-Cola Bottling Plant near the Shenzhen Reservoir, the East Lake Hotel to the east of the Reservoir was chosen as a residential and dining place for the plant's expatriate staff (fieldwork, 1982). With regard to the development of Chiwan as a rear service base for the South China Sea offshore oilfields, the existence of the Shenzhen Bay Hotel nearby will reduce the need for the extensive construction of infrastructure that has been required in other rear bases in South China — for example, in Zhanjiang where the Chinese oil company has had to develop a special area with Spanish bungalows for its expatriate employees.

The presence of these expatriate clients has the effect of reducing the adverse economic consequences of 'seasonality' which plagues the tourist industry all over the world (Baron, 1975). The tourist industry of the Shenzhen SEZ is fortunate to have their patronage which allows it to maintain a steady flow of income in the off-peak season.

If the expatriates represent the upper end of the 'domestic' sector of the tourist industry in Shenzhen, the drivers, cadres and representatives of other Chinese provinces and districts who come to Shenzhen on short business trips, together with those who come to Shenzhen for shopping and family visits, will represent the lower end of the tourist industry. Although many of them will stay with their friends or in government lodgings, some will stay in the inns run by communes and local enterprises. With the growing importance of the Shenzhen SEZ as China's window on the outside world, this patronage will become a regular phenomenon and the tourist industry of Shenzhen should not only proceed along the lines of international tourism but should also serve the less profitable but equally essential lower end of the business. Indeed, complaints from immigrant workers of the lack of recreational facilities and the monotony of life in the Shenzhen SEZ could, to a certain extent, be eliminated if less expensive tourist resorts were to be constructed and opened to all kinds of tourists, local and external alike.

Finally, tourism is not necessarily an internal concern. The latest enterprise of tourist operators in Shenzhen is to organize sightseeing tours from Shenzhen to Hong Kong, Zhongshan and Zhuhai for the residents of Shenzhen (*Shenzhen Special Zone Daily*, 3 August 1984). The growing prosperity of Shenzhen and the rise in incomes (which may include some foreign currency) of the more industrious workers and the self-employed will increase local demand for sightseeing outside Shenzhen. After a modest start, the flow of tourists between Hong Kong and Shenzhen has now become a two-way traffic.

If the Shenzhen mode of tourism development should turn out to be a workable scheme of reform, it could perhaps provide a development model, on a bigger basis, and on a grander scale, for Guangdong and other parts of China. This model may help to further the current expansion of China's tourist industry as a channel for earning foreign exchange.

6. Agricultural Land-use Patterns and Export Potential

TIANXIANG ZHENG, QINGQUAN WEI AND DAVID K. Y. CHU

WHILE Chinese cities cannot produce a significant proportion of the food consumed within the city limits, the Chinese municipalities can do so by incorporating within the municipal limits rural counties, communes and production brigades. Municipal self-sufficiency in vegetables, and to some extent in grain, meat and other agricultural produce, is a common objective of Chinese urban planning (Skinner, 1978). However, this goal has not yet been completely fulfilled, as is shown by the fact that about 30 per cent of Chinese cities rely on vegetables imported from production areas beyond the municipal boundaries (personal communication). As a result over Rmb 100 million is spent annually on the transportation of easily perishable vegetables and other agricultural produce over long distances thereby taking up much of the available railway space. But self-sufficiency is especially difficult to attain in such cities as Shenzhen where the population is increasing very rapidly.

In 1978 Shenzhen was a small frontier town with a population of less than 20,000. By 1981 its urban population had risen to 48,000 (fieldwork, August 1981). In addition, within the area there are about 50,000 people with temporary resident status and another 40,000 travellers in transit (fieldwork, August 1981). In other words, in Shenzhen at least 140,000 people require food, and because of rapid industrial development and tourism, this trend of increasing demand is expected to continue. The supply of vegetables, meat and agricultural products other than grain is falling behind the rise in demand in spite of the fact that in 1979, 2,000 vegetable farmers were transferred from the Shantou region to Shenzhen in order to increase the area of vegetable fields by 1,200 mu (1 ha = 15 mu). In 1981, a further 2,500 vegetable farmers were transferred from the Guangzhou region in order to increase the area of vegetable fields by another 2,500 mu (fieldwork, August 1981). Despite the increases in cultivated acreage, prices of vegetables, fish, meat and other secondary agricultural products have soared, and this has given rise to growing discontent among the residents of Shenzhen. How is the supply of secondary agricultural produce in Shenzhen to be increased at the lowest cost? Moreover, since Shenzhen is adjacent to Hong Kong — a huge market for agricultural produce — how can the potential for exporting agricultural produce to Hong Kong from Shenzhen be realized? This chapter attempts first to develop a model for the cropping patterns of the peri-urban areas of Chinese cities and second to apply this model to Shenzhen in the hope of creating a rational land-use pattern for the achievement of self-sufficiency in vegetable production. Finally, the possibilities for exporting agricultural produce from Shenzhen to the nearby Hong Kong market are discussed.

A Model of Peri-urban Agricultural Land Use in China

The most important reason for growing vegetables near the city where they are to be consumed is the minimization of transportation costs. As early as 1826, Von Thünen propounded a concentric ring theory for agricultural land use (Fig. 6.1). The innermost ring is to be used for free cash cropping. This ring is then surrounded by rings of forestry, the crop rotation system, the improved system, the three-field system and stock farming. This peri-urban agricultural land-use pattern was much influenced by the mode of land transport at that time — the horse-drawn wagon. The perishability and bulk of agricultural produce were the chief determinants of transportation costs. Land use organized in accordance with von Thünen's theory minimized transportation costs.

Technological advances made in the means of transportation and refrigeration have reduced the usefulness of Von Thünen's theory at city and regional levels in most developed countries today (Peet, 1969). Regional specialization and long-distance haulage enable European and American farmers to exploit the comparative advantages of particular localities regardless of their proximity to cities. Only in some developing countries where modern means of transportation are not generally available is Von Thünen's theory still of some importance (Griffin, 1973). Despite the fact that considerable progress has been achieved in developing more transport in China since 1949, the existing network is still far from adequate. In order to relieve the pressure upon this network, the Chinese government has adopted self-sufficiency in secondary agricultural produce for the large and medium-scale cities as a national policy (*Nanfang Daily*, 26 November 1981). For this reason, the Von Thünen agricultural land-use pattern may still be of relevance to China. One can visualize the peri-urban agricultural land use in the form of four concentric rings (Fig. 6.2). The innermost ring is labelled the Inner Suburban Zone and it is surrounded by the Outer Suburban Zone, Incorporated Counties Within Municipal Boundaries (ICWM) and Adjacent Counties Outside the Municipality (ACOM) respectively. Each of these rings has its own agricultural system and the transferability of its product is the chief determining factor in its location.

The position of each cropping zone corresponds with the characteristics

Fig. 6.1 Von Thünen's Theory of Agricultural Land Uses

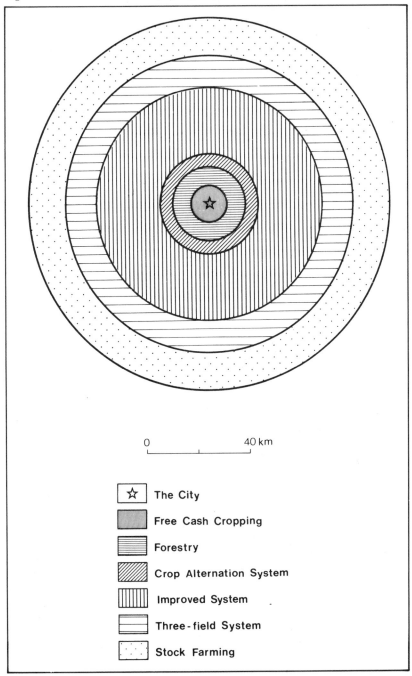

0   40 km

☆ The City

▦ Free Cash Cropping

▤ Forestry

▨ Crop Alternation System

▥ Improved System

▤ Three - field System

⦂ Stock Farming

*Fig. 6.2 The Four Concentric Rings of Peri-urban Agricultural
Land Uses in China*

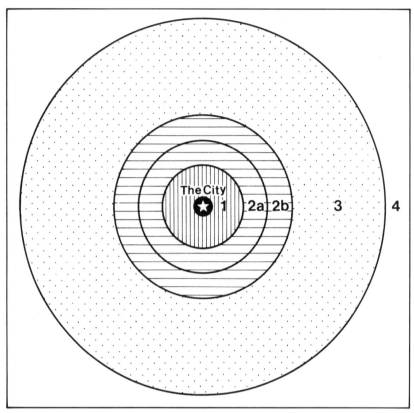

Notes: 1. Inner Suburban Zone — dominant crop: leafy vegetables
        — other crops: green fodder and flowers
        — the unmarketable parts of leafy vegetables could be used
         for pig and poultry rearing.
   2. Outer Suburban Zone — dominant crop: non-leafy vegetables
        — other crops: fruit trees, grain, oil-bearing seed
        — 2a: where non-leafy vegetables and fruit trees are more
         important
        — 2b: where grain and oil-bearing seed are more important.
   3. Incorporated Counties Within Municipal Boundaries (ICWM)
        — dominant crops: grain and oil-bearing seed
        — pigs are important
        — wherever possible cash crops are grown.
   4. Adjacent Counties Outside the Municipality (ACOM)
        — dominant crops: grain and oil-bearing seed
        — pigs are important
        — forestry and cash crops are possible.

of the various crops, and the transferability and perishability of the harvested products. Leafy vegetables are heavy and bulky. Since only fresh leafy vegetables can command high prices, they must be put on sale in the market within hours of being harvested. Hence, they must be grown near the city and so the Inner Suburban Zone is the most suitable area for their cultivation. Non-leafy vegetables and processed vegetables are less perishable and therefore do not require such rapid transportation. The Outer Suburban Zone would be the most economical location for their cultivation. Like leafy vegetables, fresh milk deteriorates rapidly and good transportation is necessary for its production. Dairy farms providing fresh milk should be sited in the Inner Suburban Zone whilst those producing cheese and processed milk, which do not spoil easily, may be sited in the Outer Suburban Zone.

Grain and oil-bearing seed are less perishable than milk and vegetables and their yield per unit area is comparatively low. Unless there is an abundance of arable land, suburban agriculture should concentrate on the production of fresh vegetables and milk for urban use rather than on less perishable products such as grain and oil-bearing seed. At most, farmers in the suburban zones should be asked to produce enough grain and oil-bearing seed for their own consumption, and the supply of grain and oil-bearing seed for the city should be the responsibility of the ICWM and the ACOM. Similarly, cash crops for light industries would best be located in the ICWM and the ACOM rather than in the suburban zones, for these crops are usually less perishable and may be subjected to long-distance transportation.

Fruit trees are perennial and more resistant to drought than vegetables. The sandy area, foothills and fringe area between the Inner Suburban Zone and the Outer Suburban Zone are the best places for orchards. Moreover, they serve as wind-breaks and green belts and can be integrated with tourism. Their distribution is thus not necessarily restricted. On the other hand, forests supplying wood products must be large in scale, and lumber is not perishable: therefore, forests should be in the ACOM.

Animal husbandry and aquaculture are equally important in all of these four zones. In the Inner Suburban Zone, there is plenty of non-marketable, inedible vegetable matter. It is estimated that one mu of land producing leafy vegetables can supply enough fodder to support one pig (fieldwork, 1981). Inside the city, there is ample left-over food (domestic and industrial) for the support of a few large-scale poultry and pig farms. Within the Outer Suburban Zone, in the ICWM, the production of grain and oil-bearing seed could be integrated with the rearing of pigs and chickens.

The above analysis describes the local characteristics of the peri-urban agricultural belts that might surround a Chinese city. However, the exact size and width of these belts have yet to be determined. It is important to ascertain the appropriate size and width of the peri-urban agricultural belts with respect to the population of the city, for this can facilitate the planned and balanced development of these two sectors. For the calculation that follows, it is assumed that all the arable land of the Inner Suburban Zone is devoted to year-round cultivation of leafy vegetables. The size of the zone is estimated as follows:

$$S_1 = \frac{P.g}{K_1}$$ (E.1)

or

$$S_1 = \frac{P.h_1.I}{K_1.Y_1}$$ (E.2)

S_1 = proper size of the Inner Suburban Zone (mu)

P = urban population of the city

g = year-round vegetable fields needed for each urban resident (mu)

K_1 = arable land as a percentage of the total land

h_1 = average annual per capita vegetable consumption (catty)

I = vegetables supplied by year-round vegetable fields as a percentage of total vegetables required

Y_1 = annual yield per unit area of the vegetable fields (catty per mu)

If the Inner Suburban Zone takes the shape of concentric rings with the city as the centre, the radius of the Inner Suburban Zone would be:

$$\gamma_1 = \sqrt{\frac{S_1+S}{\pi}}$$ (E.3)

γ_1 = radius of the Inner Suburban Zone

S_1 = proper size of the Inner Suburban Zone (mu)

S = urban area (mu)

π = 3.1416

To determine the proper size of the Outer Suburban Zone is more complicated because there are varying types of crop combinations:

$$S_2 = \frac{T_1+T_2+T_3+T_4}{K_2}$$ (E.4)

$$T_1 = P.g.f.$$ (E.5)

$$T_2 = \frac{P.h_2}{Y_2}$$ (E.6)

$$T_3 = \frac{P_2.h_3}{Y_3}$$ (E.7)

$$T_4 = \frac{P_2.h_4}{Y_4}$$ (E.8)

S_2 = proper size of the Outer Suburban Zone (mu)

T_1 = seasonal vegetable fields (mu)

T_2 = orchards (mu)

T_3 = fields for grain (mu)

T_4 = fields for oil-bearing seed (mu)

K_2 = arable land as a percentage of the total land

P = urban population of the city

g = year-round vegetable fields needed by each urban resident (mu)

f = ratio of seasonal vegetable fields to year-round vegetable fields

h_2 = average annual per capita fruit requirement (catty)

Y_2 = annual fruit yield per unit area (catty per mu)

P_2 = population of the Inner Suburban and Outer Suburban Zones

h_3 = average annual per capita grain requirement (catty)

Y_3 = annual grain yield per unit area (catty per mu)

h_4 = average annual per capita oil-bearing seed requirement (catty)

Y = annual yield per unit area of oil-bearing seed (catty per mu)

By substituting E.5, E.6, E.7 and E.8 into E.4 one can obtain:

$$S_2 = \frac{P.g.f.}{K_2} + \frac{P.h_2}{Y_2 K_2} + \frac{P_2 h_3}{Y_3 K_2} + \frac{P_2 h_4}{Y_4 K_2} \qquad (E.9)$$

The radius of the Outer Suburban Zone can then be determined as follows:

$$\gamma_2 = \sqrt{\frac{S_2 + S_1 + S}{\pi}} \qquad (E.10)$$

The proper size of the ICWM depends on the amount of grain required by the city and the amount of grain required to satisfy the needs of the farmers in this zone. The average annual rate of consumption for a city of one million people is 500 million catties of grain and 30 million catties of peanuts. (This is estimated by the food quota of 500 catties of grain per capita per year (about 250 kg per year) and 30 catties of peanuts per capita per year as observed by the authors.) If the annual yield per mu of grain amounts to 1,000 catties and the yield of peanuts amounts to 300 catties, a city of one million people would require 600,000 mu of arable land for the satisfaction of its grain and oil-bearing seed requirements. The farmers of the ICWM could use 30 to 40 per cent of their land for the production of grain and oil-bearing seed for the city, and this zone must comprise 2 million mu of arable land before the city can attain self-sufficiency in the production of grain and oil-bearing seed.

Estimating the Size of Peri-urban Agricultural Land-use Belts of Shenzhen

The target population of Shenzhen by the year 2000 is now fixed at 800,000 with a planned density of 10,000 people per sq km. The urban area (S) of

Shenzhen to be reserved for development thus amounts to 80 sq km. In Guangdong Province, about 0.03 mu of year-round vegetable fields will produce enough vegetables for one urban dweller (g) (*Nanfang Daily*, 26 November 1981) and the ratio between P_2 and P is 2 to 8. (Standard set by the Chinese government on 7 December 1963.) Annual consumption per capita is 600 catties of grain (h_3) and 30 catties of peanuts (h_4) (estimated by the current consumption level as experienced in Guangzhou). Assuming that the ratio of seasonal vegetable fields to year-round vegetable fields (f) is equal to 1, and that the annual average per capita fruit consumption (h_2) is equal to 90 catties, the area of the Inner Suburban Zone of Shenzhen should be:

$$S_1 = \frac{P.g}{K_1} = \frac{800,000\times0.03\text{mu}}{16\%} = 150,000 \text{ mu (or 100.5 sq km)}$$

According to E.3, the radius of this zone is estimated as follows:

$$\gamma_1 = \sqrt{\frac{S_1+S}{\pi}} = \sqrt{\frac{100+80}{3.1416}} = 7.57\text{km}$$

The Outer Suburban Zone of Shenzhen is estimated by using E.9:

$$S_2 = \frac{P.g.f.}{K_2} + \frac{Ph_2}{Y_2K_2} + \frac{P_2h_3}{Y_3K_2} + \frac{P_2h_4}{Y_4K_2}$$

$$= \frac{800,000\times0.03\times1}{16\%} + \frac{800,000\times90 \text{ catties}}{3,000 \text{ catties per mu}\times16\%}$$

$$+ \frac{160,000\times600 \text{ catties}}{1,000 \text{ catties per mu}\times16\%} + \frac{160,000\times30 \text{ catties}}{300 \text{ catties per mu}\times16\%}$$

$$= 994,925 \text{ mu or 666.6 sq km}$$

According to E.10, the radius of the Outer Suburban Zone of Shenzhen should be:

$$\gamma_2 = \sqrt{\frac{S_2+S_1+S}{\pi}} = \sqrt{\frac{666.6+100+80}{3.1416}} = 16.42\text{km}$$

However, as the area of Shenzhen is limited by topographical constraints, and by the border with Hong Kong, the suburban agricultural belts of Shenzhen can only assume a semi-concentric ring pattern. The estimated radii must be adjusted in order to give the same area. Therefore, when Shenzhen is fully developed, the radii of the Inner Suburban Zone and the Outer Suburban Zone should be 10.70 km and 23.32 km respectively if self-sufficiency in vegetables is adopted as the planning criterion (Fig. 6.3).

In comparing the above findings with actual conditions in Shenzhen, several points should be noted. First, the total area of the Shenzhen SEZ is 327.5 sq km. The northern boundary of the Shenzhen SEZ could serve as the limit of the Inner Suburban Zone, for the total area required by urban

*Fig. 6.3 The Theoretical Agricultural Land-use Pattern
of Shenzhen in the Year 2000*

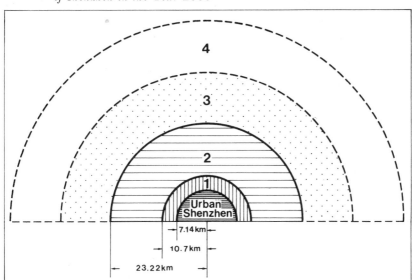

Notes: 1. Inner Suburban Zone: the SEZ.
2. Outer Suburban Zone: southern part of Bao'an.
3. Incorporated County: northern part of Bao'an (ICWM).
4. Adjacent Counties outside the Municipality: Dongguan and Huiyuan Counties (ACOM).

Shenzhen (80 sq km) and its Inner Suburban Zone (100 sq km) is still less than the total area of the Shenzhen SEZ. It is accepted that some land in the Shenzhen SEZ must be reserved for tourism, housing estates and roads: these uses would require the remaining area of the zone. Second, as the above calculation illustrates, the proper size of the Outer Suburban Zone for Shenzhen is 666.6 sq km which is only about half the area of Bao'an County, the only incorporated county within the Shenzhen Municipality boundaries (Fig. 6.4). The Outer Suburban Zone of Shenzhen cannot include the entire area of Bao'an County for it is obviously too large. However, Bao'an County would not be large enough to shoulder the whole responsibility of providing grain and oil-bearing seed to Shenzhen in the future. It may therefore be necessary to incorporate neighbouring Dongguan and Huiyang Counties into Shenzhen Municipality in order to maintain an adequate flow of grain and oil-bearing seed to Shenzhen. Finally, the rugged relief of the eastern portion of Shenzhen means that the peri-urban agricultural belts of Shenzhen could not be symmetrical semi-circular rings. Instead, they would be longitudinal belts stretching from the border between Hong Kong and Shenzhen toward the north-west.

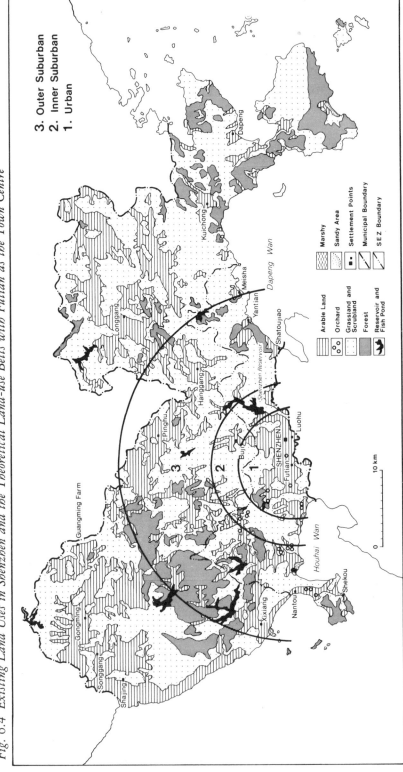

Fig. 6.4 Existing Land Uses in Shenzhen and the Theoretical Land-use Belts with Futian as the Town Centre

The Potential of Shenzhen as an Export Base for Agricultural Produce

Factors Affecting the Development of Agriculture

In contrast to other municipalities, the agricultural sector of Shenzhen should perhaps not aim at self-sufficiency alone. Shenzhen is situated next to Hong Kong which is a huge market for agricultural produce. Because of limited land and water resources, Hong Kong has a relatively low degree of self-sufficiency in the production of pigs (14 per cent), chickens (3 per cent), fish (5 per cent), and vegetables (35 per cent). However, Shenzhen has plenty of potentially arable land and a climate suitable for agricultural production. If these physical endowments and locational advantages are wisely exploited, both Shenzhen and China will benefit.

Shenzhen Municipality has an area of 2,020 sq km of which 40 per cent is low-rise uplands (between 20 and 40 m in elevation), 30 per cent is hilly, 20 per cent is flat plain and 10 per cent is water and tidal mud-flat (Fig. 6.5). The diverse topography provides a good foundation on which to develop varying types of agriculture. The fertile plains are used for paddy fields. Conversion to high-yield vegetable plots or to fish ponds is possible. Most of the hilly area is located on either side of the Kowloon–Canton Railway, and the foothills of this area would be good for cultivating tropical and subtropical fruit trees or for ranches. It is estimated that over 400,000 mu could be allotted to these purposes. Except for those which are already reserved for urban development, the low-rise uplands could be used for vegetable fields, orchards, and dairy farms. The tidal mud-flats next to the Zhujiang (Pearl River) are excellent oyster-beds. There are now over 50,000 mu of oyster-beds but there is still room for expansion if development in this area can be adequately controlled.

The annual rainfall of Shenzhen amounts to 1,900 mm. There is plenty of sunshine and high temperatures prevail throughout the year. Yet the high temperature in summer, drought in winter, and strong winds and torrential rain during the typhoon season may be hazardous to vegetable farming, especially in the lowlands beside the river. This could be partly remedied by combining fish ponds with vegetable farming. The vegetable plots could be raised with the soil dug from the fish ponds. This soil is very fertile, and would improve vegetable yields. The unmarketable parts of the vegetables could be used to feed cows and pigs whose droppings could then be fed to the fish. Irrigation water could be pumped directly from the fish ponds and the unabsorbed water would drain back into the fish ponds. This would result in the maximum utilization of water and nutrients which would be continuously recycled.

Aside from highly favourable physical conditions for agricultural development, Shenzhen has an excellent locational advantage over other

Fig. 6.5 The Topography of Shenzhen and Hong Kong

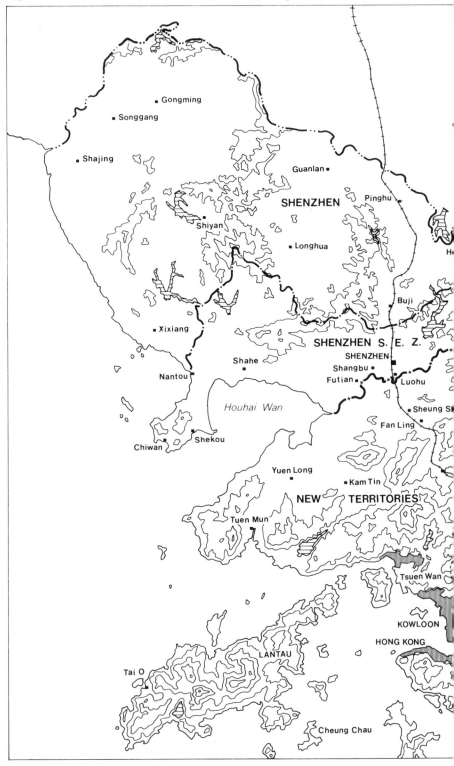

contour interval 100,300,500,700,900 metres

parts of China for exporting fresh agricultural produce to Hong Kong. Its proximity to Hong Kong ensures significant savings in transportation costs and reduced wastage. For instance, in 1980, the total number of pigs exported from various parts of China to Hong Kong amounted to 2,390,000 of which 5.2 per cent died during transport (fieldwork, August 1981). Yet, in the same period, Shenzhen exported 9,400 pigs to Hong Kong without a single death (fieldwork, August 1981). The transportation of vegetables from the Guangzhou area to Hong Kong suffers from the same problem. From March 1981 to October 1981, the total transportation costs of exporting vegetables from Guangzhou to Hong Kong was between Rmb 40,000 and 50,000, excluding wastage during transport (3.5 per cent) (fieldwork, August 1981). The average yield of leafy vegetable fields in the Guangzhou region is 10,000 catties per mu (fieldwork, August 1981). If transportation costs and wastage are included, the real yield is reduced to 6,000 catties per mu. Because of a lack of skilled manpower in Shenzhen, the actual yield of the vegetable fields is generally below 6,000 catties per mu (fieldwork, August 1981). However, skilled farmers imported from the Shantou and Guangzhou region could easily attain an average yield of 8,000 catties per mu and occasionally 10,000 catties per mu (fieldwork, August 1981). In this case, it would become more economical to export vegetables from Shenzhen than from the Guangzhou region.

The reduction of railway congestion between Guangzhou and Shenzhen would be a further advantage of the export of fresh agricultural products from Shenzhen rather than from Guangzhou. In 1980, 400,000 tonnes of fresh agricultural produce passed through this section of railway *en route* to Hong Kong, and in the same period about 400,000 tonnes of goods destined for Shenzhen were delayed because of congestion (fieldwork, August 1981). Had Shenzhen itself exported these 400,000 tonnes of agricultural produce to Hong Kong, this railway capacity could have been used instead for transporting badly needed goods to Shenzhen. One can safely predict that in the future the congestion of the railway between Guangzhou and Hong Kong will increase. It is therefore necessary to shift the agricultural export base from Guangzhou to Shenzhen.

Politically, it is not desirable to allow the income of Bao'an County to lag far behind that of the SEZ. If the average annual vegetable yield is 8,000 catties per mu in Shenzhen, at US$272.3 per tonne (*Shenzhen Special Zone Daily*, 12 June 1981), the income from one mu of vegetable fields could be as high as US$1,000. The annual yield of rice fields in Shenzhen is about 800 catties per mu (with husk) (fieldwork, August 1981), and this income can hardly compare with that earned by growing vegetables. Consequently, if the farmers are allowed to grow vegetables and flowers, and to develop aquaculture and animal husbandry instead of growing rice, their income will rise rapidly. This is illustrated by the experience of the Fung Wong Brigade, Shajing People's Commune (fieldwork, August 1981). In 1979, before the farmers were allowed to specialize in vegetable production, the value of each man-day was Rmb 2.7 per day. In 1980, when they were allowed to specialize in vegetables for export, the income rose to Rmb 5.5 per day, which is approximately equal to that of a worker in the Shenzhen SEZ. In other words, allowing the Shenzhen farmers to grow more vegetables has the pleasing political effect of narrowing the income gap between the SEZ and Bao'an County.

Policy Recommendations

There are 530,000 mu of arable land in Shenzhen (fieldwork, August 1981). The total sown area in 1980 was 788,499 mu of which 81.9 per cent consisted of paddy-fields, 15.9 per cent cash crops and 2.1 per cent vegetables (fieldwork, August 1981). In other words, most of the arable land was sown with rice and less than 17,000 mu was allotted to vegetables. This was partly because of the former widespread policy of striving for self-sufficiency in grain. Prior to 1978, over 100 million catties of rice per year were bought from Shenzhen and shipped to other parts of China (fieldwork, August 1981). In recent years, because of the abolition of monoculture, a rapid population increase and the encouragement of diversification of the rural economy, the quota of grain has been gradually reduced. Nonetheless, in 1981, Shenzhen still had the task of supplying 40 million catties of grain annually for inland consumption or export (fieldwork, August 1981). In other words, up to 1981 Shenzhen was not only self-sufficient in grain but was also a centre for exporting grain. This undoubtedly suppressed Shenzhen's capacity to act as an export base for fresh agricultural products. For example, Shenzhen contributed only 1.4 million catties of vegetables for export to Hong Kong in 1980 (fieldwork, August 1981), a figure which represented only 15 per cent of its total exports in 1927 (Foshan Revolutionary Committee, 1976) or 0.1 per cent of the total consumption of vegetables in Hong Kong in 1980. This indicates that there is plenty of potential for increasing exports from Shenzhen.

The easiest way to maximize economic benefits and improve the living standards of Bao'an farmers is to eliminate the annual demand for more than 40 million catties of rice from Shenzhen and to encourage the farmers to grow more vegetables for home consumption and for export. Since the yield of paddy-fields is about 800 catties per mu, this would spare a total area of 50,000–60,000 mu of arable land for vegetable cultivation. As shown above, at an average yield of 8,000 catties per mu and an income therefore of over US$1,000 per mu, converting the 60,000 mu of paddy-fields to vegetable fields will bring in an annual revenue of US$60 million. This will undoubtedly bolster the local economy. As shown in Fig. 6.6 and Table 6.1, it would be best to position these 60,000 mu of newly converted vegetable fields in the vicinity of the existing vegetable fields which are clustered in the west and north-west of the Outer Suburban Zone of Shenzhen.

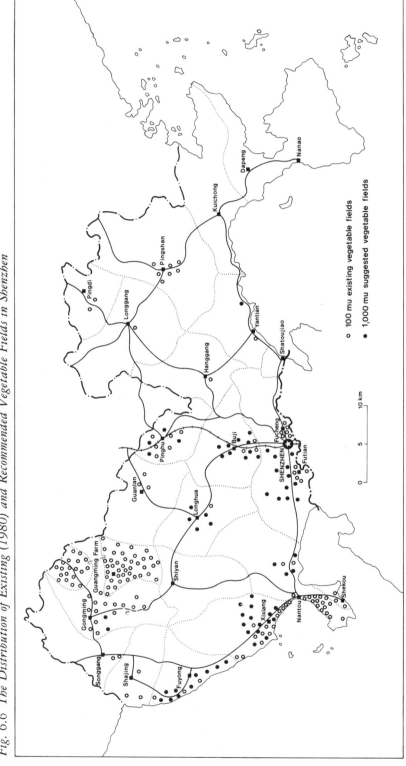

Fig. 6.6 The Distribution of Existing (1980) and Recommended Vegetable Fields in Shenzhen

Table 6.1 A Summary of the Distribution of Existing and Recommended Vegetable Fields

District	Total Arable Land (mu)	Existing Vegetable Fields (1980) (mu)	Recommended Vegetable Fields (mu)	Total Area* of Existing and Recommended Vegetable Fields (mu)	Existing and Recommended Vegetable Fields as a Percentage of Total Arable Land
Shenzhen SEZ	28,000	3,200	16,800	20,000	71.4
Xixiang Commune	30,950	1,400	13,600	15,000	48.5
Fuyong Commune	37,947	800	9,200	10,000	26.4
Congming Commune and Guangming Farm	57,000	7,800	2,200	10,000	17.5
Buji Commune	16,527	300	9,700	10,000	60.5
Pinghu and Longhua Commune	32,000	1,000	9,000	10,000	31.2
Total	202,424	14,500	60,500	75,000	37.1

Note: *It should be noted that the private plots tilled by individuals are not included.

The reason for selecting these fields for conversion is simple: their proximity to existing vegetable fields will facilitate the transfer of technology and the exploitation of economies of scale. As these conversions will be at the expense of paddy-fields, there will not be any surplus grain for procurement by the Chinese government. It is anticipated that after the conversion Shenzhen Municipality will become a grain deficit region. The purchase of grain from adjacent counties or the enlargement of Shenzhen Municipality by incorporating the adjacent counties to form a bigger municipality are thus possible alternatives whereby Shenzhen could obtain its grain supply.

The 20,000 mu of vegetable fields which we have proposed for the Shenzhen SEZ (Table 6.1) will be of a transitional nature. With rapid urban encroachment and population growth, plus the shortage of local labour, abandoned paddy-fields have already become a subject for concern (fieldwork, 1983). In fact, it has been anticipated since 1983 that Shenzhen will become a grain deficit area. However, this is not a result of land-use conversion but simply of abandonment due to relatively low productivity in grain cultivation. The conversion of paddy-fields to other agricultural uses should thus be accelerated; otherwise more and more paddy-fields will simply be left fallow. Though commonplace in Western cities (Sinclair, 1967), this phenomenon may not necessarily be repeated in socialist China for the country as a whole has an almost unlimited supply of cheap farm labour. The ploughing of these fields for vegetable production until they are converted to urban use will give the imported hired temporary farm labourers a higher income than paddy growing in their home counties and will also increase the export value of Shenzhen. At the very least, it would increase the supply of vegetables to the local market and help to reduce the price of vegetables in the SEZ.

At the same time, Shenzhen could further expand its fish ponds, dairy farming, animal husbandry and poultry rearing and cultivate more fruit trees. The existing 53,000 mu of fish ponds developed through joint ventures between the Shenzhen government and Hong Kong merchants could be extended to 100,000 mu. Given that 600 catties of fish per mu are produced annually, this area would yield 30,000 tonnes of fish for export per annum (fieldwork, August 1981). Guangming Dairy Farm has introduced 3,651 dairy cattle and in 1983 it produced and exported 7,400 tonnes of milk (*People's Daily*, 29 March 1984); there is still potential for further development. Furthermore, by improving the grasses on the hilly slopes, the 200,000 mu of meadows could support 40,000 head of beef cattle (estimated at one head of cattle per five mu of grassland). The newly converted vegetable fields could support an extra 60,000 pigs on their non-marketable remains. Finally, by fuller utilization of the hilly area, the 50,000 mu of existing orchards could be expanded to about 100,000 mu or more (fieldwork, August 1981). All these suggestions point to the direction in which the agricultural economy of Shenzhen should expand.

In short, Shenzhen Municipality has much potential for developing fresh agricultural produce for export. With enough investment, grain supplies from other regions, advanced agricultural technology, and a rational land-use plan, Shenzhen Municipality could become not only self-sufficient in the production of vegetables and other agricultural products with the exception of grain, but also a significant export base of agricultural produce for foreign exchange earnings. The foreign currency thus earned could be used in the pursuit of other targets for modernization in China. The role played by the agricultural sector of Shenzhen Municipality should not be underestimated.

PART III: PLANNING — INFRASTRUCTURE, LABOUR AND THE ENVIRONMENT IN SHENZHEN

7. Physical Planning

ANTHONY G. O. YEH

THE transformation of Shenzhen from a small market town to one of the largest special economic zones in China involves much development and construction. Good forward planning is essential to provide the necessary infrastructure and an orderly and functional physical environment to attract foreign investment. The importance of physical planning in the development of the Shenzhen SEZ has long been recognized by the Chinese government. Indeed, the planning and development of Shenzhen started even before its designation as an SEZ. Basic planning and construction work in the Shekou Industrial Zone, which is owned by the China Merchants' Steam Navigation Co. Ltd. (CMSN) of Hong Kong and is now one of the planning districts in the Shenzhen SEZ, started in 1979, one year before Shenzhen gained official status as an SEZ. To facilitate and co-ordinate future comprehensive development, two plans with different purposes have been prepared, namely, the Shenzhen SEZ Social and Economic Development Plan (hereafter referred to as the social and economic plan) and the Shenzhen SEZ Outline Master Plan (hereafter referred to as the master plan). The former deals with the future population and economic structure of the SEZ and the latter deals with land use and physical development. In addition, provisional regulations on land control in the SEZ have been adopted to manage and administer land development by foreign investors. This chapter will discuss the physical planning process and land administration of the Shenzhen SEZ and will examine some related planning issues.

Planning Administration

Planning in the Shenzhen SEZ is carried out by the Planning Department of the Shenzhen SEZ Construction Company, a quasi-government agency that handles land development and construction projects run by both the Shenzhen government and foreign investors. It is of the same status as the Municipal Government Office, the Shenzhen SEZ Development Company, and the Police, Procuratorates and Courts of the People's Government of Shenzhen Municipality (Fig. 7.1). It is called a company rather than a department because it has to be responsible for its own profits and losses — a common requirement under China's new economic policy. Besides the Planning Department, there are a number of departments and subdivisions under the Shenzhen SEZ Construction Company that are related to planning and development control in the zone, for example, the Architecture Department and the Building Construction Company. The functions of the Building Construction Company include the organization of construction teams after a building permit has been obtained from the Planning Department, quality control of construction work, and the issue of construction permits. All construction work in the SEZ must go through the Building Construction Company.

The main functions of the Planning Department are to carry out planning and to issue land-use certificates and building permits. Apart from the administration office, there are three major divisions in the Planning Department:

(a) the Planning Division which is responsible for the preparation of master plans, detailed layout plans of the planning districts, and special-subject plans such as waterworks, electricity, drainage and recreation; it is also responsible for land-use control through the issue of land-use certificates;

(b) the Building Control Division which scrutinizes all building plans to check whether they conform to the specifications in the land-use certificates and the building standards of China before making recommendations for the issue of building permits by the Planning Department; and

(c) the Surveying and Cartographic Division which carries out all surveying work in the municipality and provides socio-economic, land-use, hydrological, topographical and geological information for planning.

The Planning Process

Although Shenzhen is an SEZ, its planning procedure is similar to that of other parts of China and follows the stipulations laid down by the Provisional

*Fig. 7.1 The Organization of the People's Government of Shenzhen
Municipality and the Departments Responsible for Planning and
Land Development Control*

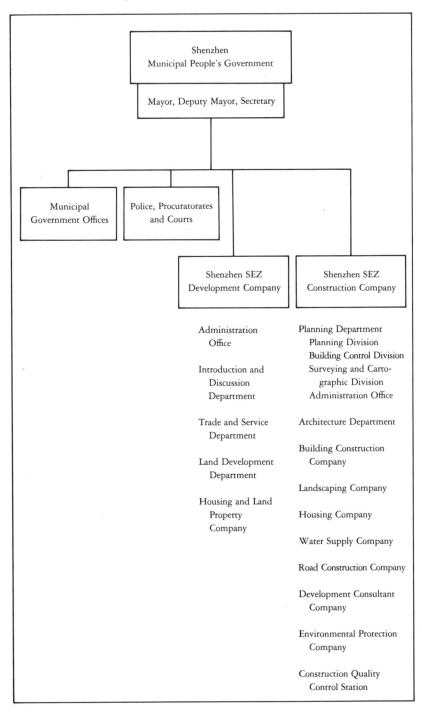

Source: Fieldwork, 1983.

Regulations for Plan Preparation and Approval adopted by the National Committee on Capital Construction in 1980. A two-tier approach is used in planning. At the top level is the master plan that outlines the general land-use pattern of the area. Below it are the detailed layout plans for districts that will be developed within the next five years as specified in the master plan. The master plan of the Shenzhen SEZ has first to be approved by the municipal government before proceeding to the Guangdong Provincial Government for assessment. Because of the special nature of the Shenzhen SEZ, it is also necessary to obtain final approval from the State Council. The detailed layout plans for districts within the Shenzhen SEZ, however, do not have to be approved by the provincial government and only need the approval of the municipal government, that is, the People's Government of Shenzhen Municipality.

The master plan consists of descriptions and maps and describes the nature and direction of urban development and the planned target population. It also prescribes the planning standards and requirements for various land uses and public facilities. It is basically a policy statement that recommends the manner of distribution of land use. The map section of the master plan shows the distribution of general land-use categories — residential, industrial, communications, storage, public utilities and services, and open space — and special land uses such as for prisons, military camps, and historical and nature conservation areas.

Four types of information are collected and analysed in the preparation of the master plan. They concern:

(a) the history and physical environment of the city as revealed in its topography, weather, hydrology, geology, seismic information and the origin and historical development of the city;

(b) the population and economic resources of the city including the distribution, quantity and quality of natural resources such as minerals, water, energy and agriculture; the population of the area; its land utilization potential; the number and distribution of factories and institutions; external communications and transportation; various types of warehousing and storage; and the staff and student numbers of secondary and technical schools and scientific research institutes;

(c) existing buildings and their condition — the number, density and distribution of housing units; and the distribution of public buildings and open space; and

(d) the urban environment and other information such as the quantity and distribution of air, water, and solid waste pollution.

Two time periods are specified in the master plan of the Shenzhen SEZ: a long-term plan for a period of twenty years and a short-term plan for a period of five years. The maps of the master plan are normally drawn to a scale of 1:25,000 or 1:10,000. They are usually accompanied by a series of special-subject plans which cover the engineering aspect of infrastructure development related to the plan. Examples of special-subject plans are: (a) a communication and transportation plan; (b) a water supply and drainage plan; (c) an electricity and gas supply plan; (d) a site preparation plan; and (e) an open space, parks and scenic area plan.

The detailed layout plans are prepared for districts that are designated for development within the next five years. Each of these provides detailed planning of land-use distribution and the road layout within a planning district. The maps of the detailed layout plans are normally drawn to a scale of 1:500, 1:1,000 or 1:2,000.

A draft master plan for the Shenzhen SEZ was prepared by the Planning Department in 1981. Three years later the final master plan had still not been approved by the Guangdong Provincial Government and the State Council. Nevertheless, it serves as a guideline for the preparation of detailed layout plans for districts with rapid growth and it also provides an instrument for the interim control of development. Without the draft master plan, it would be difficult for the Shenzhen SEZ to regulate the rapid development that is already under way.

The Master Plan and Planning Strategy

The object of the development of the Shenzhen SEZ is the attraction of foreign investment, and the general planning strategy therefore seeks to create an environment conducive to foreign investment in industry, housing, and tourism, and to maximize the utilization of land and natural resources within the boundaries of the zone. Since the very beginning of its work, the SEZ authority has recognized that success in the attraction of industrial development would depend upon the provision of adequate infrastructure. For example, in the development of the Shekou Industrial Zone, one of the first areas in the Shenzhen SEZ to be developed, the provision of basic infrastructure, the so-called 'five linkages and one levelling', was strongly emphasized (see Chapter 11).

The master plan of the Shenzhen SEZ was prepared by taking into consideration the topography of the area and the geographical location of the zone in relation to Hong Kong. Topographically, the Shenzhen SEZ can be divided into a hilly area and a lowland area. The 50 m contour more or less demarcates the boundary between these two types of land. The hilly region mainly occupies the northern part of the zone and the area east of the Shenzhen Reservoir. As the area is hilly and relatively inaccessible, it is generally not suitable for urban development. Tourism and quarrying are the major developments planned for this area. Most of the lowland area lies close to the border with Hong Kong along the coastal plain of Shenzhen Bay (Deep Bay) and occupies the central and western part of the SEZ. Because of its proximity to Hong Kong and the level topography, the lowland area is planned for urban development in industry, commerce and housing.

The target population of the Shenzhen SEZ is set at around 800,000 by the year 2000. Table 7.1 shows its planned land-use distribution. As one of the major objectives in setting up the zone was industrial development, it is not surprising that a relatively high percentage of land is allocated to industries and warehouses.

Geographically, the master plan divides the Shenzhen SEZ into three regions. The planning districts of each region and their development characteristics are summarized in Fig. 7.2 and Table 7.2 respectively.

Table 7.1 Planned Land-use Distribution

Land Use	Land Area (in sq km)	Percentage of Total Area
Residence	20.0	20.41
Industry	15.0	15.31
Warehouse and storage	6.5	6.63
Public and community facilities	13.0	13.27
Public utilities	4.0	4.08
Tourism	4.0	4.08
Open space	11.0	11.22
External communications	4.0	4.08
Roads and public squares	14.0	14.29
Others	6.5	6.63
Total	98.0	100.00

Sources: Chinese SEZ Handbook, 1984; and *New Evening Post* (Hong Kong), p. 17.

The Eastern Planning Region

This region lies to the east of the Shenzhen Reservoir. It is hilly and is not suitable for large-scale urban development. The road system is poorly developed. Planning for the development of the eastern region emphasizes the utilization of its natural resources such as water, beaches, reservoirs and minerals. The beautiful beaches along Dapeng Bay (Mirs Bay) are very close o Hong Kong and thus have great potential as a weekend water-sports resort for people from Hong Kong. A joint venture between Shenzhen and a Hong Kong firm has already developed Xiaomeisha for camping and swimming. The Shenzhen Reservoir, which at present supplies 30 per cent of Hong Kong's water supply, will be developed into a country park for passive recreation. It is not planned for use for active recreation for fear that the water would become polluted.

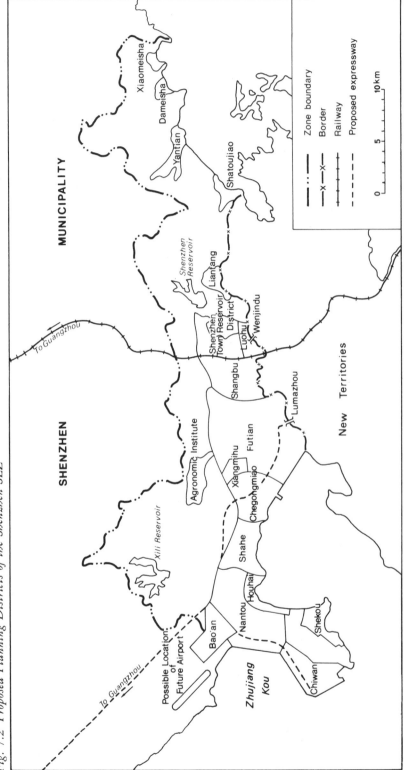

Fig. 7.2 Proposed Planning Districts of the Shenzhen SEZ

Table 7.2 Major Functions and the Target Population of Planning Districts

Regions		Planning Districts	Major Functions	Usable Land (ha)	Target Population	Average Density (persons/ha)
Eastern		Shatoujiao	commerce, residence	260		
		Yantian	fishery, agriculture, industry	578	30,000	30
		Dameisha and Xiaomeisha	tourism	172		
	Eastern	Luohu (Lowu)	commerce, residence, industry	200	110,000	550
		Shenzhen Town	commerce, residence, industry	400	40,000	100
		Liantang	industry	300	15,000	50
		Reservoir District	tourism, residence	440	30,000	68
Central	Central	Shangbu	industry, residence, warehouse	1,000	60,000	60
	Western	Futian New Town	comprehensive	3,000	300,000	100
		Chegongmiao	comprehensive	600	25,000	42
		Xiangmihu	tourism	210	1,000	5
		Agronomic Institute	scientific education and research	400	4,000	10
Western		Shekou Industrial Zone	mainly industry	230	50,000	217
		Shahe	mainly industry	1,200	40,000	33
		Houhai	comprehensive, education	600	30,000	50
		Xili Reservoir	tourism	300	3,000	10
		Chiwan Port District	industry, port, supporting base for South China Sea oil industry	500	30,000	60
		Nantou, Bao'an County Town	industry, comprehensive	610	32,000	52

Another planned development in the eastern region is the power station at Yantian. Water will be pumped at night to a reservoir by surplus night-time electricity from Hong Kong. In the daytime, water will flow down from the reservoir to generate electricity for the SEZ.

A quarry has been developed at Wushigu through a joint-venture arrangement. China provides land and workers while Hong Kong businessmen furnish the machinery, technology and labour training and supply other basic materials. A conveyor belt will be built across the border to simplify the process of transporting the rocks from the SEZ to Hong Kong. Rocks from the quarry are mainly for use by the construction industry in Hong Kong.

The Central Planning Region

The central region is bounded by the Shenzhen Reservoir in the east and approximately by Chegongmiao in the west. Major planning districts of the region include Shenzhen Town, Luohu, Shangbu and Futian. Because of its proximity to Hong Kong, it will be the major focus of urban development in the immediate future.

The vast coastal plain of the central region provides ample opportunities for urban development. The planning strategy is to redevelop the old market town of Shenzhen and to develop light industries and residential housing estates along the coastal plain. At present most of the urban growth is concentrated in the Shenzhen Town and Luohu district: this was the original urban area and is the major customs check-point between Hong Kong and China.

Most of the buildings in Shenzhen Town were built thirty years ago and are now rather dilapidated. A merchant in Hong Kong has expressed interest in redeveloping the area by demolishing some of the old housing and constructing in its place a Chinese product exhibition and shopping complex where traditional artefacts and products from different provinces of China will be displayed and sold.

The Luohu district will be developed as a commercial, residential and hotel centre because it is the customs check-point on the Chinese side of the border. It provides transit services for passengers and businessmen on their way to Hong Kong or to other parts of China. Two large commercial complexes (the Luohu Building and the Shenzhen International Commercial Building), both of them joint investment ventures of Hong Kong investors and the Shenzhen District Property Company, are under construction.

The Shangbu district is planned chiefly for light industry and administration. The Office of the People's Government of Shenzhen Municipality recently moved to its new building in Shangbu: this will be the main administrative centre for the SEZ. Most of the land will be devoted to light industry or residential housing estates. Futian district is to be developed by a large real estate company from Hong Kong. The original planned population was 400,000 but this has recently been reduced to 300,000. The district will be used as a commercial and residential area.

The Western Planning Region

The western region extends from Chegongmiao in the east to the Zhujiang Kou (Pearl River Estuary) in the west. It includes the Xili Reservoir Holiday Camp, Shahe, Nantou, Shekou and Chiwan. The planning emphasis of this region is mainly on industry — in particular, heavy industry.

Most of the development in Shekou is administered by the Hong Kong branch of the CMSN. The CMSN was established in 1872 and was one of the earliest state-owned enterprises in China. Its Hong Kong branch was authorized by the State Council of the People's Republic of China to develop Shekou district into an industrial zone producing goods for export, using resources and funds raised by the company. Site preparation work at the Shekou industrial zone started in July 1979. With only a few exceptions, most investments in the Shekou industrial zone are in joint ventures. These include the manufacture of containers, iron and steel, shipbreaking, aluminium rolling, oxygen and acetylene production and flour milling (Wong, 1982). Shekou also provides port facilities for the SEZ. It has a wharf that can handle 3,000-ton cargo lighters as well as cargo ships with a draught of less than 5 m. At present, this wharf is also used by the passenger hovercraft that connect Shenzhen with Hong Kong.

Chiwan, to the south-west of Shekou, will be developed into a ship repair and maintenance base for offshore oil drilling in the South China Sea. For this reason a deep-water wharf that can handle ships of up to 10,000 tons is under construction.

No definite detailed layout plan has been drawn up for Shahe and Nantou, but the Shenzhen University is now being built in the area and fish culture is being practised at Qianhai Bay. At present, most development of the western region is concentrated around Shekou and Chiwan.

Regulations for Development Control

In China, there are no binding regulations or laws to control land development. The master plan is only a guideline and has no legal status. It is up to individuals and production units to follow such guidelines in land development. Any proposal for development not conforming to the master plan will be dealt with mainly by persuasion. Individuals or production units violating the plan will be publicly criticized, but at present no legal action can be taken to punish the violators.

This system of persuasion and self-control may work well in other parts of China but it will not make foreign investors feel confident in property investment in the SEZ. Although the master plan is designed to regulate land use, the lack of a regulated system of land administration means that there is no guarantee that land will be developed as planned. Foreign investors need some form of guarantee that their properties can be under their control and operation for a certain number of years before they will feel confident to invest in the Shenzhen SEZ. It is for this reason that the Provisional Regulations on Land Control in the Shenzhen SEZ were prepared. They were passed by the Thirteenth Session of the Standing Committee of the Fifth Guangdong Provincial People's Congress in November 1981 together with three other sets of regulations on the registration of enterprises, labour and wages, and visas. The Provisional Regulations on Land Control laid down on paper the authority of the Shenzhen government in planning, land management and development control, and set the rents for land use in the SEZ for foreign investors.

The land development control regulations have six major characteristics. Firstly, all proposals for the use of land must be submitted to the Shenzhen People's Government for approval. Private transactions and negotiations with a landowner without the prior approval of the government will not be honoured.

Secondly, a leasehold system is established in the SEZ. The lease period depends on the amount of investment and practical needs. The maximum lease period for the major land uses is shown in Table 7.3. Upon the expiry of the lease, it is renewable subject to the approval of the special zone authority.

A land-use fee is levied according to use, location and lease period (Table 7.3). Not unexpectedly, the cheapest standard annual land-use fee is for industrial purposes. This corresponds with the original intention, in setting up the SEZ, of attracting industrial development. Tourism and commercial land use have the highest standard annual land-use fees. Special preferential treatment is granted to educational, cultural, scientific, technological, medical, health and public welfare land use. Projects involving the most advanced technology and non-profit making projects may be exempted from land-use fees. All land-use fees are to be adjusted once every three years.

Thirdly, foreign investors have to obtain a land-use certificate from the Shenzhen People's Government before land development can proceed. The application for the certificate has to be accompanied by the contracts or agreements signed with the Shenzhen SEZ Development Company and related information on the scale and nature of the proposed land use. The land will be delineated and a land-use certificate will be issued by the Planning Department after it has been verified that the application conforms with the master plan, and once the land-use fees have been paid.

Fourthly, the Provisional Regulations on Land Control in the Shenzhen SEZ guard strictly against land speculation. Article 4 prohibits private land

Table 7.3 Lease Periods and Land-use Fees

	Maximum Lease Period (years)	Standard Annual Land-use Fees	
		Original Rmb/sq m	Revised (1984) Rmb/sq m
Industrial	30	10–30	6–30
Commercial	20	70–200	40–200
Residential	50	30–60	18–60
Educational, scientific, technological, medical and health	50	*	*
Tourism	30	60–100	35–100
Agriculture and animal husbandry	20	*	*

Note: *These will be determined on individual application.

Source: Provisional Regulations on Land Control in Shenzhen Special Economic Zone (Guangdong Provincial Administration of Special Economic Zones); and *Wen Wei Po*, 22 June 1984.

transactions and Article 5 explicitly states that private land transactions are forbidden and that the land-use certificate refers only to the right to use the land and not to ownership of the land. 'It is forbidden to buy and sell land, or to do so in a disguised way, to let or transfer land without prior permission, or to mine, use or damage underground resources and other resources' (Article 5). Article 13 specifies that 'overseas investors must engage in construction on the land for their use according to the purpose as stipulated in the contracts or agreements, and are not allowed to convert the land for other purposes at will'.

Fifthly, a time limit is set for development to take place. Within six months after the land-use certificate becomes effective, building and construction plans have to be submitted for approval, and within nine months construction must take place. Otherwise, if there are no justifiable reasons for delay, the land-use certificate will be revoked and the fees paid will not be refunded. Apart from preventing land speculation, the regulations also try to make sure that development will take place as scheduled.

Finally, land developers have to bear the cost of curbing environmental pollution. Any discharge and treatment of solid waste, gas and waste water from land leased by the foreign investor has to meet the discharge standards and treatment requirements of China. The leaseholder must pay treatment fees if treatment is required. The costs of linking any power supply, water supply, drainage, sewers, gas pipes and telecommunications equipment with the SEZ network also have to be paid by the leaseholder.

In 1983, in view of the primitive state of development of the SEZ when land levelling and infrastructure construction were still under way and the operation and production conditions for industrial and commercial development were not yet complete, a 30 to 50 per cent reduction of the standard land-use fees up to 1985 was offered. The SEZ was divided into three zones for the purpose of reducing land-use fees: (a) the Luohu and Shekou industrial districts; (b) the Shangbu, Reservoir and Shatoujiao districts; and (c) the other areas excluding districts developed by joint venture (Shenzhen SEZ Development Company, 1983, p. 19). The rates of reduction in standard rents for these three zones were 30 per cent, 40 per cent and 50 per cent respectively. In addition, fees for uncultivated land such as slopes, hillsides and swamps will be exempted for one to five years according to their use. Land-use fees will be adjusted once every three years with increases of not more than 30 per cent.

Land Development Procedure

Permission for the use of land in the Shenzhen SEZ has to be obtained from the Planning Department of the Shenzhen SEZ Construction Company. The process of land development in the SEZ has been summarized in Fig. 7.3.

Foreign investors who need land for their investment projects have first to approach the Shenzhen SEZ Development Company with details of their investment proposals. These details must include items of investment, the amount of investment, the form of investment (such as sole investment, joint investment and co-operation), the land area required, and the proposed location of the project. Prospective investors in the Shekou and Shahe industrial zones can contact the CMSN and the Shahe Overseas Chinese Enterprise Company (Shenzhen) respectively direct. An agreement will be signed if the investment proposal is accepted by the Shenzhen SEZ Development Company and this will lead to the signing of a contract at a later stage.

With the agreement or contract and the investment proposal in hand, the investor can then apply for a land-use certificate from the Planning Department. The Planning Department will assess the proposal to see whether it conflicts with the master plan. If there is no proposal as to the location of the project, the Planning Department will try to find the best location for the development according to the master plan. After payment of the land-use fees determined by the Planning Department, a land-use certificate will be issued.

The investor then has to go to the Architecture Department to obtain approval of his architectural plan. Once approval has been obtained from the Architecture Department, the investor will then proceed to the Building Control Division of the Planning Department to apply for a building permit. A building permit will be issued if the building plan meets the building

Fig. 7.3 The Land Development Procedure in the Shenzhen SEZ

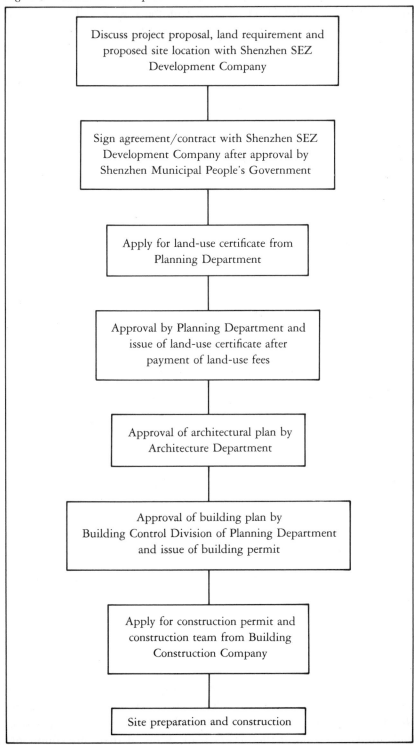

Source: Fieldwork, 1983.

standards of China. With the building permit in hand, the investor will approach the Building Construction Company who will arrange the construction permit and recruit a construction team to start site preparation and building construction. All construction work in the SEZ has to be arranged by the Building Construction Company.

The land administration and development control process of the Shenzhen SEZ is a lengthy one, but it benefits and protects both the government and the investor. On the one hand, the process ensures that every stage of land development will be under the control of the SEZ and will conform to planning and building standards acceptable to China. On the other hand, it protects the rights of the developers in using the land and ensures that their development will not be jeopardized by unplanned and chaotic land development in the zone.

Planning Issues

For the past thirty years China has been a relatively closed society and has had little experience in dealing with foreign investors, especially those from a different economic system. The setting up of SEZs may provide an opportunity for China to observe and learn, from the operation and management of modern industrial and commercial enterprises, about the Western capitalist economy. The active construction of the basic infrastructure, the preparation of the social and economic development plan and the master plan, and the passing of the four sets of regulations on the registration of enterprises, land use, visas, and labour and wages, are positive steps taken by the Chinese government in its strategy for attracting foreign investment to the SEZ.

The master plan seeks to enforce control over development and to co-ordinate the provision of infrastructure and public utilities, without which development in the Shenzhen SEZ will be haphazard and disorderly. The four sets of regulations on the registration of enterprises, land use, visas, and labour and wages are intended to provide a secure environment for foreign investment. They may be more significant than the provision of infrastructure in attracting foreign investment because they provide a framework within which the foreign investor will feel confident to invest.

All these efforts exerted by the SEZ may not, however, lead to the development that is anticipated. Experiences in some developed countries indicate that good planning is not sufficient to promote development. There are some problems and issues that will probably be encountered in developing the zone. Some of these problems are of direct relevance to the planning and implementation of the master plan. Some of them are commonly experienced in developing special economic districts in other parts of the world, and some are unique to the Shenzhen SEZ because of its special characteristics.

The Uncertainty of the Planning Environment

The target population of the master plan is 800,000 which is more than eight times the population of 1982. A large number of industrial and commercial enterprises will be needed to provide sufficient employment for all these people. With the large population base of China, it is not difficult to attract people to the SEZ. However, it may be difficult to attract the foreign investment that will be required to support such a large population, especially as this new industrial area will have to compete with other more established industrial districts in South-east Asia as well as with Hong Kong. The viability of the SEZ depends greatly on how much foreign investment it can attract.

The attraction of employment to newly developed areas such as new towns and growth poles is always a difficult problem for planners to solve. Most new towns in England were set up as an act of faith in the hope that jobs would follow after the infrastructure had been provided (Schaffer, 1970, p. 133). Tuen Mun New Town, one of the more recent new towns of Hong Kong, is not far from the Shenzhen SEZ and only 32 km away from the industrial core of Hong Kong. But even with the influx of a population of 600,000, it has not been successful in attracting industry. Compared to the Shenzhen SEZ, Tuen Mun is better equipped with roads, infrastructure and public utilities. It also has the advantages of proximity to the well-established industrial core of Hong Kong and of operating under a free economy. Despite much promotion and publicity of the advantages of setting up factories in Tuen Mun, the movement of industries to the area is still unsatisfactory. Many factory owners do not want to take the risk of moving to a new location. As the Shenzhen SEZ is a new industrial area operating under a socialist economy that is very different from the capitalist economy, foreign investors may hesitate to involve themselves. Despite careful planning, the development of the zone is vulnerable to fluctuations in foreign investment. An over-provision of infrastructure for anticipated developments that do not materialize may be costly to the Shenzhen SEZ which has only limited resources.

Although physical planning cannot guarantee the success of the SEZ in attracting foreign investment, if used carefully it can help to safeguard against the financial losses which would be the consequence of a shortfall in investment. Phased development control can be used to guide the sequence and timing of land development. It has been used in the planning of many newly developed areas of various scales ranging from industrial estates to new towns. The provision of infrastructure and public utilities for industrial development takes time and money. In order to launch production in the shortest possible time, reduce the size of investment, and prevent over-provision and under-utilization of infrastructure, it is usual for industrial estates to be developed in stages (UNIDO, 1978b, p. 53). In new town planning in the United Kingdom, development corporations are required to submit a plan for development in stages in addition to the general land-use and transportation plan (Corden, 1977, p. 77).

Another measure that can be used to guide the timing of development is phased zoning. Land designated for development, but presently not in the process of development, is only permitted to be developed if the developer can provide his own infrastructure such as sewers, waste water treatment, parking areas and roads. This may be used to prevent leap-frog development which would ultimately be damaging to the SEZ.

The Fluidity of the Planning Environment

As well as being subject to the level of foreign investment, planning policy in the Shenzhen SEZ is also vulnerable to decisions that are made outside its territory. The drafting of the master plan and its implementation are not entirely under the control of the Planning Department of the Shenzhen SEZ. For example, the original planned population of the Futian district, one of the largest districts in the SEZ, was not very large. However, when a real estate company from Hong Kong showed interest in developing the area and approached the authorities in Beijing, the planned population was increased to 300,000 and it became one of the largest projects in the SEZ. Another example of the fluidity of the planning environment is the expressway linking Hong Kong and Guangzhou that passes through the Shenzhen SEZ near Futian. A route for the expressway was not contained in the original draft of the master plan because it was considered too expensive to be built by the Chinese government and would involve financing not only from the SEZ but also from other counties lying along the route of the expressway. However, after a letter of intent had been signed between the land developer from Hong Kong and the Chinese government, the expressway was added to the master plan.

Some of the developments in the Shenzhen SEZ, like the Futian district and the Hong Kong–Guangzhou expressway, were initiated by foreign investors. As the purpose of the SEZ is to attract foreign investment, it is very difficult for the local administration to turn down development proposals by foreign investors, especially those that the central government in Beijing has approved. This, however, may lead to difficulty in implementing the master plan because development proposals by foreign investors may not conform to it and major alterations of the master plan may then be required. Furthermore the location of development and the pace of development may depend too much on outside investors over whom the Planning Department in Shenzhen has little control.

As most foreign investment in Shenzhen either comes from Hong Kong or passes through Hong Kong, and some of the housing projects built with foreign investments are aimed at the Hong Kong market, road links with Hong Kong are very important. Plans to open two new entry-points to Hong Kong are being prepared. One is in the east at Shatoujiao and the other in the west at Luomazhou. However, these entry-points affect not only the development of the SEZ, but also developments in Hong Kong, especially of road transport. Whether these two sites are suitable locations for check-points between Shenzhen and Hong Kong has still to be decided by the Hong Kong government. If the Hong Kong government decides to locate them at other places then the road network connecting the proposed check-points and related planned development in the master plan will have to be altered accordingly. Co-ordination and co-operation with the Hong Kong government is necessary if the master plan is to be implemented successfully.

Massive Land Development by Private Developers

In the first days of the development of the Shenzhen SEZ, land levelling work and infrastructure development were mainly undertaken by the SEZ itself. This work requires enormous amounts of capital. From 1979 to 1981, a total of Rmb 286 million (US$147 million) was invested site preparation and capital construction. Rmb 540 million (US$278 million) was invested in 1982 to undertake large-scale development and to speed up construction (Shenzhen SEZ Development Company, 1983, p. 16). However, the return of capital investment from land-use fees and tax collected from foreign investors is rather slow. A new approach that attempts to minimize capital outlay by allowing foreign investors to develop large tracts of land is currently being adopted. The Futian development is an example of this new approach. A Hong Kong real estate company is being allowed to develop 3,000 ha of land for commercial, industrial and residential use. The developer will carry out all the necessary site preparation and will provide the basic infrastructure and will be allowed to subdivide this large tract of land. From a financial point of view, this approach is attractive especially when there is a shortage of capital. However, it may not be desirable for future implementation of the master plan. The absence of regulations to prevent the subdivision of large tracts of land developed by foreign investors may create negative side-effects such as traffic congestion and environmental pollution which would lead to malfunctioning of the master plan. Moreover, the timing of such development by private developers may not co-ordinate well with the development of neighbouring districts and may lead to undesirable fragmented development in the SEZ.

External Communications

Internal communications are important for the movement of goods, people and information within the Shenzhen SEZ. However, as the development of the zone depends very much on foreign investment, external communications are of paramount importance. Foreign firms in Shenzhen need to maintain international contacts and their personnel need to travel in and out of the Shenzhen SEZ easily. Good port facilities are also required to import raw materials and export finished products. One of the major obstacles to the development of the Shenzhen SEZ is its poor provision for external communications. The telephone and telegram facilities are not adequate to meet the demand from the zone's growing service sector and from foreign investors. Travelling in and out of the Shenzhen SEZ is also not convenient. Luohu, the major land entrance from Hong Kong that operates between 8.00 a.m. and 8.30 p.m., is always overloaded because it serves tourists and businessmen travelling not only to Shenzhen but to other parts of China as well. In 1981, a total of 8.4 million people entered China through Luohu. It takes at least two hours to pass through immigration and customs counters that are always crowded. To facilitate the movement of people and goods to and from Hong Kong, it is important to shorten the time and the procedure for crossing the border. This can be done by opening up more check-points along the border as well as by separating travellers and businessmen going to the Shenzhen SEZ from those that are going to other parts of China.

Population Composition

The master plan of the Shenzhen SEZ allows for a population of 800,000. Given the large population base of China, there will be no problem in meeting this target. What may be more difficult is controlling the inflow of people into the zone and providing them with jobs. Population inflow has to be co-ordinated with development, otherwise unemployment will occur.

Experience in other developing countries shows that similar special economic districts such as export processing zones, free trade zones and industrial estates often attract poor job-seeking migrants whose arrival creates housing and unemployment problems in the areas where these zones are located. Attempts have been made by the Chinese government to control the inflow of population into the Shenzhen SEZ. A border fence, 84.6 km long and well-illuminated, has been constructed on the northern boundary to separate the SEZ from other parts of China. There are six check-points to control the movement of people and goods in and out of the zone. To control the quality of the labour force in the SEZ, technical personnel and skilled workers are to be recruited and selected from all over the country through the SEZ Labour Services Company. However, these two measures cannot ensure that there will not be illegal immigration into the SEZ because of its attractive wages and living standards. There is also concern about the age structure and sex ratio in relation to the future development of the SEZ and the present large percentage of temporary construction workers (Zheng, *et al.*, 1981).

Neither the social and economic development plan nor the master plan of the Shenzhen SEZ gives any indication of the future population composition of the zone. Shenzhen will attract people not only from other parts of China but also from Hong Kong and other countries. Since the setting up of the SEZ, most of the housing projects sponsored by foreign investors have been located within a short distance of the Shenzhen Town and Luohu districts. These housing projects are built mainly for people in Hong Kong or from overseas, as their prices are beyond the reach of local residents. At present the prospective buyers of these housing units are mainly foreign investors who need to provide living quarters for their management staff brought in from Hong Kong or overseas, plus Hong Kong and overseas Chinese who buy properties for their relatives in Shenzhen and China. The Futian development, with a planned population of 300,000, is also directed at the Hong Kong market in the hope that the cheaper house prices of the zone will eventually attract people from Hong Kong to use Shenzhen as a dormitory town.

At present, there is a wide gap between the standard of living and life-styles of local Chinese and people from Hong Kong and overseas. It is difficult to plan for two different groups of people with differing life-styles and it is important at the planning stage to establish an optimum mixture of these two types of people. Without a planned population mixture, it is difficult to determine the number of housing units and facilities that will be needed for local Chinese residents and the number of housing units to be built for people from Hong Kong and overseas.

Closely related to the problems of population mixture are the problems of planning standards and social integration.

Planning Standards

Planning standards for the provision of community facilities such as recreation areas, community halls and commercial facilities are related to the standard of living and life-style of the planned population. The current planning standard used in China for its residential districts relates to the life-style of local Chinese. It may not be applicable to people from Hong Kong and overseas. As the future population will be a mixture of local Chinese and people from Hong Kong and overseas, it is necessary to design a planning standard for the SEZ that will suit the characteristics of the future population. The authorities have still to decide which planning standard is to be used in the Shenzhen SEZ — whether to use the Chinese planning standard, or a standard acceptable to foreign investors, or a combination of both.

Social Integration

The mixture of population will not only complicate the setting of planning standards, but will also create problems of social integration. The question of whether people with different life-styles can live together without conflict is a major planning consideration. The experience of new towns and housing estates in other parts of the world suggests that the mixing of social groups, especially of those that are very different in character, may lead to hostility and conflict rather than to a more interesting and varied community life (Keller, 1966). However, this is not to suggest that the SEZ should not have a mixture of local Chinese and people from Hong Kong and overseas. Plans are needed to arrange the different social groups in a harmonious way. Social homogeneity on one level may contribute to heterogeneity on a higher level (Michelson, 1976, p. 123). The extent to which a social group should remain homogeneous and the extent to which heterogeneity could exist have to be carefully decided and planned.

The problems of a planning standard and of social integration may not be visible at present because the scale of development is still relatively small. They may become more apparent as the Shenzhen SEZ continues to develop towards its target population.

Conclusion

The development of the Shenzhen SEZ has been very rapid. Its population grew from 68,000 in 1978 to 104,000 in mid-1982. Like the new towns of Hong Kong, the Shenzhen SEZ can best be described as a large construction site. Building construction, road-works, and site preparation are common scenes in the zone. Shenzhen is the fastest growing SEZ in China and attracts most of the foreign investment. From their setting up until 1983, the four SEZs attracted approximately US$3,000 million worth of intended foreign investment, and a large proportion of it (US$1,700 million) was invested in the Shenzhen SEZ (*People's Daily*, 29 March 1984; *Chinese SEZ Handbook*, 1984, p. 244). Its annual growth in industrial output is 86 per cent, which is the highest among the SEZs and higher than for most cities in China (*People's Daily*, 29 March 1984). The rapid growth of the Shenzhen SEZ is closely related to Hong Kong as over 80 per cent of its foreign investment has come from Hong Kong.

Planning is a continuous process and constant feedback from the process of implementation of a plan is necessary to make that plan viable. This is especially important in the physical planning of the Shenzhen SEZ because China has little experience of developments that involve foreign investors. The preparation of the social and economic development plan and the master plan and the establishment of land-use control regulations are already major steps towards the management of land development in Shenzhen. The land development control regulations bear mainly on land use, but regulations on land subdivision, height and bulk restrictions, and population density control, which are commonly found in land development control regulations in other countries, are lacking in the current planning system of the Shenzhen SEZ. However, these may be exercised through the land development procedure which the Shenzhen SEZ authority can negotiate with foreign investors.

Although a new policy of allowing private developers to develop large tracts of land has been adopted in the Shenzhen SEZ to lessen the financial burden of site preparation and infrastructure provision, the SEZ has still to provide most of the basic infrastructure, housing for local workers and standard factory buildings. Considering the large amount of capital involved, it may be desirable for the SEZ to develop in stages to maximize the utility of the infrastructure and to avoid an over-provision.

China has attempted to control population movement into the Shenzhen SEZ by constructing a fence on the northern border of the zone to separate it from other parts of China. Hopefully this can control the rate of population increase derived from immigration into the zone. As housing for local workers is mainly provided by the government, the control of population migration into the zone may reduce the problem of a housing shortage which has plagued the special economic districts of other developing countries.

The Shenzhen SEZ lies along the border with Hong Kong. Its development will affect the development of Hong Kong and vice versa. For example, the proposed development of Futian new town and the Hong Kong–Guangzhou expressway through Luomazhou will greatly increase the traffic load in the New Territories of Hong Kong. The development of the Shenzhen SEZ depends very much on easy entry and exit across the border with Hong Kong and this requires the co-operation of Hong Kong in opening up new customs check-points. Conversely, the development of the north-west and north-east New Territories of Hong Kong will affect the physical planning of Shenzhen. Since physical planning on both sides of the border is closely related, it is imperative that the planners of Shenzhen and Hong Kong understand the plans in both areas. Lack of co-ordination between the two parties will jeopardize physical planning and development in both the Shenzhen SEZ and Hong Kong.

A good master plan and layout plan that provide an adequate fundamental infrastructure, a sufficient supply of cheap power and water, as well as good internal and external transportation and communications, will undoubtedly facilitate industrial development. However, they are not in themselves sufficient for the attraction of foreign investment. Political and social stability, sound and long-term economic development policies, efficient administrative organizations, and abundant high-quality but low-cost labour are other very important factors for a successful special economic district (Vittal, 1977, p. 31).

Good physical planning must be well co-ordinated with other development programmes. There are five possible reasons for the failure of other industrial estates to achieve their goals which may be equally applicable to the Shenzhen SEZ (UNIDO, 1978a):

(a) unrealistic objectives which are difficult to achieve given local resources and conditions;

(b) an absence of co-ordination with other development programmes; for example, between the provision of electricity and water supplies and communications systems as against industrial development;

(c) an inadequate provision of supporting institutions — where, for instance, a location offering land and infrastructure lacks the support of financial institutions, vocational training, management training and extension services — so that the efficiency of industrial operation is unsatisfactory;

(d) a lack of adequate pre-planning in site selection; and

(e) vacillating government attitudes and policies towards the programme, causing unnecessary delays in development and prompting investors to go elsewhere.

The development of the Shenzhen SEZ depends very much on the inflow of outside capital over which the zone administration has very little control. However, despite some shortcomings in its planning, the Shenzhen SEZ has tried its best to provide an orderly planned environment that is conducive to foreign investment. More significantly, it has established a planning system and land-use regulations that may be used as a guideline for the future planning and development of other Chinese SEZs. The planning and implementation of the master plan in the Shenzhen SEZ has provided an invaluable challenge and experience for the planners of China, especially now that the government has announced its interest in developing fourteen more coastal ports as economic development zones with similar characteristics to the SEZs.

8. Population Growth and Related Issues

David K. Y. Chu

WITH the development of the special economic zone, Shenzhen has had to face many problems arising from rapid population growth, industrialization and urbanization. The scale of these problems in Shenzhen is much larger than in other export processing zones owing to the greater size of the zone and to the fact that the original infrastructure was very poor. The task of developing the Shenzhen SEZ is, in fact, comparable to building a new industrial, commercial and administrative city from scratch.

This chapter will outline the problems related to population growth and discuss some solutions proposed and undertaken by the Shenzhen SEZ authority.

Recent Experiences of Population Growth in Shenzhen

Since 1978, the Shenzhen SEZ has experienced very rapid change in terms of population size and composition. The area now designated as the Shenzhen SEZ was previously a rural frontier zone, with a very small urban population, under the administration of Bao'an County. The largest urban settlement before 1978 was Shenzhen Town and the second largest was Nantou Market. Together they contained most of the urban population of the area which amounted to 27,366 people (Zheng, *et al.*, 1981), or 40.15 per cent of the total Shenzhen SEZ population (about 68,166 — the 1978 population figure cited by Zheng, *et al.*, 1981). In other words, before 1978, the zone was predominantly agricultural and almost 60 per cent of its people were classified as rural. The character of the zone began to change in 1979 when it was announced that Shekou would be the site for an industrial estate to be operated by the China Merchants' Steam Navigation Co. Ltd. of Hong Kong. Construction workers, technicians and engineers recruited mainly from Shanxi Province were among the first wave of immigrants to enter the zone (fieldwork, 1981). Other newcomers included those cadres who were transferred to the area to prepare and to carry out the upgrading of the Bao'an County administration to municipal status (February 1979) and the designation of Shenzhen as an SEZ (December 1979).

By the end of 1980, the total population figure recorded in the Shenzhen SEZ was 84,057 of which 57.4 per cent was classified as urban (Zheng, *et al.*, 1981). This denoted a 23.3 per cent increase in population over a period of two years and, for the first time, the urban population overtook the rural population in size, giving the area an urban character. This trend of growth continued. In mid-1982 when the national census was taken, the population of the Shenzhen SEZ had grown to 104,000 (*Wen Wei Po*, 9 July 1982). Owing to the different definition of urban population employed in the census, the rural-urban ratio obtained in the census was not directly comparable with previous figures. A year later, it was estimated that the total population with permanent residence had increased to 123,000 (computed according to statistics given in the *Shenzhen Special Zone Daily*, 7 November 1984) and the percentage share of the rural population in 1982 had further shrunk to about 30 per cent (Ng, 1983a), if the conventional Chinese definition of urban is employed.

One should note that these population figures do not reflect the actual population living in the Shenzhen SEZ, for they cover only those with permanent residence. Workers, visitors and the relatives of Shenzhen residents with temporary status are not included in these figures. For example, those people with temporary residential status amounted to 50,000 in 1981 (Zheng, *et al.*, 1981) and about 86,000 by the end of 1982 (computed according to statistics given in *Wen Wei Po*, 28 January 1983). In other words, as far as population and social planning are concerned, the temporary residents of the Shenzhen SEZ have become an element that cannot be overlooked. Indeed many of these temporary residents will eventually settle down in Shenzhen and obtain permanent citizenship in the zone. This can be exemplified by the recent granting of permanent citizenship to 25,000 construction workers and engineers belonging to the construction battalion of the People's Liberation Army working in the Shenzhen SEZ. Following the policy of streamlining the Army in September 1983, these workers and engineers were organized into five local construction companies, one engineering company and one machine-installation company (*Shenzhen Special Zone Daily*, 26 September 1983).

The Targets of Population Growth

The Planning Department of the Shenzhen SEZ is vested with the responsibility for setting the target population and its spatial distribution in the zone. In May 1981 when the first draft of the master plan of the Shenzhen SEZ was formulated, it was proposed that the population should reach 300,000 by 1990 and 500,000 by the year 2000 (fieldwork, May 1981). As the first draft of the master plan had not taken account of the possibility of massive joint-venture land development schemes, such as the proposed joint venture between the Shenzhen Municipal Government and the Hopewell Group of Hong Kong over an area of 32 sq km in Futian, the first draft of the master plan of the Shenzhen SEZ was scrapped. Another draft of the master plan was formulated in the second half of 1981. The eventual target of population growth was double that of the first draft: 400,000 by 1990 and one million by the year 2000. This twofold increase is mainly due to a desire on the part of the Hong Kong partners of the massive land development joint-venture projects to make profits. For their purposes, the Shenzhen SEZ would ideally become a replica of urban Hong Kong with multi-storey buildings, a high population density and an intensive use of every square inch of land. For example, the Hopewell Group of Hong Kong proposed that within the 32 sq km at Futian, as many as 700,000 people should be housed. The Planning Department of the Shenzhen SEZ thought otherwise and insisted on a much lower population target in order to preserve a more pleasant living environment. Consequently, a target population of only 400,000 was allocated for Futian in the preliminary version of the second draft of the master plan (fieldwork, April 1982). The Futian case clearly demonstrated the conflict of interests between the planners and the commercial developers of the Shenzhen SEZ.

The second draft of the master plan for the town was then released and discussed by many scholars, town planners and administrators, both local and from overseas. By the time it was finalized (September 1982), the target population of the Shenzhen SEZ for the year 2000 was set at only 800,000. The target population figures for many districts were then reduced, with the biggest cut at Futian, from 400,000 to 300,000. As shown in Table 8.1, the population targets of some other zones were also reduced and only that for Chegongmiao was increased (fieldwork, September 1982).

Natural growth, currently running at about 2 per cent or even lower (Ng, 1983a), will not be a major source of population growth. The main source will be the skilled labourers, technicians, engineers and their families who are being brought in to support the newly developed industrial and commercial enterprises. Another possible source is the transfer from other parts of China of the relatives of Chinese from Hong Kong and overseas. For example, in mid-1982 240 such households, making a total of 889 people, moved into the Shenzhen SEZ (*Wen Wei Po*, 9 July 1982).

In view of the dependence of population growth in the Shenzhen SEZ on economic development, the timing and speed, as well as the spatial distribution, of future population growth is thus subject to the ability of the Shenzhen SEZ to attract overseas investors. If the Shenzhen SEZ is to be highly successful, population growth will exceed the planned targets. The inevitable uncertainty over the future of the zone means that the population targets of the Shenzhen SEZ are at best very fluid projections. This in turn will seriously affect the growth of an infrastructure and the planning of other social facilities.

Table 8.1 Population Targets in Various Districts of the Shenzhen SEZ by the Year 2000

	Original Target	New Target	Difference
Daxiaomeisha	10,000	10,000	0
Yantian	20,000	10,000	−10,000
Shatoujiao	10,000	10,000	0
Liantang	15,000	15,000	0
Luohu	120,000	110,000	−10,000
Shenzhen Town	40,000	40,000	0
Reservoir	30,000	30,000	0
Shangbu	100,000	60,000	−40,000
Futian	405,000	300,000	−105,000
Xiangmihu	10,000	1,000	−9,000
Chegongmiao	20,000	25,000	+5,000
Agronomic Institute	10,000	4,000	−6,000
Shahe	50,000	40,000	−10,000
Houhai	30,000	30,000	0
Shekou	50,000	50,000	0
Xili	3,000	3,000	0
Chiwan	50,000	30,000	−20,000
Nantou-Bao'an	42,000	30,000	−12,000
Total	1,015,000	798,000	−217,000

Problems and Some Solutions

The Shortage of Labour

As happens in the suburban fringes of many other fast-developing cities, the farmers of the Shenzhen SEZ are easily lured to more lucrative employment in the non-farming sector, leading to a marked decrease in agricultural production because of the shortage of labour. Land is abandoned and left untilled. Consequently, the Shenzhen SEZ has had to import farmers in order to keep the farmland in production. Some 2,000 vegetable farmers were hired from the Shantou district in 1979 and another 2,500 vegetable farmers were hired from the Guangzhou area in 1980. But the problem is still not solved (see Chapter 6). According to the initial draft of the economic plan, the Shenzhen SEZ will need as many as 32,000 farmers in 1990. (On the revised draft plan, the projected agricultural working population for 1990 has been reduced to 15,000, which is more realistic.) Even without further loss, the existing 14,000 farmers active in Shenzhen will not be sufficient to maintain the level of farming production in the near future. The problem of a shortage of labour in the agricultural sector persists, for the wages and returns in the farming sector are much lower than those in the commercial and industrial sectors.

A shortage of labour is a problem not only in the agricultural sector, but also in the industrial and commercial sectors. These sectors do not lack unskilled labourers who are easily recruited from the local farming sector and nearby counties, but they are short of skilled and semi-skilled workers. Such workers can easily find employment in their local towns and in established inland industrial and commercial enterprises. Although the wages are higher in the Shenzhen SEZ than in other parts of China, higher living costs in Shenzhen, the lack of local recreational facilities and the disruption of social ties (for the relatives of residents of the Shenzhen SEZ cannot come to the zone without permission, and this is not easily obtained), all discourage them from leaving their familiar working and social environment to go to work in Shenzhen. Realizing the inertia of skilled and semi-skilled workers, the Shenzhen SEZ authority has offered them many incentive schemes in the hope that these will persuade them to move. Such schemes include better housing, medical benefits and the granting of permanent urban status to these workers and their children, irrespective of their former status, whether rural or temporary urban (*Shenzhen Special Zone Daily*, 26 August 1982). To what extent the incentive schemes will be effective remains to be seen. But it seems certain that these schemes will have a positive effect on the supply of skilled and semi-skilled workers.

The Problem of Rising Expectations

Foreign investment, massive construction of infrastructure, a shortage of labour and the rapid growth in export trade and tourism together with the system of awarding bonuses and prizes to diligent workers have all helped to increase the income of the residents of the Shenzhen SEZ. The average monetary wage for workers and staff members of state-owned enterprises in the Shenzhen SEZ jumped from Rmb 571 in 1978 to Rmb 1,359 in 1982, an increase of 138 per cent (*Shenzhen Special Zone Daily*, 10 March 1983). Farmers in the Shenzhen SEZ are now receiving an annual average income of Rmb 685, an increase of 320 per cent over 1978 (*Shenzhen Special Zone Daily*, 10 November 1983). The wages of workers in joint-venture enterprises are even higher. There are, in general, four categories of labour in these enterprises. Probationary labourers are paid HK$500 per month. Contract labourers are employed for a period of three months to one year at a wage rate of HK$600 per month. Skilled labourers are paid HK$700–HK$800 per month, while the most highly paid technicians receive around HK$1,000–HK$1,200 per month. In general, workers engaged in these enterprises receive about 70 per cent of the nominal wages paid by their employers in renminbi whilst the remaining 30 per cent of their wages is handed over to the local authorities for medical and other collective welfare schemes (fieldwork, 1984). Nevertheless, even after this deduction, they are still amongst the most highly paid workers in the Shenzhen SEZ.

Rises in income promote expectations for more commodities, better housing, more educational opportunities, and easier access to hospitals and recreational centres. The problem becomes even more critical when there are not only rising expectations amongst the existing population but also when the population itself is expanding.

Rising Living Costs

There are ample supplies of televisions, sewing machines and bicycles in the Shenzhen SEZ — probably because the zone is the gateway for the legal and illegal importation of these items. In fact, the prices of these goods are lower than in other areas of China and about 10 per cent lower than in Guangzhou (Huang, 1983).

The pressure of rising costs is most apparent in the prices of staple foods, daily necessities and transport. When the central government plans were formulated, it was impossible to foresee this situation and allocate more commodities to the Shenzhen market. Acute shortages of official supplies were recorded from 1979 to 1981 so that the citizens of Shenzhen had to buy most of their daily needs from free markets at higher prices, thereby triggering off an inflationary spiral. For example, between 1978 and 1981, average vegetable prices rose by 30 per cent and monthly charges for food in the canteens of government offices rose by 66.7 per cent. Consequently, it was estimated that in 1981 each adult needed a sum of at least Rmb 51.12 per month to survive in the Shenzhen SEZ (*Shenzhen Special Zone Daily*, 19 July 1982), almost triple the amount for 1978. Fortunately, the inflationary spiral was arrested in 1982. The basic cost of living for an adult declined to Rmb 50.14, a drop of 2 per cent compared with 1981. Huang (1983) attributed this decline to the additional supplies at cheap official prices allocated to the Shenzhen SEZ market from other parts of China, so that people bought less from the free market.

The Increasing Demand for Housing

It is a commonplace that housing provision in China varies markedly from that in a capitalist society, in the sense that housing is regarded as a social provision monitored by the state. However, with rising incomes and a growing population, the demand for better housing is very widespread, although this demand will not be reflected in the prices of housing as in a capitalist society. Instead, this demand is likely to be channelled to the managers of enterprises in the form of workers' opinions or otherwise.

In view of growing overcrowding in existing housing and the poor conditions in the temporary huts, the Shenzhen SEZ authority will have to spend some of its scarce resources on the provision of housing. In 1982, over Rmb 80 million was allocated for housing construction to build over 210,000 sq m of new houses (*Shenzhen Special Zone Daily*, 20 December 1982). The 1982 figure was welcomed as representing more than the total sum spent on the construction of housing between 1978 and 1981. As the new flats constructed in 1982 could house only 2,000 families, one might estimate that only about 4,000 families or about 20,000 people (taking a family of five members) were provided with new houses in the last four years. This estimate of 20,000 people rehoused is only a small fraction of the actual increase of population from 30,000 people in 1978 to 210,000 in 1982, including both temporary and permanent residents. It is no wonder then that most of the population of the Shenzhen SEZ live in very crowded conditions and a significant proportion of workers have to live in temporary huts and mat-sheds.

As most of the workers in Chinese enterprises (state-owned and collective-owned alike) are given living quarters with enormous rent subsidies, they normally accept whatever they are allocated. Workers employed by the joint-venture enterprises or foreign wholly owned enterprises, however, do not enjoy this privilege. Overseas investors do not regard housing provision as their responsibility. In attempting to resolve this dilemma, the Shenzhen SEZ authority has decided that workers should be allowed to purchase their own flats or houses from the commercial real-estate developers. The China Merchants' Steam Navigation Co. Ltd., the developer of the Shekou Industrial Zone, is now selling some of its flats, originally constructed for investors and other buyers from overseas, to workers in Shekou at discounted prices with mortgage arrangements. The author was told that these flats would cost a Hong Kong buyer HK$200,000, but would cost a local worker only HK$50,000 (fieldwork, April 1982). As there is as much as 300,000 sq m of private housing to be completed in 1983 and another 220,000 sq m under construction (*Shenzhen Special Zone Daily*, 6 December 1982), the arrangement pioneered in the Shekou Industrial Zone might help to ease the shortage of housing in the Shenzhen SEZ.

The Need for More Educational Opportunities

In view of the fact that most of the new migrants to the Shenzhen SEZ are adults, the need for primary schools and secondary schools is not as pressing as the need for technical institutes and universities. It is very important to provide the means to upgrade the technical knowledge of the adult population as well as to offer educational opportunities for local youths. Furthermore, the economic system and the nature of the SEZ are so different from the educational environment in inland China that, ideally, there should be courses tailored to the needs of the SEZ. Consequently, the Shenzhen

University was established and took in its first batch of students in 1983 (*Shenzhen Special Zone Daily*, 28 March 1983). Part-time courses will also be offered in the future, according to a spokesman. Undoubtedly, with the establishment of the Shenzhen University, the future supply of educated personnel for the SEZ will be better guaranteed.

The Shortage of Medical and Recreational Facilities

Between 1979 and 1982, the expansion of medical facilities fell far behind the increase in population. Only one hospital (with 200 beds) and four clinics are available. This is definitely not enough to meet the demands of a city of 100,000 people (Ng, 1983b). In 1982, a sum of Rmb 8 million was allocated to enlarge the hospital (*Ta Kung Pao*, 26 February 1983), but this sum is obviously too small to provide medical facilities for the expanding population of the zone. Equally, recreational facilities are lacking. Workers complain that there are not enough opportunities for them to relax and enjoy their free time. The tourist resorts such as those at Xili Reservoir are obviously too expensive for local youths. Consequently, the only inexpensive way for them to spend their leisure is to watch television programmes broadcast from the Hong Kong television stations. However, the Shenzhen SEZ authorities suspect that those programmes may be harmful to the mental health of Shenzhen citizens as their society is still very different from the capitalist society of Hong Kong.

Rising living standards indicate that the livelihood of the expanding population of the Shenzhen SEZ has greatly improved. However, the social infrastructure seems not to be expanding fast enough to keep pace with population growth and increasing expectations — although the Shenzhen SEZ authorities have already had some success in resolving this dilemma. As the projected population is several times larger than the existing one, it is essential that more attention be given to this problem.

Social Stratification

Although the actual composition of the target population by 1990 and by the year 2000 has never been fully revealed, based on existing evidence one could predict that the future population of the Shenzhen SEZ will be heterogeneous.

Overseas investors, and expatriate technicians, managerial employees, and their families will be given many privileges that are not available to local residents. Added to them, there will be an unknown number of people who will live in Shenzhen residential estates and work in Hong Kong. They will enter and leave the Shenzhen SEZ freely; while staying in Shenzhen, they will live in a style of their own with a higher standard of living than local inhabitants. Being wealthy capitalists, or well-paid white-collar workers and engineers, some of them could afford to live in their own houses or bungalows, such as those on top of the hills overlooking the Shenzhen Reservoir, and have private limousines as their means of transport. Together with their less well-off fellows who may live in multi-storey private flats and own small private cars, they will make up the wealthier stratum of the Shenzhen SEZ.

Those workers in Shenzhen, irrespective of their origin (local countryside or other parts of China), who are hired by the capitalist-socialist joint ventures or foreign wholly owned enterprises and receive higher wages and sizeable bonuses, probably live in their own flats and enjoy a high standard of living. They may be joined by some enterprising local self-employed people who may specialize in a particular trade or farming business, and thus earn a more comfortable living through hard work and entrepreneurship. Together they will form a middle stratum in the Shenzhen SEZ community.

By contrast, the poorest group is composed of workers who are employed in the socialist sector. Wage-earners have relatively low rates of pay and they are only sustained by many official subsidies such as subsidized housing, an electricity subsidy and a food subsidy — with the additional advantage that their jobs are perhaps the most secure. Cadres in the government of the Shenzhen SEZ also belong to this group, although they are supposed to be among the most influential elements of the community.

Divided by different terms of employment, the separation of three groups of citizens in the Shenzhen SEZ is real and could be regarded as a by-product of the new economic system. Anthony Yeh in Chapter 7 quoted Keller's contention that 'mixing social groups, especially those that are very different in characteristics, may lead to hostility and conflict rather than a more interesting and varied community life'. The social implications of social stratification should not be underestimated. In what sense the Shenzhen SEZ could foster a unified sense of belonging among the three different social groups is a question that the Shenzhen SEZ government ought to consider carefully.

Conclusion

This chapter has attempted to outline some of the issues related to population growth in the Shenzhen SEZ. The selection of issues is by no means exhaustive, yet they are all very important and are of immediate concern if the population is to expand as planned. The Shenzhen SEZ is by far the largest SEZ in the world and the building of a city with nearly one million residents within two decades is very rare indeed. That the Shenzhen SEZ should encounter many problems is not at all surprising and its solutions to such problems are thus of great referential value to planners within and outside China.

9. Forecasting Future Transportation Demand and the Planned Road Network

DAVID K. Y. CHU

THE design of a transport system must take into account many features peculiar to the area in question. Amongst the most important factors relevant to a transport network are: population targets; the distribution of population; the socio-economic characteristics of the population; and the relationships between residential areas and industrial, shopping and other functional areas. Other factors which will influence an evaluation of the system include the physical relief of the area, external communications and the financial situation of the local government. This chapter will analyse the demands for transport within the Shenzhen SEZ in the light of all these factors and will put forward suggestions for the enhancement of the proposed network of roads for internal communication.

The Pattern of Future Passenger Flows

The Target Future Population of the Shenzhen SEZ

Before 1980, Shenzhen was just a small frontier town with an urban population of 23,000 and an urban area of 1.7 sq km. However, since its designation as one of the four Chinese SEZs, its population has grown rapidly. By 1985, its urban population is expected to reach 250,000. It will further grow to 400,000 by 1990 and to about 800,000 by the year 2000. By then, the urban built-up area will amount to 98 sq km. Following such rapid increases of population and urban area, it is to be expected that there will be a corresponding expansion of demand for transport. If the transport network and other transport facilities fail to meet the growth in demand, the economy of Shenzhen will be seriously hampered.

The Spatial Distribution of Population

Given that the socio-economic characteristics of the planned population are homogeneous, the number of journeys generated (Gi) by each district is proportional to the size of its population. Fig. 9.1 shows the spatial distribution of the 800,000 people who will be living in the Shenzhen SEZ in the year 2000. As shown in the figure, of the eighteen major planning districts, the five districts in the centre of the zone, namely, Futian, Shangbu, Luohu, Shenzhen Town (Jiucheng) and Reservoir, are the most heavily populated, containing as much as 68 per cent of the planned total urban population. Towards the west, eight districts account for another 27 per cent whilst the eastern portion is the least populated with only 5 per cent of the planned population residing there. The five central districts will therefore generate the bulk of passenger journeys, followed by the western and eastern districts.

Socio-economic Characteristics

According to the latest plan, 40 per cent of the future population will be employed in the industrial sector and 25 per cent will be in the service sector. The remaining 35 per cent of the population will be regarded as dependent, for example, children of various ages, retired persons and housewives. To forecast the number of work journeys generated by district, one need thus only take into account 65 per cent of the population, that is to say those who are economically active. However, when social, recreational and shopping journeys are considered, one must take the whole adult and teenage population into account.

Furthermore, it is understandable that with growing affluence and rising living standards, people tend to use motorized transport more frequently in order to save time and energy. Zhang Kedong (personal communication based on his study for the Shenzhen Planning Department) suggested that the existing level of utilization of motorized transport (40 per cent for work journeys, 20 per cent for school journeys, and 30 per cent for social, shopping and recreational journeys) may not reflect future needs. Zhang's projections for the use of motorized transport in the future are 80 per cent for work journeys, 50 per cent for school journeys and 80 per cent for social, shopping and recreational journeys, so that the annual number of journeys with motorized means of transportation per resident of the Shenzhen SEZ will increase from 357 in the year 1980 to 830 in the year 2000.

Traffic Generation (Gi)

Zhang Kedong (1981a) estimated that a worker normally makes two journeys, and a cadre normally makes two and half journeys, per working day. He thus generalized that a working person will make 2.3 journeys per working day. In China there are usually 306 working days in a year. Zhang concluded that a figure of 703.8 journeys per worker per year could be used for forecasting purposes.

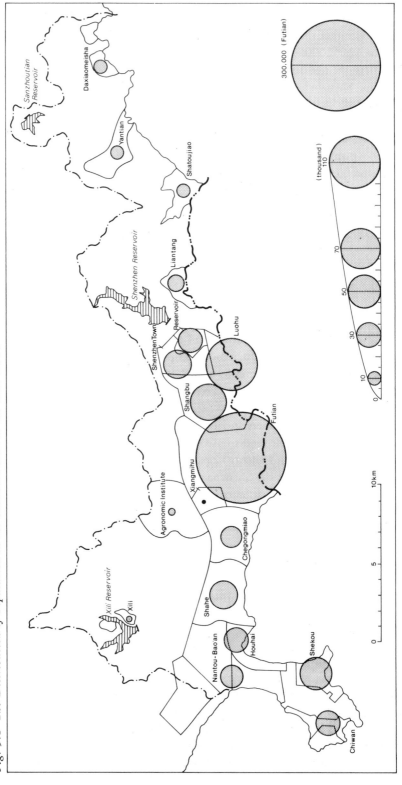

Fig. 9.1 The Distribution of Population in the Shenzhen SEZ in the Year 2000

Among the dependent population, 7.5 per cent will be of school age (Zhang, 1981a). There are many school holidays, and the school year is only 240 days long. Zhang proposed 2.5 journeys per day for each student, totalling 600 journeys per student per year.

By excluding rainy days, Zhang suggested a 300-day year for social, shopping and recreational purposes. From empirical evidence, he proposed that 2 journeys for each adult per day will be enough for planning purposes. In other words 600 journeys would be used as the planning criterion for this purpose.

Accordingly, one may use the aforementioned criteria to forecast the future passenger transport demand generated in each district by multiplying the number of journeys (by purpose) by the target population size of each district (Table 9.1).

Journey Absorption (Dj)

While the number of journeys generated could be estimated according to the target population of each planning district, it is more difficult to locate where the journeys should end. For forecasting purposes, many assumptions and arbitrary measures must be employed. Theoretically, the destinations of journeys are very much affected by the siting of different land uses (Mitchell and Rapkin, 1954; and Blunden, 1971). The land-use plan (Fig. 9.2) of the Shenzhen SEZ would thus be the chief source of information.

Commercial services and public services are of two major types: one serves the whole of the Shenzhen SEZ while the other serves the locality. From the master plan, it is not difficult to locate the chief commercial and public services centres: Futian, Luohu, Shenzhen Town (Jiucheng), Nantou-Bao'an and the municipal government in Shangbu. However, it is impossible to differentiate between the local services centres and local government offices. For the sake of computation, it is assumed arbitrarily that 50 per cent of service sector employment is of a local nature and the other 50 per cent is inter-district.

As seen in the master plan and some district plans, schools are sited very close to the residential areas. It is thus assumed that most of the school journeys will end inside the planned functional districts and will not be inter-district.

Like school journeys, the majority of social visits are over short distances and intra-district. Long-distance social journeys are usually multi-purpose, for example, mixing shopping and recreation. As observed above, shopping facilities are hierarchical. This is also true for recreational resorts. People tend to frequent the local facilities more often than those of a higher order in the hierarchy. Assuming that most people can only go to the municipal shopping and recreational centres during their weekends and holidays, a

Table 9.1 The Number of Journeys Generated by Activities and Purposes

District	Target Pop. 2000 AD	No. Working in Industries (40%)	Total Work Journeys (Industries) ('000)	No. Working in Services (25%)	Total Work Journeys (Services) ('000)	Students (7.5%)	School Journeys ('000)	Adults & Teenagers (92.5%)	Social/ Recreational Journeys ('000)
Daxiaomeisha	10,000	4,000	2,815.2	2,500	1,759.5	750	450	9,250	5,550
Yantian	10,000	4,000	2,815.2	2,500	1,759.5	750	450	9,250	5,550
Shatoujiao	10,000	4,000	2,815.2	2,500	1,759.5	750	450	9,250	5,550
Liantang	15,000	6,000	4,222.8	3,750	2,639.3	1,125	675	13,875	8,325
Luohu	110,000	44,000	30,967.2	27,500	19,354.5	8,250	4,950	101,750	61,050
Shenzhen Town	40,000	16,000	11,260.8	10,000	7,038.0	3,000	1,800	37,000	22,200
Reservoir	30,000	12,000	8,445.6	7,500	5,278.5	2,250	1,350	27,750	16,650
Shangbu	60,000	24,000	16,891.2	15,000	10,557.0	4,500	2,700	55,500	33,300
Futian	300,000	120,000	84,456.0	75,000	52,785.0	22,500	13,500	277,500	166,500
Xiangmihu	1,000	400	281.5	250	176.0	75	45	925	555
Chegongmiao	25,000	10,000	7,038.0	6,250	4,398.8	1,875	1,125	23,125	13,875
Agronomic Inst.	4,000	1,600	1,126.1	1,000	703.8	300	180	3,700	2,220
Shahe	40,000	16,000	11,260.8	10,000	7,038.0	3,000	1,800	37,000	22,200
Houhai	30,000	12,000	8,445.6	7,500	5,278.5	2,250	1,350	27,750	16,650
Shekou	50,000	20,000	14,076.0	12,500	8,797.5	3,750	2,250	46,250	27,750
Xili	3,000	1,200	844.6	750	527.9	225	135	2,775	1,665
Chiwan	30,000	12,000	8,445.6	7,500	5,278.5	2,250	1,350	27,750	16,650
Nantou-Bao'an	30,000	12,000	8,445.6	7,500	5,278.5	2,250	1,350	27,750	16,650
Total	798,000	319,200	224,653.0	199,500	140,408.3	59,850	35,910	738,150	442,890

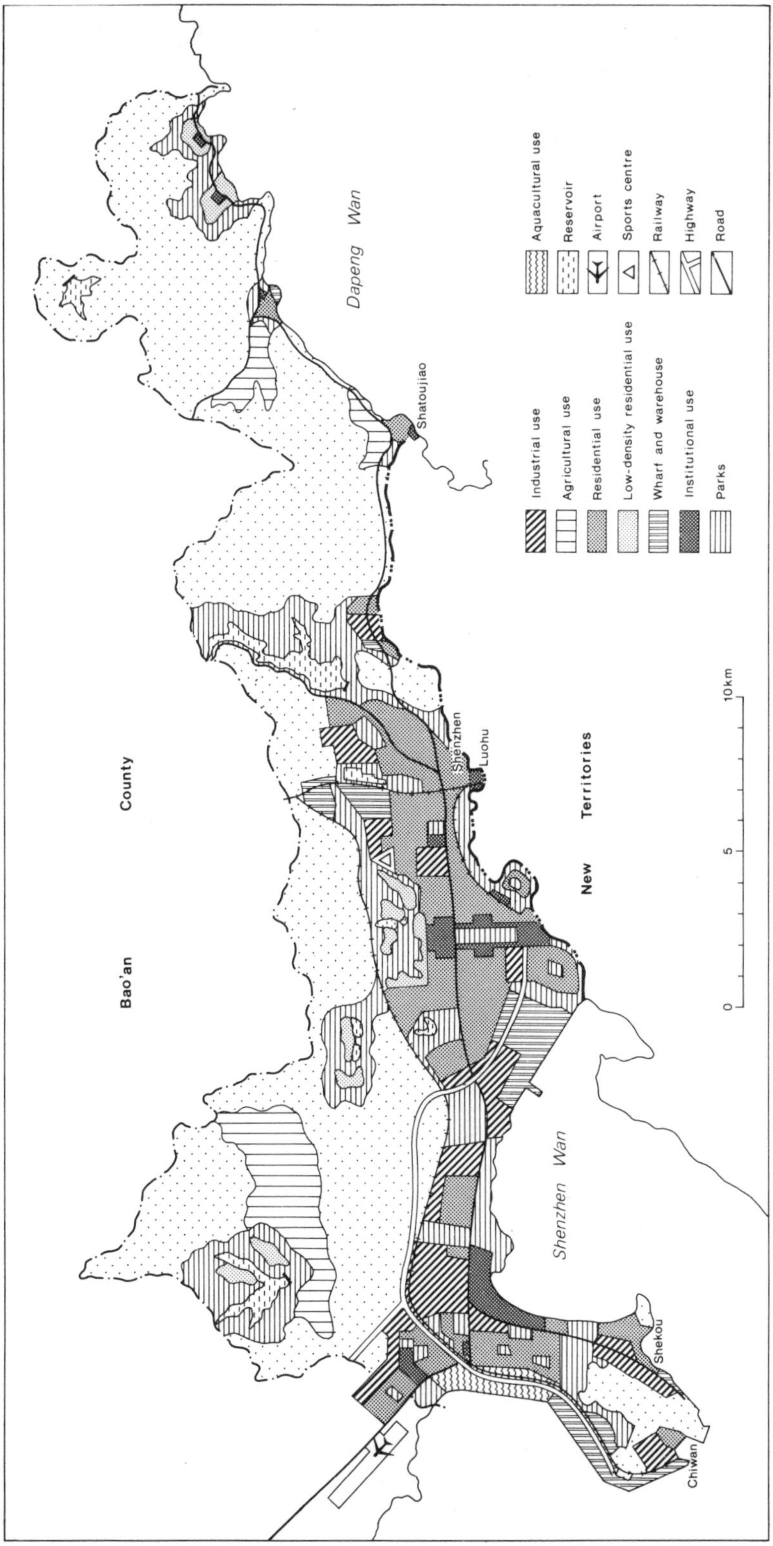

Fig. 9.2 The Provisional Plan of Land Uses in the Shenzhen SEZ

Industrial use
Agricultural use
Residential use
Low-density residential use
Wharf and warehouse
Institutional use
Parks

Aquacultural use
Reservoir
Airport
Sports centre
Railway
Highway
Road

Bao'an   County

New   Territories

Dapeng   Wan

Shatoujiao

Shenzhen
Luohu

Shenzhen Wan

Shekou

Chiwan

0   5   10km

quarter of the journeys for shopping and recreational purposes will be assigned for visiting municipal, as opposed to local, centres.

The weighting of the relative attractiveness of the industrial areas, commercial and institutional areas and recreational resorts presents another problem. Lacking any better information, the sizes of industrial, commercial, and institutional areas are employed as indicators, but equal weighting is assigned to Daxiaomeisha, Reservoir District, Futian, Xili Reservoir and the Sports Centre at Shangbu, for their sizes may not reflect their relative attraction.

Table 9.2 summarizes the estimates of journey destinations. The basis is that the SEZ is planned as 'a belt-shaped city with a distribution of unit groups, matching its narrow and long geographic features. Unit groups are linked up together by afforestation belts as constituted by gardens, parks and roads according to their topographical features. Every unit group has a complete set of public facilities . . . a suitable balance for work and residence in each case' (*Wen Wei Po*, 1982, p. 41). These estimates, though extremely crude, appear reasonable and thus are employed for the investigation of future optimal flows of passengers.

As the distance (d_{ij}) separating each functional district can be measured along the trunk route on the master plan, with the centroid of each district fixed at the prospective activity centre, a distance matrix can then be compiled. The optimal passenger flows among districts could be obtained from:

$$\min Z = \sum_{i=1}^{n} \sum_{j=1}^{m} d_{ij} \quad t_{ij}$$

$$\sum_{j=1}^{m} t_{ij} = G_i$$

$$\sum_{i=1}^{n} t_{ij} = D_j$$

$$t_{ij} \geqslant 0$$

This is the transportation problem of linear programming and it can be solved by a set computer algorithm. The resultant optimal flows of passengers are summarized in Table 9.3 and Fig. 9.3.

The Pattern of Future Freight Flows

Three different types of cargo may be considered in forecasting the future pattern of freight flows in the Shenzhen SEZ: goods for household consumption, the import and export of manufacturing plant, and the construction materials required for infrastructural improvement and extension.

Table 9.2 The Number of Journeys Absorbed by Area

District	Size of Industrial Area (sq km)	No. of Work Journeys ('000)	Size of Commercial/Institutional Area (sq km)	No. of Service Journeys* ('000)	Weights for Shopping	Weights for Recreational	No. of Shopping/Recreational Journeys ('000)
Daxiaomeisha							
Yantian	0.05	779.5				0.5	11,558
Shatoujiao							
Liantang	0.62	9,665.9					
Luohu	0.15	2,338.5	0.61	18,701	0.61		14,100
Shenzhen Town	1.27	19,779.4	0.39	11,956	0.39		9,015
Reservoir						0.5	11,558
Shangbu	1.57	24,476.4	0.17	5,212	0.17	0.5	15,487
Futian	0.32	4,988.8	1.01	30,963	1.01	0.5	34,904
Xiangmihu							
Chegongmiao	2.67	41,625.5					
Agronomic Inst.							
Shahe	1.57	24,476.4					
Houhai							
Shekou	2.30	35,857.2					
Xili						0.5	11,558
Chiwan	0.82	12,783.9					
Nantou-Bao'an	3.07	47,861.5	0.11	3,372	0.11		2,543
Total	14.41	224,653.0	2.29	70,204			110,723

Note: * Only those travelling to office/service centres of municipal significance are included.

Table 9.3 Resultant Optimal Flows of Passengers as Estimated by the Linear Programming Model ('000)

From \ To	Daxiaomeisha	Yantian	Shatoujiao	Liantang	Luohu	Shenzhen Town	Reservoir	Shangbu
Daxiaomeisha	1,388	780		2,036		880		
Yantian	1,388			2,815		880		
Shatoujiao	1,388			2,815		880		
Liantang	2,081			2,000		3,543		
Luohu					26,116	1,163		22,346
Shenzhen Town	1,846				3,519	9,131	3,705	2,130
Reservoir						11,085	4,163	
Shangbu					3,305	1,973	473	
Futian						11,237	3,218	20,699
Xiangmihu								
Chegongmiao	3,469				2,199			
Agronomic Institute								
Shahe								
Houhai								
Shekou								
Xili								
Chiwan								
Nantou-Bao'an								

Note: Figures have been rounded.

Futian	Xiangmihu	Chegongmiao	Agronomic Institute	Shahe	Houhai	Shekou	Xili	Chiwan	Nantou-Bao'an
		6,282							
		16,891							
45,904		10,006		24,476		17,674			27,311
227		282							
		7,038							
907		1,126							
9,069									11,260
6,069						8,446			733
5,977						9,738		4,338	
264							5,360		845
2,639						4,163	8,446		
							1,620		13,628

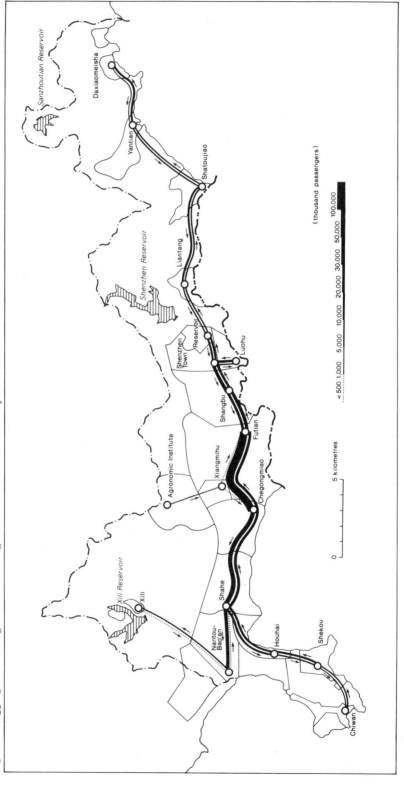

Fig. 9.3 Aggregate Passenger Flows Among the Functional Districts of the Shenzhen SEZ

It is necessary to forecast them separately because their origins and destinations are different. As there will be little agricultural land left in the Shenzhen SEZ by the year 2000, food and fuel will necessarily be supplied mainly by the neighbouring counties of Dongguan and Huiyang. On the one hand, Nantou-Bao'an and the check-point at the north of the Reservoir District will be the chief entry-points for these goods for household consumption. The destination of these goods will be the residential districts. The imports and exports of manufacturing plant, on the other hand, will tend to use the gateways at Futian and Wenjindu. Most of the factories of the Shenzhen SEZ are involved in export processing rather than in producing for domestic consumption. Some raw materials, parts and semi-finished products will be transported from Hong Kong to Shenzhen and finished products will then be returned from Shenzhen to Hong Kong. These two gateways will thus be the entrances and exits for these cargoes. The receiving points of these cargo flows will be the industrial zones of the Shenzhen SEZ. As construction materials will be unloaded at the Mamiao Wharf in the east of Shatoujiao, it is anticipated that the flow of construction materials will be from Mamiao to the various construction sites in the Shenzhen SEZ.

According to Zhang (1981a), about four tonnes of domestic goods are consumed by each resident annually. In other words, with a population of 800,000 in the year 2000, about 3.2 million tonnes of food, clothes and other household supplies will be required. Assuming that goods required in the eastern part of Shenzhen will be supplied from Huiyang and in the western part from Dongguan, the pattern of flow of goods for domestic consumption can be estimated.

The tonnage of imports and exports by the manufacturing plants will depend very much on the type and scale of industries to be developed in the Shenzhen SEZ. With no better information available, Zhang (1981a) proposed using Shashi in Hubei Province as an analogy (an industrial city with 1.5 million tonnes of industrial transport demand in 1975). As the planned industrial areas in the Shenzhen SEZ are twice as large as those in the city of Shashi, and most of the Shenzhen SEZ factory buildings will be of a multi-storey type, the total tonnage for export and import will thus be several times larger. A total tonnage of 10 million tonnes (5 million tonnes import and 5 million tonnes export) is thus used for forecasting purposes.

According to Zhang (1981a), 21.3 per cent of Foshan's total freight transport will consist of construction materials when the expansion of the city ceases. By the year 2000 Shenzhen will have used up its 98 sq km of planned built-up area. Using Foshan's pattern as an analogy, the tonnage of construction material will be around 3.5 million tonnes in the year 2000 (3.5 million tonnes forms 21 per cent of 16.7 million tonnes).

Table 9.4 summarizes the pattern of forecasted freight flows generated or absorbed by the Shenzhen SEZ's functional districts in the year 2000 and Fig. 9.4 shows the projected optimal flows of freight under the aforementioned assumptions.

Table 9.4 The Volume of Freight Traffic Generated or Absorbed by District

District	Target Population	Domestic Goods Consumed (tonnes)	Industrial Area (sq km)	Industrial Goods ('000 tonnes) Import	Export	Planned Built-up Area (ha)	Construction Materials ('000 tonnes)
Daxiaomeisha	10,000	40,000				172	54.73
Yantian	10,000	40,000				578	183.91
Shatoujiao	10,000	40,000				260	82.73
Liantang	15,000	60,000	0.62	215.9	215.9	300	95.45
Luohu	110,000	440,000	0.15	52.2	52.2	200	63.64
Shenzhen Town	40,000	160,000	1.27	442.2	442.2	400	127.27
Reservoir	30,000	120,000				440	140.00
Shangbu	60,000	240,000	1.57	546.7	546.7	1,000	318.18
Futian	300,000	1,200,000	0.32	111.4	111.4	3,000	954.55
Xiangmihu	1,000	4,000				210	66.82
Chegongmiao	25,000	100,000	2.67	929.7	929.7	600	190.91
Agronomic Inst.	4,000	16,000				400	127.27
Shahe	40,000	160,000	1.57	546.7	546.7	1,200	381.82
Houhai	30,000	120,000				600	190.91
Shekou	50,000	200,000	2.30	800.8	800.8	230	73.18
Xili	3,000	12,000				300	95.45
Chiwan	30,000	120,000	0.82	285.5	285.5	500	159.09
Nantou-Bao'an	30,000	120,000	3.07	1,068.9	1,068.9	610	194.09
Total	798,000	3,192,000	14.36	5,000.0	5,000.0	11,000	3,500.00

Analysis of Data

Based on the forecasted flows of passengers and freight, a few points deserve discussion.

(a) The total freight/passenger flows of the Shenzhen SEZ can be divided into three categories. The first category is the through traffic between Hong Kong and the area north of the Shenzhen SEZ. This includes the traffic along the railway and the projected super-highway between Guangzhou and Hong Kong. It is not only desirable but also inevitable that the through traffic should be separated from the traffic generated inside the Shenzhen SEZ. In fact, the Shenzhen master plan seems to have taken this into account already. This is a wise move, for the traffic generated inside the Shenzhen SEZ should be large enough to justify a system of its own. The second category is the inter-district transport within the Shenzhen SEZ, and it is with this category that this chapter is chiefly concerned. The third category is the traffic inside each functional district. It appears that the third type is by no means unimportant but that it should be less significant than the second category. Nonetheless, it should be borne in mind that a good inter-district network must be supplemented by a good intra-district network if the city's economy is to prosper.

(b) Looking at the future road plans (Fig. 9.5) and the aggregated flows of passengers (Fig. 9.3) and freight (Fig. 9.4), one wonders if the future road plan has taken account of the future transport pattern. As shown in Figs. 9.3 and 9.4, the greatest transport load that the inter-district network will bear will be on the sections between Futian and Chegongmiao, and Chegongmiao and Shahe (Table 9.5). However, as the future road plan indicates, these roads of Futian will converge into only two east–west bound routes in Chegongmiao. This could lead to heavy congestion at the point of convergence and would not help to solve the heavy demand on the route between Chegongmiao and Futian. Somewhere in the area between the northern boundaries of Shahe and Chegongmiao and the existing road from Shenzhen to Nantou, a road or two should be constructed to connect the Futian network to the north and south of Dalingxia. Such roads would serve to divert traffic from the point of convergence.

(c) Another bottle-neck for traffic will be at the boundary between Luohu and Shenzhen Town where the east–west traffic meets north–south traffic. Congestion has already built up during peak hours under current conditions. It may be anticipated that the situation will worsen when the population of Shenzhen increases. Two solutions seem possible. One is to separate the east–west traffic from the north–south traffic by building flyovers. The other is to divert the east–west traffic to the north of

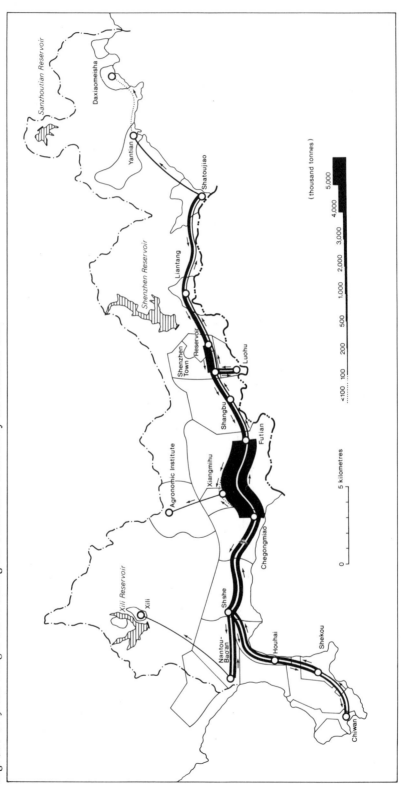

Fig. 9.4 Projected Freight Flows Among the Functional Districts of the Shenzhen SEZ

Fig. 9.5 The Provisional Plan for the Transport Network of the Shenzhen SEZ

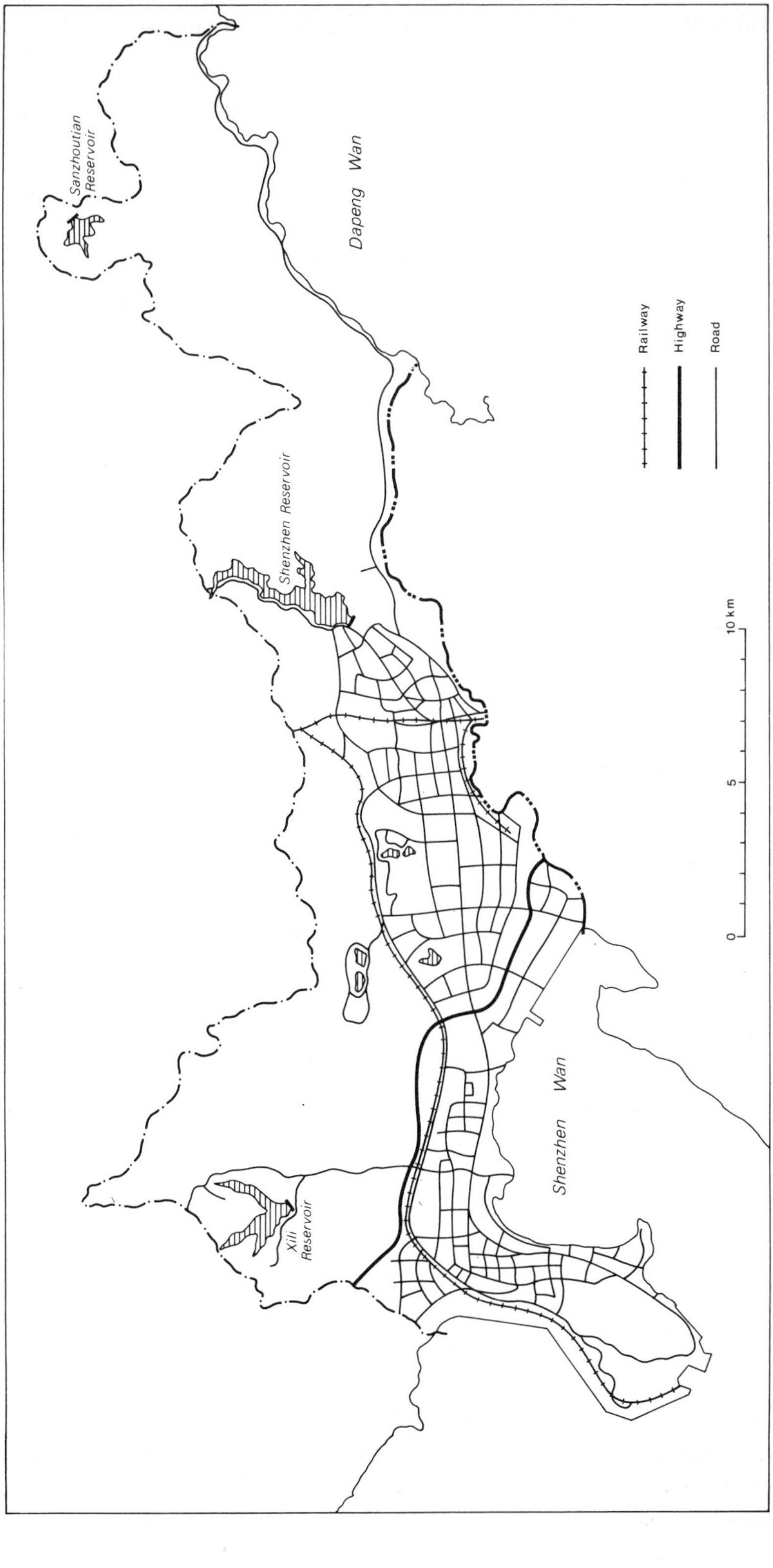

Table 9.5   The Projected Utilization of Road Sections

Road Section	Mileage (in km)	Passenger '000/yr	Passenger -km (million)	Freight '000 tonnes	Tonnes -km (million)
Daxiaomeisha–Yantian	5	3,694.9	18.5	—	—
Yantian–Daxiaomeisha		10,170.5	50.9	95.0	0.5
Yantian–Shatoujiao	8	6,610.3	52.9	—	—
Shatoujiao–Yantian		8,783.0	70.3	219.0	1.8
Shatoujiao–Liantang	8	10,305.2	82.4	2,984.0	23.9
Liantang–Shatoujiao		7,395.5	59.2	120.0	1.0
Liantang–Reservoir	5	6,181.8	30.9	3,104.5	15.5
Reservoir–Liantang		5,314.1	26.4	395.5	2.0
Reservoir–Shenzhen Town	2.5	17,266.7	43.2	4,260.5	10.7
Shenzhen Town–Reservoir		12,709.6	31.8	215.5	0.5
Luohu–Shenzhen Town	1.5	29,791.2	44.7	927.5	1.4
Shenzhen Town–Luohu		9,032.7	13.5	1,431.5	5.9
Shenzhen Town–Shangbu	2.5	30,758.7	76.9	3,524.0	8.8
Shangbu–Shenzhen Town		25,874.7	64.7	270.0	0.7
Shangbu–Futian	3.5	23,173.5	81.1	3,165.0	11.1
Futian–Shangbu		40,822.7	142.9	275.0	1.0
Chegongmiao–Agr. Inst.	8	—	—	143.0	1.1
Agr. Inst.–Chegongmiao		1,126.1	9.0	—	—
Futian–Xiangmihu	3	—	—	67.0	0.2
Xiangmihu–Futian		226.8	0.7	—	—
Chegongmiao–Xiangmihu	3	—	—	4.0	—
Xiangmihu–Chegongmiao		281.5	0.8	—	—
Futian–Chegongmiao	6	102,640.7	615.8	5,043.5	30.3
Chegongmiao–Futian		29,686.0	178.1	4,375.5	26.3
Chegongmiao–Shahe	11	69,460.8	764.1	3,796.0	41.8
Shahe–Chegongmiao		24,017.8	264.2	3,566.0	39.2
Shahe–Houhai	5	56,245.2	281.2	2,867.5	14.3
Houhai–Shahe		14,948.8	74.7	3,079.5	15.4
Houhai–Nantou-Bao'an	3.5	43,466.9	152.1	1,358.0	4.8
Nantou-Bao'an–Houhai		263.9	0.9	2,433.0	8.5
Houhai–Shekou	3	26,119.5	78.4	1,638.5	4.9
Shekou–Houhai		12,778.5	38.3	108.5	3.3
Shekou–Chiwan	4	4,338.3	17.4	564.5	2.2
Chiwan–Shekou		6,801.7	27.2	285.5	1.1
Nantou-Bao'an–Xili	9	5,782.0	52.0	107.0	1.0
Xili–Nantou-Bao'an		263.9	2.3	—	—

Shenzhen Town. For the second solution, an extension of the planned highway from Shuiwei to Liantang would probably be necessary.

(d) One other possible bottle-neck is the junction between Houhai and Nantou-Bao'an where again the east–west traffic meets the north–south traffic. Flyovers to separate these two streams of traffic seem the only solution.

(e) As in most Chinese cities, including Hong Kong, most of the inter-district passenger transport will be carried by public vehicles. The multiplication of forecasted journeys by the distance between the origin and the destination of journeys gives an estimate of the capacity of the inter-district transport system that will be required. The result reveals that the system needs to deal with as many as 3,448 million passengers per km annually. Given a bus of 50 passengers running for 3,650 hours a year at an average speed of 30 km per hour, the Shenzhen SEZ needs a minimum fleet size of 630 buses to cope with the inter-district transport demand. If a lorry with an average load of 10 tonnes and average speed of 20 km per hour works 3,650 hours a year, the minimum number of lorries required will be 382. However, one must take into account the fact that the transport demand in both directions may not be equal, and that many vehicles must return empty in order to transport another consignment. In other words, more vehicles would be needed than the minimum forecasted.

(f) As pointed out at the beginning of this chapter, motorized inter-district transport will only account for a part of the motorized transport demand. When people become more affluent, some intra-district journeys will demand motorized transport. Additional buses or mini-buses will be needed to cope with this demand. Furthermore, with the growing affluence of the citizens of the Shenzhen SEZ and the increasing number of tourists, taxis and other personal transport vehicles will become a significant element of the Shenzhen SEZ transport system which should not be overlooked.

Conclusion

This chapter attempts to forecast the future transportation demand of the Shenzhen SEZ through an analysis of the spatial and socio-economic characteristics of the planned population and the planned land uses. The methodology employed is the cost-minimizing type which assumes that the population will go to the nearest industrial/commercial area to work and to the nearest shopping centre/resort to spend their leisure time. However, this assumption may not be valid in all cases. Furthermore, the inadequacy of data has led to the employment of many arbitrary measures, subjective estimates and analogies which in turn affect the usefulness of the forecast.

As more information becomes available, the forecast can be adjusted accordingly and it is hoped that this study will at least provide some food for thought for the transport planners of the Shenzhen SEZ.

10. Environmental Considerations

KIN-CHE LAM AND STEVE S.I. HSU

THE Shenzhen SEZ was the first SEZ to be instituted in China and is also the largest. According to the latest revised development plan, the Shenzhen SEZ is going to be developed into a modern industrial, residential and commercial complex that will accommodate 800,000 people by the year 2000. The scale and pace of development are unprecedented in modern China and reflect the anticipation of a period of rapid urbanization and industrial growth. The amount of waste and polluted discharge will certainly increase as a result of these changes. Likewise, changes in the landscape and a reduction in surface vegetation will alter the environmental quality. A thorough understanding of these changes and their effects on the inhabitants is urgently needed so that the benefits of development will not be offset by environmental repercussions.

This chapter highlights the environmental problems that may arise from such development, describes the present environmental policy and control measures, and discusses how the environment in Shenzhen can best be managed.

An Overview of the Development of the SEZ

Before 1979, Shenzhen was a small township engaged mainly in agricultural activities. As described in Chapter 7, most of the anticipated development is to take place in the central and western portions of the SEZ, concentrating in the following areas: Luohu, Shangbu, Futian, Houhai, Shekou and Chiwan. The three facets of development that may have a bearing on the environment are population growth, agricultural development and industrial development. These will be evaluated in the following paragraphs.

Population Growth

Given the space (98 sq km) available for development, the population density will not be particularly high and overcrowding is not likely to be a problem. However, the rapid increase in population will be followed by a dramatic increase in the demand for food, water, energy resources and disposal facilities for domestic sewage and waste. Waste disposal has rarely been a problem in other Chinese cities. This is partly due to the traditional attitude of frugality and the necessity to make the maximum use of scarce resources, and also to the fact that, in other parts of China, the city proper is functionally so closely interwoven with the countryside that municipal waste, sewage and manure are efficiently recycled. Unfortunately, the Shenzhen SEZ is separated administratively, and to a lesser extent functionally, from the countryside to the north. Unlike other cities in China, the SEZ cannot rely too much on its rural counterpart to assimilate its waste. This problem is further compounded by the fact that China has neither sufficient capital nor the experience to use modern waste treatment and disposal technology.

Agricultural Development

To meet the needs of the increasing population, agriculture is likely to develop very rapidly in the SEZ and in the adjoining area to the north. Even in the last four years since the establishment of the Shenzhen SEZ, some remarkable changes have occurred in the agricultural sector. There has been a significant decrease in paddy cultivation but a dramatic increase in market gardening and pond fish culture. The number of large pig and poultry farms is also on the increase.

A trend underlying these changes is that agriculture tends to become more and more specialized, compartmentalized and sophisticated. For example, pigs are no longer kept by ordinary farmers as a sideline business but are bred in their hundreds in large feedlots. This line of development is undesirable environmentally for two reasons. Firstly, agriculture is gradually losing its traditional valuable role of waste assimilation. Secondly, large-scale pig and poultry farming can become an environmental nuisance, as the experience of Hong Kong illustrates.

Industrial Development

There were very few industries in Shenzhen before 1979. In spite of the fact that most of the investment in the last few years has gone to housing and tourism projects, the Chinese government wishes rather that industry should become the mainstay of the SEZ because industry can help to modernize China. Very high priorities have thus been accorded by the Shenzhen authority to the promotion of industrial development.

The Chinese government particularly welcomes industries using advanced techniques and equipment and those that are not a pollution risk. Because industrial development in the SEZ is still in the initial stage, most of the industrial undertakings are small or medium in size and are of the following major types: electronics, foodstuffs, textiles and garments, building materials, machine-building and feedstuffs (Fig. 10.1). The major industrial districts are Shangbu, Shahe and Shekou (Fig. 10.2).

Most of the existing industries are not likely to produce heavy pollution loads. The large bleaching and dyeing factory, located at Kuichong, was one of the very early industrial projects in the Shenzhen Municipality and was negotiated at a time when the industrial policy had not taken shape. When this factory was put into operation in 1982, the Shenzhen authority was not happy with the pollution it caused to a nearby stream. It has now become rather firmer in turning down proposals to set up polluting industries in the SEZ.

However, the opening of oilfields in the South China Sea has suggested the use of Shenzhen as a rear service base and as a centre for the petrochemical industries. In spite of the adverse effects which a petrochemical complex could have on the environment, the Shenzhen government has decided to set aside Chiwan and Mawan (to be reclaimed off the coast of Nantou) for these functions.

At the moment, the major source of fuel in the SEZ is coal, the combustion of which has caused SO_2, smoke and dust problems in some cities in China. Although the SEZ is now apparently free from these problems, there is no guarantee that the air quality will not deteriorate as more industries are established. To meet the escalating demand for energy, plans have been made to build a 1.2 million kW coal-fired power-plant at Shajiao and a 1.8 million kW nuclear plant on the shores of Daya Bay, both outside the boundaries of the Shenzhen SEZ (Fig. 10.3). When these are completed, industries may shift from coal to electricity, a change that is environmentally desirable.

Physical Setting

The physical setting affects the dispersion characteristics of air and water pollutants and has, therefore, to be considered in the environmental assessment of any development project.

Topography and Climate

The Shenzhen SEZ resembles a basin surrounded by hills of about 500 m on the north, south and east banks. The climate of Shenzhen is very similar

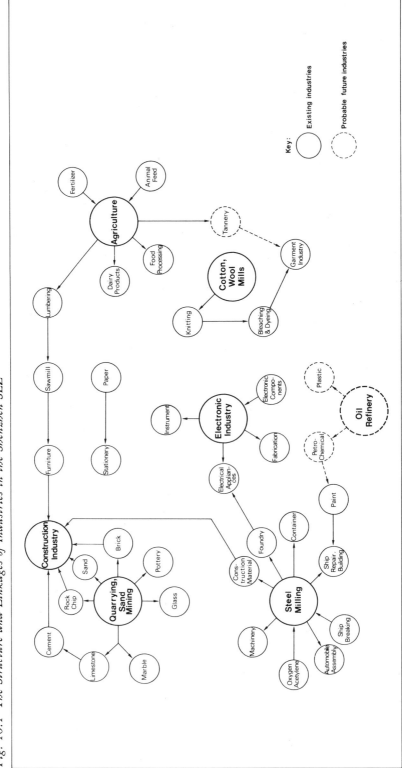

Fig. 10.1 The Structure and Linkages of Industries in the Shenzhen SEZ

Fig. 10.2 Population Distribution and Industrial Allocation in the Shenzhen SEZ

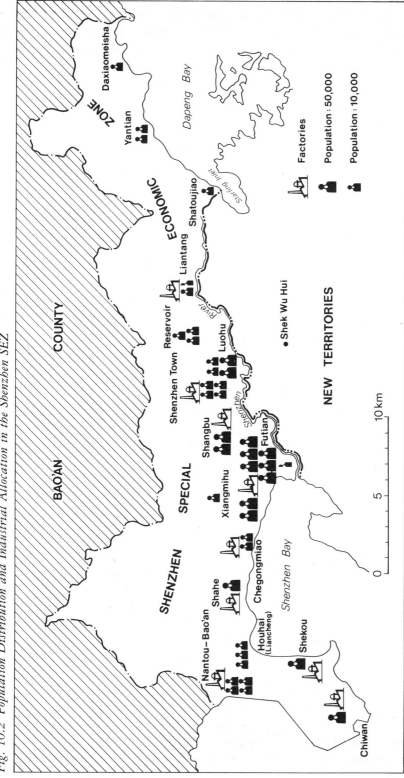

to that of Hong Kong. It has a mean annual temperature of 22.3°C with a maximum of 37°C in summer and a minimum of −2.5°C in winter. Annual rainfall averages 1,800 mm, a large portion of which is brought by tropical cyclones and local thunderstorms during the summer.

Being located on the South China coast and in the subtropical region, Shenzhen experiences a monsoonal climate characterized by a cool dry winter and a hot moist summer. In winter, under the influence of continental high-pressure systems, the prevailing winds come primarily from the east. In summer, a continental low-pressure cell draws warm moist air from the ocean and west winds are predominant. However, under light synoptic conditions, small-scale circulations such as land and sea breezes may also occur. Sea breezes are expected to blow from Shenzhen Bay (Deep Bay) towards the basin during the day, while land breezes blow in the opposite direction at night.

Streams and Water Bodies

Streams in the SEZ are generally short with steep gradients in the upper course but very gentle gradients in the lower stretches. Streams in the eastern portion of the SEZ flow into Dapeng Bay whereas those in the central and western portions flow into Shenzhen Bay. Of these streams, the longest is Shenzhen River which forms the political boundary between China and Hong Kong. Shenzhen River drains an area of 312 sq km, of which two-fifths lie in the New Territories and the rest in China. Because the lower stretch of the river is a tidal stream, water pollutants are sometimes carried backwards and forwards with the tide.

In spite of its name, Shenzhen Bay (Deep Bay) is not deep at all. The mean depth is about 3 m and the tidal range is 2.8 m. On the basis of tidal dilution alone, the mean retention time for the water in the bay is about 14½ hours. Given such a short retention time, the bay is able to accept very large pollution loads from inflowing streams if mixing in the bay and the Zhujiang (Pearl River) Estuary is complete. Evidence from the movement of oyster larvae, however, suggests that much of the water which flows westward during the ebb tide returns during the flood, so that in reality the retention time is much longer than that indicated by the tidal dilution calculation.

On the other hand, Dapeng Bay (Mirs Bay) to the east is deeper but fairly enclosed. The predominant flow of water into the bay is from the south-east. These factors could mean that the exchange of water with the open sea is rather slow and the mean retention time is estimated to be 20 to 50 days. Hence, the assimilative capacity of the water body is low and accumulation of pollutants can occur in more sheltered areas such as Starling Inlet.

Possible Environmental Effects of the Development of the SEZ

Owing to the lack of reliable data on existing and future development activities in the SEZ, it is not possible to predict environmental changes with precision. Thus, the following analysis will focus on the pros and cons of different development options from the environmental stance, and highlight the constraints placed upon development by the requirement to maintain a healthy and acceptable environment.

Air Quality

According to an environmental base-line study conducted by the Shenzhen Environmental Protection Office (EPO) in 1980–2, concentrations of SO_2, NO_2, O_3 and particulates in the Shenzhen SEZ are well within the Chinese national air quality standards (Liu, 1983). The effects of future development on the air quality will be largely determined by the nature and quality of the emissions and the atmospheric dispersion conditions. With regard to the former, it is anticipated that there will be no high-level stationary emission sources in the SEZ. The coal-fired power-plant at Shajiao and the nuclear power-plant at Daya Bay are both located away from the SEZ (Fig. 10.3) so that their effects on ground-level pollution in the zone will be minimal. Low-level emissions come largely from industries, most of which use coal at present. As mentioned in the preceding section, there will be a shift from coal to electricity. This shift is environmentally desirable because the location of the emission is thereby transferred out of the SEZ and the pollutants are discharged at a high altitude.

Both the topography and climate suggest that airborne dispersion in the SEZ is likely to be better in winter than in summer. This is due to the fact that, in winter, the north-easterly wind (3 m/s) moves the polluted air away from the highly populated area towards the open sea to the south-west. In summer, however, low-speed winds (1 m/s) blowing from the south-westerly direction may accumulate air pollutants in the eastern part of the basin due to the slow dilution effect. Other factors being equal, this means that airborne concentrations in the basin will be three times higher in summer than in winter.

Temperature inversion, the other important climatic parameter affecting dispersion, should also be considered. In a basin such as the Shenzhen SEZ, it is known that temperature inversion may retard vertical airborne dispersion, thereby trapping polluting and toxic gases in the air layer between the ground surface and the plume height. Should this occur, severe air pollution will result. In Shenzhen, most of the temperature inversion days occur in spring and winter, particularly in the morning on calm clear days. It is estimated that this occurs on about 57 days in a year (Table 10.1).

Fig. 10.3 Location of the Daya Bay Nuclear Plant and the Shajiao Coal-fired Power-plant

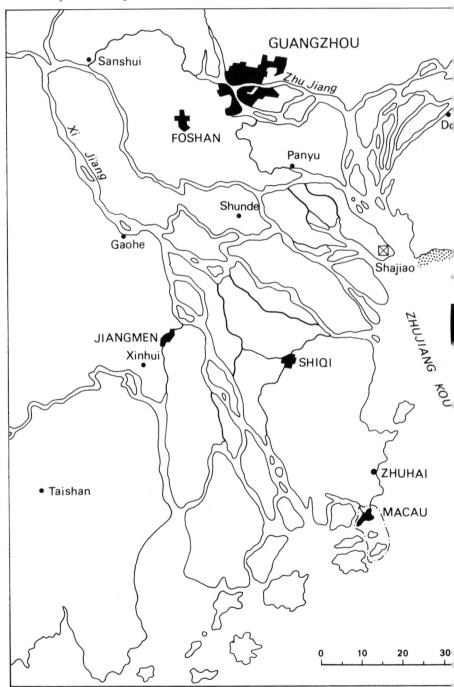

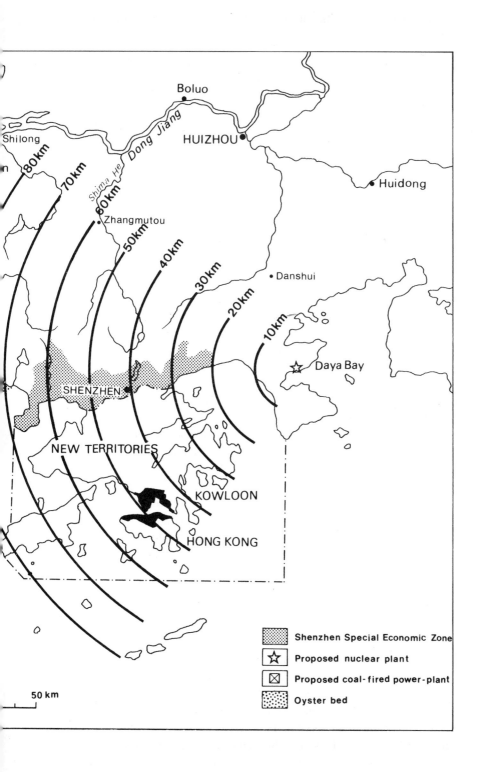

Boluo

Shilong

Shima He Dong Jiang

HUIZHOU

Huidong

80km

70km

60km

50km

40km

30km

20km

10km

Zhangmutou

Danshui

Daya Bay

SHENZHEN

NEW TERRITORIES

KOWLOON

HONG KONG

50 km

Shenzhen Special Economic Zone

Proposed nuclear plant

Proposed coal-fired power-plant

Oyster bed

Table 10.1 The Number of Days with Inversions Below 600 m, 1950–68

Month	Number of Days with Inversions		Percentage
	Total	Average	
January	174	9.2	29.5
February	175	9.2	32.6
March	225	11.8	38.6
April	151	7.9	26.5
May	60	3.2	10.2
June	13	0.7	2.3
July	65	3.4	0.8
August	18	1.0	3.1
September	20	1.1	3.5
October	16	0.8	2.7
November	49	2.6	8.6
December	123	6.5	20.9
Year	1,029	54.2	14.8

Consequently, winter-time airborne dispersion is poor in terms of temperature inversion frequency. Nevertheless, the strong winter monsoons may often provide better horizontal dilution which may offset the unfavourable dispersion.

Taking population distribution, industrial location, topographical influence and climatic conditions into account, a schematic air quality map is constructed and presented in Fig. 10.4. It can be seen that the Shekou district and the central portion of the Shenzhen SEZ, including Shangbu, Futian, Shenzhen Town and its eastern hillsides, may become heavily polluted. The eastern part of the SEZ, including Meisha, Shatoujiao and the suburbs of the basin are expected to be lightly polluted, whilst the areas between Shekou and Shenzhen Town may be moderately polluted.

River Water Quality

With the exception of the Shenzhen River, there is very little information on the condition of the streams in the Shenzhen SEZ. Given the low population, scattered agriculture and negligible industry, the water quality of the upper courses of the streams in the zone is expected to be good (*Shenzhen Special Zone Daily*, 27 June 1983). So too is the water quality of the streams above the reservoirs. However, when these streams flow through small settlements on the shore, the water quality deteriorates.

The most severe water pollution is found in the lower stretch of the Shenzhen River, particularly the section between Wenjindu and Yumincun,

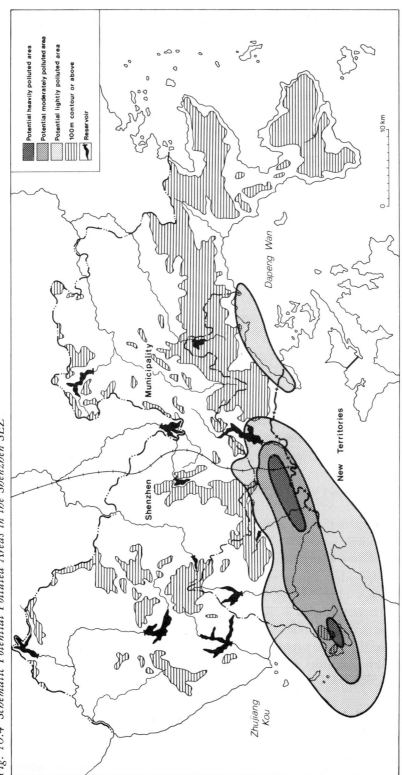

Fig. 10.4 Schematic Potential Polluted Areas in the Shenzhen SEZ

where the flow is sluggish and the water is black. During the dry season, organic muds are exposed on the river banks, producing an offensive smell. Since the Shenzhen River is the main watercourse entering Shenzhen Bay, it is one of the principal determinants of the inshore portion of the bay.

As mentioned earlier, the Shenzhen River receives pollution from both the north-eastern New Territories of Hong Kong and the Shenzhen SEZ. There is no information on the pollution load from the Chinese side, but the total organic load from the Hong Kong side alone amounts to 20,250 kg biochemical oxygen demand (BOD)/day, 85 per cent of which is agricultural in origin (pig and poultry manure). The rest is contributed by domestic sewage (10 per cent) and industrial effluents (5 per cent). Industries on the Hong Kong side include bleaching and dyeing, food manufacturing and rattan. On the Chinese side, there are about fifteen Hong Kong-based tanneries which, because of the tightening of environmental controls in Hong Kong, took refuge in Shenzhen in the mid-1970s.

Compared with the existing pollution load from Hong Kong alone, the increase in BOD load due to industrial development is likely to be small since very few of the existing or planned industries produce effluents high in BOD. However, the projected population increase in that part of the SEZ that falls within the Shenzhen River catchment area (500,000 people by the year 2000) will add a further 27,000 kg BOD/day to the river. Population growth in the north-eastern New Territories on the Hong Kong side will also add a substantial but as yet unknown quantity of organic load. The quality of the Shenzhen River will, therefore, deteriorate further unless appropriate measures are taken to alleviate the contamination. Although both the Hong Kong and Shenzhen governments have planned to build sewage treatment plants (at Shek Wu Hui, Shangbu and Futian), such measures alone are not sufficient to reduce the pollution level to an acceptable one. As the pollution of the Shenzhen River is exacerbated by tidal flow, it appears that the tidal section of the river will have to be realigned and paved to facilitate water flow. This aspect is now being seriously considered by the joint China–Hong Kong Expert Working Group.

Two other aspects of development in Shenzhen may have important bearings on river water quality. Firstly, the development of holiday resorts and recreation areas in the upper courses of rivers and around reservoirs has to be carefully controlled, for otherwise the water supply will be contaminated. Secondly, the environmental consequences of the development of pig and poultry industries should be fully explored to avoid the kind of stream pollution that has troubled Hong Kong.

The Quality of Marine Waters

The maintenance and improvement of the quality of marine waters in Dapeng Bay and Shenzhen Bay is another major issue affecting development in Shenzhen. Unless these water bodies are protected, the maricultural activities in Shenzhen Bay and the flourishing tourist industry in Dapeng Bay will be jeopardized.

As indicated by the presence of coral communities, water quality in Dapeng Bay is generally good. In fact, the pollution loads discharged into Dapeng Bay are small, and are spread over a long irregular coastline. The largest concentration of domestic and agricultural discharges arises around Shatoujiao and enters Dapeng Bay via Starling Inlet. Visual inspection suggests that there are localized problems immediately offshore of Shatoujiao, but that the rest of the inlet is unpolluted despite its shallow and closed nature. The water quality of Dapeng Bay is likely to remain clean for three reasons. Firstly, there are no known development plans which may adversely affect water quality. Secondly, a sewage treatment plant, providing secondary treatment, has been planned for Shatoujiao to improve the quality of the discharge into Starling Inlet. Thirdly, the bleaching and dyeing factory at Kuichong has recently been in financial trouble and is unlikely to expand. Moreover, the Shenzhen SEZ authority is now very aware of the pollution problem of this factory and will not favour its further expansion.

On the other hand, water quality in Shenzhen Bay is a major cause for concern because it is already poor in certain parts. Of the five sites sampled by Morton and Wu (1975), Tsim Bei Tsui on the Hong Kong side showed the highest values for BOD, phosphate and nitrate concentrations. Dissolved oxygen levels were generally low but at times supersaturated, showing that algal growth is active in the bay. The agricultural development and planned population growth will increase the discharge of phosphate and nitrate tremendously. The extent to which these increased nutrient loads will cause algal growth depends on whether local hydrographic dilution rates exceed the growth rates of algae. Although no direct measurements of the latter exist for Shenzhen Bay, they are probably in the order of several days so that the main body of the bay is unlikely to suffer from very severe algal blooms. However, any substantial increase in nutrient loads should be viewed with caution, and its environmental effect should be evaluated by mathematical modelling.

The Possible Environmental Impact of the Nuclear Plant at Daya Bay

About two-thirds of the total energy produced by a nuclear reactor is usually wasted, leaving only one-third for power generation. The large amount of waste heat is normally discharged through air or water. From the geographical position and climatic condition of the nuclear plant at Daya Bay, it is predicted that a once-through water cooling system will be installed. This method requires that large quantities of fresh sea water be pumped into a condenser and then discharged back into the sea at a higher temperature.

Daya Bay is a semi-enclosed bay that limits water exchange with the surrounding areas. The sea temperature within a few kilometres of the plant will be raised noticeably. This will perhaps affect the aquatic ecosystem considerably.

The raising of the sea surface temperature will also result in frequent fog, especially in winter, and such foggy weather will affect sea transportation.

The authorities concerned should, therefore, study thoroughly and acquire a complete understanding of these environmental considerations, as well as of the impact of the radioactive substance that will be released, before setting up the plant.

Environmental Control

The Shenzhen authority is not unaware of the environmental consequences that may arise from the development of the SEZ. An Environmental Protection Office (EPO) was in fact established as early as 1980 to monitor the environment, enforce environmental regulations, evaluate development projects, and specify conditions and control measures with which investors have to comply.

In collaboration with the Zhongshan University in Guangzhou, the EPO has undertaken a large-scale environmental base-line study of the air, water, noise, soil and vegetation, and of the health of the residents. This study describes the problems which will have to be tackled and provides the reference against which future monitoring results can be compared.

At present, the Shenzhen SEZ still uses the Chinese national environmental quality objectives and emission standards (Tables 10.2 and 10.3). In comparison with Hong Kong and the USA, the Chinese standards can be considered as looser for water quality but more stringent for air quality. Since China is a vast country with appreciable variations in environmental assimilative capacity, these standards may not be appropriate for the Shenzhen SEZ. Thus, the Shenzhen government passed an environmental protection and management bill which gave the Shenzhen EPO the authority to establish its own standards and administrative procedures for managing the environment.

The major approaches to environmental management used by the Shenzhen authority are comprehensive planning and environmental assessment.

Comprehensive planning is an effective tool for managing the environment, particularly where the scale of development is large. It is well known that environmental quality can best be enhanced through sensibly planned economic and human activities that will reduce waste generation and the impact of this waste on the inhabitants. The location of heavy industries at Shekou and Chiwan is evidence that careful thought has been given to segregate industries from land uses that may be sensitive to pollution.

Table 10.2 A Comparison of Water Quality Control in China, Hong Kong[1] and the United States (unit in mg/l)

Item	China (Emission Standard)	Hong Kong (Emission Standard)[2]	USA (Quality Standard)
Cd	0.1	0.1	0.02
Cr^{+6}	0.5	—	0.1
As	0.5	—	0.1
Pb	1.0	—	0.1
Hg	0.05	0.1	—
Susp. Solids	500.0	30.0	—
BOD_5	60.0	20.0	—
COD	100.0	50.0	—
Sulphides	1.0	1.0	—
Phenol	0.5	0.5	0.002
CN	0.5	0.1	0.4
pH	6–9	6–10	6.5–8.5

Notes: 1. The standards are the preliminary suggestions by the Environmental Resources Ltd. (1977).
2. For direct or sewered discharges to Class S1 INLAND WATERS, and for new or varied discharges to OTHER INLAND WATERS (Class S2).

Table 10.3 A Comparison of Air Quality Control in China, Hong Kong[1] and the United States (unit in mg/m³)

Petroleum	Short-term[2] China (Emission Standard)	Hong Kong (Emission Standard)	USA (Ambient Standard)	Long-term[3] China (Emission Standard)	Hong Kong (Emission Standard)	USA (Ambient Standard)
CO	3.0	4.0	46.0	1.0	0.5	11 (12hr)
SO_2	0.5	0.75	1.31	0.15	0.5	0.105
NO_2	0.15	0.30	0.47	—	0.16	—
Pb	—	—	—	0.007	—	0.0015 (30 day)
Dust	0.5	—	—	0.15	—	0.1
Petroleum (as C)	1.5	—	—	—	—	—

Notes: 1. Preliminary suggestions by the Environmental Resources Ltd. (1977).
2. Averaged over a 1-hour period.
3. Averaged over a 24-hour period, except where otherwise specified.

Environmental assessment is a positive means of preventing environmental problems that would otherwise be expensive or difficult to control. In the SEZ, detailed environmental assessment studies have been undertaken for large stationary sources of emission such as the Shajiao power-station. For certain industrial investment projects, investors have also to submit environmental impact studies to the EPO for approval. If approved, environmental protection measures have to be taken to the satisfaction of the EPO in the design, construction and operation stages of these projects. Recently, a laundry run by a commune at Shahe was ordered to close because it had not complied with the EPO requirements.

Conclusion

The outsider's impressions of the Chinese environment have changed significantly since the latter half of the 1970s. In the first half of the 1970s it was widely believed that the Chinese environment was a Maoist miracle: the country was clean and green; soil erosion was checked by massive afforestation; pests were effectively controlled by biological methods; and wastes were thoroughly recycled. However, since the downfall of the 'Gang of Four', a great deal of information concerning environmental problems in China has gradually emerged. These reports show that environmental pollution in China is at least as serious as in any large modernized nation. Environmental deterioration in China is not a consequence of affluence, as it is in Hong Kong, but rather of industrial inefficiency. Fortunately, Chinese society is so structured that wastes are efficiently recycled and re-utilized. China's modernization programme will have considerable bearing on industrial efficiency, waste generation and the social structure. It would be interesting to research the effect of these factors upon the environmental quality of China.

In the light of the preceding discussions, the authors suggest that careful consideration should be given to the following issues.

(a) The Shenzhen SEZ authority should carefully select the types of industry which are necessary for economic growth and conducive to modernization. Polluting industries should be avoided as far as possible otherwise some of the polluting industries of Hong Kong may infiltrate the SEZ in reaction to the tightening of environmental legislation in Hong Kong.

(b) Despite the fact that comprehensive planning has been repeatedly emphasized, incompatible land uses are still sometimes found next to each other. In Shekou, for example, the holiday resort on the beach is not far from an industrial zone.

(c) The Shenzhen and Hong Kong authorities should work together to investigate environmental problems of common interest. Both parties should exchange data and share the responsibility for a clean environment.

(d) Owing to the lack of sufficient data, it is difficult to make judgements on the environmental consequences of development. Final decisions on the various development options must await the results of mathematical modelling. It is suggested that mathematical models should be developed for the dispersion of air pollutants in the SEZ and water pollutants in Shenzhen Bay without further delay.

11. The Investment Environment

KWAN-YIU WONG AND DAVID K. Y. CHU

IN determining where to put his money, the investor will normally assess carefully the investment environment of various locations. Two different approaches are widely used in the evaluation of an investment environment. One is quantitative and the other qualitative. The quantitative approach is generally regarded as more objective in nature (Mun and Ho, 1979). It employs a rating scale and assigns numeric scores to selected economic and political factors as the basis for the screening of the investment environment of a country. Stobaugh's method of analysing the investment climate is a popular example of this approach. Based on eight screening factors, namely capital repatriation, foreign ownership, discrimination and controls against foreign business, currency stability, political stability, willingness to grant tariff protection, availability of local capital and annual inflation for the last five years, a country's investment climate can be summed up to a certain numerical value (Stobaugh, 1969). This approach has undoubtedly been widely used among the multinationals in assessing the investment climate of the developing countries. However, its 'objectiveness' is open to question. Indeed, the weights assigned to each factor as well as the selection of factors are totally arbitrary. At the same time, most of these models, including Stobaugh's, are designed for the developing countries in the capitalist world, and their rating scale is therefore of limited use in assessing the SEZs of the People's Republic of China. In this chapter, the authors adopt the alternative approach — a qualitative analysis of the investment environment — in the hope that through such analysis, many key concerns of entrepreneurs and potential investors can be discussed. At the same time, the economic practitioners and planners of the Shenzhen SEZ will be able to benefit from a third party assessment.

The Administrative Structure

Administratively, the Shenzhen SEZ is part of the Shenzhen Municipality which is under the jurisdiction of the Guangdong Provincial Government. However, according to the Guangdong SEZ Regulations, the Shenzhen SEZ is also managed by the Guangdong Provincial Administration of SEZs which was set up 'to exercise unified management of the special zones on behalf of the Guangdong Provincial People's Government' (Article 3). Investors wishing to open factories or embark on various economic ventures may apply to the Guangdong Provincial Administration of SEZs: they will be issued with licences of registry and certificates for the use of land after examination and approval (Article 7). Acting on behalf of the Provincial Administration of the SEZs, the Guangdong Provincial SEZ Development Company was set up to administer economic activities in the zones. Its scope of business includes fund raising and trust investment, operating enterprises or joint ventures with investors in the SEZs, acting as agent for investors in the zones in matters related to sales and purchases in China outside the SEZs, and providing services for business talks (Article 25). In short, the Shenzhen SEZ operates under the dual leadership of the Shenzhen Municipality and the Guangdong Provincial Administration of SEZs. However, this structure is further complicated by the fact that the industrial districts of Shekou and Shahe (Fig. 11.1), which are geographically and administratively part of the Shenzhen SEZ, are actually run by the China Merchants' Steam Navigation Co. Ltd. (Hong Kong) and the Overseas Chinese Enterprise Company respectively. The former is part of the Transport Department of the central government whilst the latter works under the Committee on Overseas Chinese Affairs of Guangdong Province which, besides running Shahe, also runs the Guangming Farm in Bao'an County (Fig. 11.1). Neither of these is subject to the authority of Shenzhen Municipality. Therefore, only land development, investment projects and negotiations in areas outside Shekou, Shahe and the Guangming Farm go through the Shenzhen Municipal Government. These various channels for negotiation are usually not clearly understood by potential investors, and this leads to unnecessary inconvenience and confusion.

The Early Administrative Structure

The existing governmental structure has evolved from a small frontier county administration (that of Bao'an County) with a relatively simple structure staffed by low-ranking cadre officers. In 1979, Bao'an County was upgraded to municipality status and given the name Shenzhen Municipality. There are two types of municipality in a Chinese province: one is directly under the provincial government and the other is under the prefectural government. Shenzhen Municipality belongs to the former category. Prior to 1979, six districts were located within the confines of the municipality: Luohu, Nantou, Songgang, Longhua, Longgang and Kuichong. Under the district government, there were twenty-two people's communes and one township with the same rank as the communes (Fig. 11.2). Directly under the municipal government were the eight 'fronts': the Economic Commission; Planning Commission; Construction Commission; Office of Finance and Trade; Office of Agriculture,

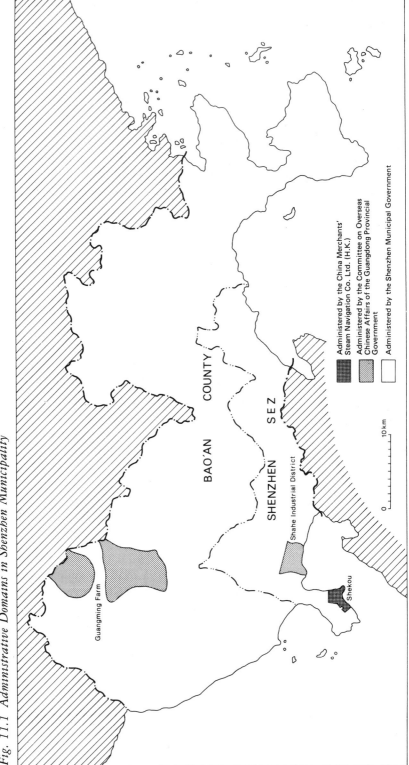

Fig. 11.1 Administrative Domains in Shenzhen Municipality

BAO'AN COUNTY

SHENZHEN SEZ

Guangming Farm

Shahe Industrial District

Shekou

Administered by the China Merchants' Steam Navigation Co. Ltd. (H.K.)

Administered by the Committee on Overseas Chinese Affairs of the Guangdong Provincial Government

Administered by the Shenzhen Municipal Government

0   10 km

Fig. 11.2 The Administrative Hierarchy of Shenzhen Municipality before 1981

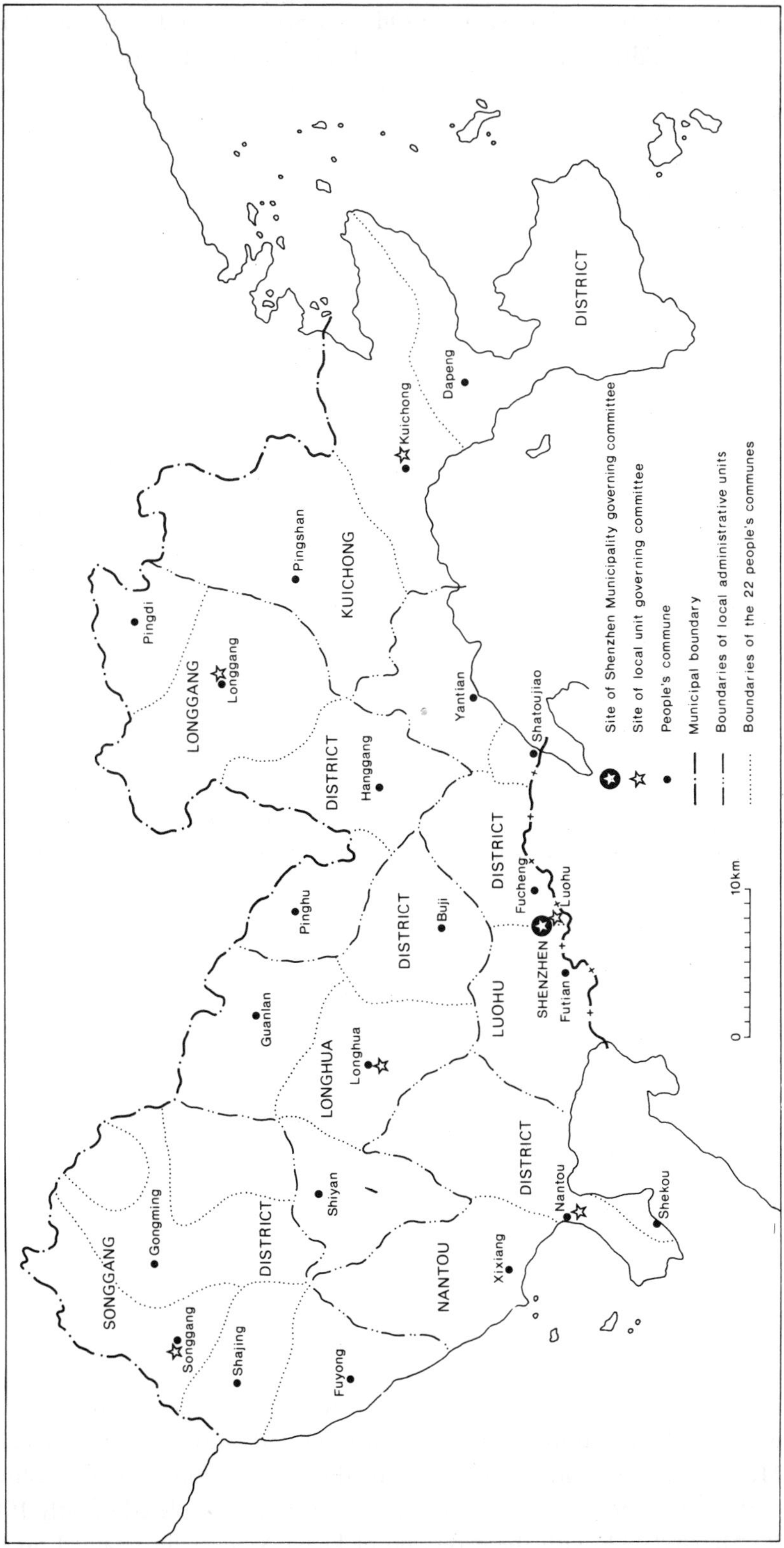

Forestry and Water Conservancy; Office of Science and Technology; Office of Culture, Education and Hygiene; and the Institute of Public Security and Justice. A third tier of the municipal government structure included numerous departments, examples of which can be found in Fig. 11.3. In addition, there were other government agencies beyond the control of the Shenzhen municipal government. These were the branch offices either of the Guangdong Provincial Government or of the central government in Beijing. The Customs Office, the Office of Foreign Affairs, the banks, China Travel Service Ltd., and the Department of Railway Communication were examples of such agencies.

Such a complex and cumbersome governmental structure has confused many investors who have insufficient knowledge of which department they should negotiate with. Divided but unclear responsibility adds to the difficulty of negotiation. Before October 1981, there was a total of six to seven deputy mayors and up to three hundred cadre officers in the Shenzhen municipal government, so that the process of negotiation was intolerably complicated and time-consuming. The first step to solve the problem was to set up the Shenzhen Overseas Economic and Technical Liaison Office which was delegated to make arrangements between investors and the appropriate government agencies. However, co-ordination among the various government agencies was still far from satisfactory and when an agreement was reached, the contract had to receive the approval of all government agencies involved, resulting in long delays and in great inefficiency.

In September 1981, Bao'an County was re-established, but its jurisdiction is now confined to the areas outside the Shenzhen SEZ. The five districts formerly subject to the Bao'an County administration were abolished. Luohu District was expanded to cover the whole area designated for the Shenzhen SEZ. Both the Bao'an county government and the Luohu district government were put under the jurisdiction of the Shenzhen municipal government. The re-establishment of Bao'an County can be regarded as an attempt to solve the problem of over-staffing in the Shenzhen municipal government and as providing an outlet for the original Bao'an staff who were found to be too junior or unqualified for a municipal or SEZ level of administration. The task given to Bao'an County for development as a source of agricultural products for the Shenzhen SEZ is perhaps more suitable for the former Bao'an County cadres.

The Reorganized Administrative Structure

In October 1981, Liang Xiang was appointed Chief Secretary of the Shenzhen Municipal Communist Party Committee and Mayor of the Shenzhen Municipality. A definite move toward the simplification and streamlining of the governmental structure soon began and was completed in early 1982. By March 1982, with the exception of Liang Xiang who retained his two

*Fig. 11.3 The Structure of the Shenzhen Municipal Government before
Reorganization*

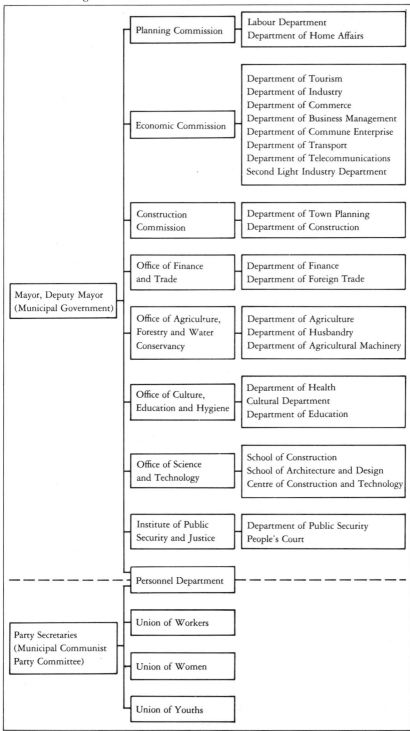

Source: Fieldwork, 1983.

positions, few officials were permitted to keep two posts at the same time. The number of deputy mayors was reduced to three (now increased to five) and the municipal government was cut to one-third of its original size, being staffed in 1982 by about 100 cadre officers. Above all, significant changes were made in the number and the title of government agencies. Among the major changes were:

(a) dissolution of the Office of Agriculture, Forestry and Water Conservancy, its responsibilities being discharged to the county level;

(b) subdivision of the Economic Commission into two new organizations: the Office of Industrial and Transportation Affairs and the Office of Overseas Economic Affairs, both under the administration of the General Office of the Shenzhen municipal government; the former is in charge of the Telecommunications, Transportation, Shipping and Aviation companies, whilst the latter takes care of the Foreign Trade Department and Companies and the Tourist Department;

(c) reform of the Office of Finance and Trade under the new name of Office of Financial and Trade Affairs (which now governs the Department of Finance, the Department of Tax and the internal trading companies);

(d) amalgamation of the former Commission of Science and Technology and the Office of Culture, Education and Hygiene into the newly founded Office of General Affairs, heading the Department of Health, the Department of Education, the Sports Development Centre and the Scientific and Technological Development Centre;

(e) restructuring of the Construction Commission as the Shenzhen SEZ Construction Company, responsible for the administration of the following units:

> Town Planning Department; Office of Environmental Protection; companies dealing with construction material, importation of construction material, fixtures, water supply, coal gas, road systems, parks and greenery, capital construction, staff and worker services, facilities installation and residence; School of Construction; School of Architecture and Design; Centre of Construction Technology; and Centre of Construction Quality Control;

(f) merging of the Personnel Department within the Communist Party structure; and

(g) replacement of the Planning Commission by the Department of Planning and Statistics which, like the Labour Services Company, lies outside the General Office of the Shenzhen municipal government.

However, there are still some offices which remain unchanged after the reorganization, and these include the Public Security Department, the Procuratorate and the Court. Fig. 11.4 shows the administrative structure of the Shenzhen Municipality after the reorganization.

Also shown in Fig. 11.4 is the restructuring of the Luohu district government which started in 1982 and was completed in September 1983. The former Luohu district government covered the entire area of the Shenzhen

Fig. 11.4 The Administrative System of Shenzhen Municipality after Reorganization in 1982–3

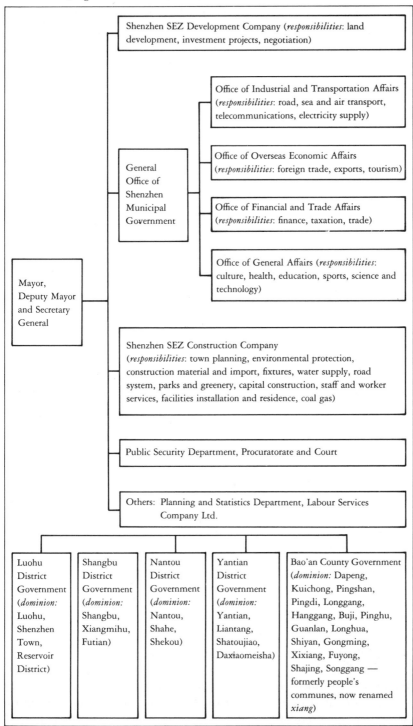

SEZ. In the new structure, it is being replaced by four urban district governments, namely Luohu, Shangbu, Nantou and Yantian district governments. The new Luohu district government is much smaller than the previous one, and its dominions include Luohu District, Shenzhen Town and the Reservoir District (*Wen Wei Po*, 4 September 1983). These four district governments are of the same ranking as the county governments.

As a result of the reorganization, negotiations for land development and the introduction of outside capital have to go through the Shenzhen SEZ Development Company which acts on behalf of the Shenzhen Municipal People's Government on these issues. The examination and approval of investment projects lies in the hands of the Office of External Economic Affairs, under the General Office of the Shenzhen Municipal Government. For infrastructure development and capital construction, the responsibility lies with the Shenzhen SEZ Construction Company (Fig. 11.5).

On the whole, after the reform and streamlining of Shenzhen's administrative structure in early 1982, the responsibilities and duties of the government agencies are more clearly defined and also more comprehensible to outsiders. With reductions in redundant staff, in auxiliary positions and in the number of departments, the new government structure can perhaps raise the administrative efficiency of the Shenzhen government and thus facilitate the development of the SEZ. Reports from many entrepreneurs and potential investors have pointed out that the administrative reform and the streamlining of investment procedures have indeed simplified the negotiation process and the implementation of contracts and agreements between investors and the Shenzhen SEZ government. However, it is also clear that the ideal progression projected in Fig. 11.5 is still far from the practical reality. Bureaucratic interference must be further reduced. Nevertheless, with the new administrative structure and better defined departmental responsibilities, the chaos of the past has gradually disappeared (fieldwork, 1983).

The Legal System

On 26 August 1980, the Guangdong SEZ Regulations were approved by the fifteenth session of the Standing Committee of the Fifth National People's Congress and thenceforth became effective. This was the first and most important set of regulations concerning the SEZs in Guangdong, and was made up of six chapters — General Principles, Registration and Operation, Preferential Treatment, Labour Management, Administration, and Appendix — with a total of twenty-six articles. Concerning the management of the SEZs, five more sets of SEZ Provisional Regulations were enacted on 17 November 1981 by the thirteenth session of the Standing Committee of

Fig. 11.5 The Present Investment Flow Chart

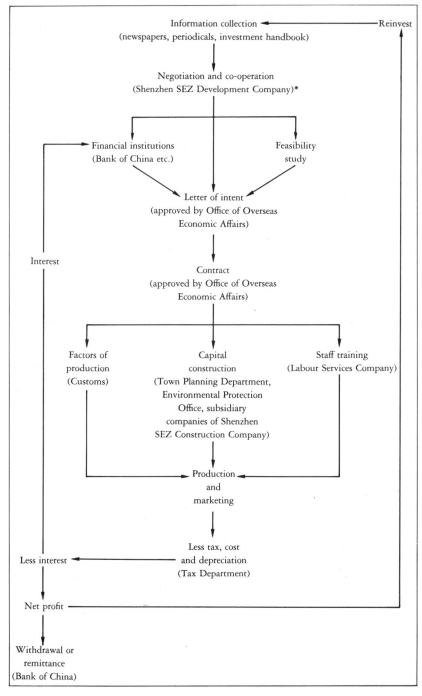

Note: * For the Shekou Industrial Zone, negotiation goes through the China Merchants'
    Steam Navigation Co. Ltd. (H.K.), while the Overseas Chinese Enterprise
    Company is responsible for the Shahe Industrial District.

Source: Fieldwork, April 1982 and September 1983.

the Fifth Provincial People's Congress of Guangdong. These are: (a) the Provisional Labour and Wage Regulations (Guangdong SEZs); (b) the Provisional Entry/Exit Regulations (Guangdong SEZs); (c) the Provisional Regulations for Business Registration (Guangdong SEZs); (d) the Provisional Land Regulations for Shenzhen SEZ; and (e) the Provisional Administration Regulations for Shenzhen SEZ.

The first three sets of regulations are applicable to all the SEZs of Guangdong, while the latter two are for the Shenzhen SEZ in particular. The first four regulations were published in December 1981, and came into force on 1 January 1982, but the fifth set of regulations on administration has not yet been published. Generally speaking, these five sets of provisional regulations for the SEZs are supplements to the Guangdong SEZ Regulations. Notwithstanding the limited coverage of these provisional regulations, they indicate a change of practice — from the traditional emphasis on personal credits to the more impersonal practice of a legal code — which is welcomed by overseas investors.

In January 1984, two more sets of regulations were passed by the Standing Committee of the Guangdong Provincial People's Congress. The Foreign Economic Contract Regulations for the Shenzhen SEZ contain seven chapters and 41 articles. They aim at protecting the rights of all parties involved in foreign economic contracts and stipulate that Chinese enterprises inside the zone and their foreign partners must follow the principle of 'equality and mutual benefits' when they embark on economic and technological co-operation. The Provisional Regulations on the Introduction of Technology for the Shenzhen SEZ contain only one chapter and 25 articles and cover such items as the ways in which foreign technology could be introduced and the transfer of patent rights. Both sets of regulations were specially enacted for the Shenzhen SEZ but they could also be applied to the other two SEZs in Guangdong. Indeed, they are important landmarks in the development of a legal system in China in general and in the SEZs in particular. This is especially true in the case of the Foreign Economic Contract Regulations because the Chinese contract law covering domestic economic activities does not apply to activities involving foreign investment. The Foreign Economic Contract Regulations (which are not provisional) are directed at business activities involving foreign investors, such as joint ventures. In other words, these regulations will set a precedent in contract matters involving foreign investors in China.

By early 1984, seven sets of regulations had been enacted; they are, however, essentially general principles and lack specific details. Besides, their scope is still limited. Other commercial laws such as the Property/Estate Law, the SEZ Customs Law, the SEZ Law of Taxation, the Regulations on Foreign Exchange, the Company Law and the Foreign-Capital-Based Banking Ordinance, which are all of direct concern to potential investors, are still in the process of drafting and are not yet ready for publication. In fact, the contract law is the most complicated among the commercial laws. Without the support of other commercial laws, the implementation of the Foreign Economic Contract Regulations is bound to be difficult as loopholes become apparent in the process of enforcement.

Without the back-up of a company law and a bankruptcy law, for example, the Foreign Economic Contract Regulations have serious limitations. This can be illustrated in the case of the winding up of LMK Nam Sang Ltd., a Hong Kong registered firm which was at the same time the owner of the LMK Nam Sang Dyeing Factory in Kuichong, Shenzhen. In the absence of a company law, the Shenzhen officials said that, because there were jurisdictional differences, the decision by foreign banks to put the Hong Kong registered LMK Nam Sang Ltd. into official receivership should not affect the LMK Nam Sang Dyeing Factory of Shenzhen. The winding up of business of the LMK Nam Sang Dyeing Factory at Shenzhen was refused despite the bankruptcy of the mother company in Hong Kong. Government officials in Shenzhen insisted on the continued operation of the dyeing factory on the grounds that the company was making a profit in Shenzhen and that the agreements for loans advanced to the mother company were signed in Hong Kong and not in Shenzhen. Finally, the secretary-general of the Shenzhen SEZ, Mr Zou Erkang, agreed that if the banks could produce documentary proof of loans made to the factory, they would agree to settle the dispute in accordance with Chinese laws with reference to Hong Kong laws. The eventual result was the transfer of ownership of the dyeing factory in Shenzhen from the bankrupted LMK Nam Sang Ltd. to Chung Koon Co. which agreed to buy the factory for HK$33.4 million (*Wen Wei Po*, 14 April 1984). The incident reveals the urgency of the need for a set of company laws for the Shenzhen SEZ. According to Mr Zou Erkang, it is hoped that a company law for the Shenzhen SEZ will be enacted by the end of 1984 (*Wen Wei Po*, 30 May 1984). Other commercial laws will also be drafted and enacted as soon as possible.

An early completion of these laws would be welcomed by overseas investors and perhaps also by Chinese enterprises. According to a survey conducted by the Guangdong Law Society (1981), quite a number of contracts signed between 1979 and 1981 were found to have loopholes, and considerable losses were incurred by the Chinese government as a result. Some of these contracts, in fact, did not conform with the laws, regulations and associated policies operating in China, and were thus invalid. It was reported that these contracts were revised and their problems solved only after lengthy and patient persuasion. With the enactment of these new sets of laws, both overseas investors and Chinese enterprises will have better guidelines before signing their agreements.

Other aspects of the legal system need to be improved as well. For example, ambiguities due to problems in translation have created many misunderstandings and arguments between investors on the one hand and Chinese officials on the other. At one time, much confusion was caused by differences in the interpretation of 'letter of intent' and 'legal contract'. All these problems are due to the fact that, at the beginning of the development of the Shenzhen SEZ, Chinese officials lacked professional knowledge and experience of commercial dealings. By early 1982, the first batch of lawyers was delegated to Shenzhen from Beijing in the hope that they might resolve these legal problems. Legal consultancy services are also provided at minimum charges so that overseas investors and the Chinese authorities can understand contracts fully before signing them. In January 1984, the Legal Consultancy in the Shenzhen SEZ was renamed the Shenzhen Lawyers' Office and it started providing a full range of legal services in April 1984.

With the enactment of the commercial laws and the greater availability of legal personnel, many mistakes made in the past should not be repeated. However, the commercial laws are no substitute for arbitration agencies. Before 1983, there was no arbitration agency or court for economic affairs in the Shenzhen SEZ. The absence of these institutions seriously hampered the proper functioning of the zone. As early as 1981, Li (1981) of the Law Department of Zhongshan University advocated the idea of setting up an arbitration system for the SEZ. He pointed out that the zone should follow the common practice of international commercial arbitration in which a third party, independent of both contractual parties, should be appointed and entrusted with the authority to mediate in any possible dispute. He further suggested that all contracts should incorporate a statement of arbitration, including (a) the place of arbitration; (b) the arbitration agency; (c) the procedures of arbitration; and (d) an agreement that decisions of the arbitration should be legally binding so that disputes could be dealt with more efficiently and pragmatically. He also advocated that the Shenzhen SEZ should have its own arbitration agency to deal with disputes quickly and with greater understanding of the SEZ environment. Only in complicated cases or cases involving a large sum of money should arbitration follow the process indicated in Article 14 of the Law of the People's Republic of China on Chinese–Foreign Joint Ventures which states that

disputes arising between the parties in a joint venture which the Board of Directors fails to settle through consultation may be settled through conciliation or arbitration by an arbitral body of China or through arbitration by an arbitral body agreed upon by the parties.

In such cases, arbitration normally goes through the Committee for Overseas Economic and Trade Arbitration in Beijing. Li's argument was endorsed by the Shenzhen SEZ government, and the Shenzhen Office of the Chinese External Trade Arbitral Committee was established on 2 April 1984. Moreover, eight well-known Hong Kong citizens have been invited to join the team of fifteen arbitrators in order to give confidence to overseas investors.

A complete set of laws and a standard contract format, together with an efficient and just arbitration agency, are required to safeguard the interests of both the investors and the Chinese government. They are also necessary conditions for economic growth, especially in terms of raising the confidence of investors and generating a more favourable investment environment. To conclude, although remarkable advances have been made since 1979, various incidents have indicated that the legal system of the Shenzhen SEZ has so far still not evolved fast enough to cope with actual needs. This situation can perhaps be improved in the near future.

The Banking and Financial Structure

Banking and Financial Institutions

All the four major banks of China — the People's Bank, the People's Construction Bank, the Agricultural Bank and the Bank of China — have branch offices in the Shenzhen SEZ. The People's Bank is a general purpose bank whilst the remaining three are regarded as specialist banks. So far only one overseas bank — the Nanyang Commercial Bank — has been permitted to establish branch offices in the Shenzhen SEZ (one office in Shenzhen Town and one in the Shekou Industrial Zone). According to a report in the *Shenzhen Special Zone Daily* (31 May 1982), about eleven overseas banking and financial institutions will be allowed to set up representative offices in the Shenzhen SEZ, amongst them the Hongkong and Shanghai Banking Corporation, Takugin International (Asia) Ltd., the Banque de l'Indochine et de Suez and the Banque Nationale de Paris. The Nanyang Commercial Bank is now functioning as a commercial bank taking deposits in Rmb as well as in Hong Kong dollars, but the representative offices of the other banks are unlikely to have similar functions. They will probably provide significant services in investment consultancy, import and export credits and the lending of foreign exchange to joint-venture projects via overseas channels. However, as the regulations for overseas banks are still in the drafting stage, the exact role that these representative offices will play is unclear.

Before 1982, most overseas investors in the Shenzhen SEZ had to rely on their own sources of capital. This explains why investment projects concluded in that period were either with large multinational corporations with strong financial back-up or with petty investors from Hong Kong investing mainly in small projects. Medium-scale investment projects in which the investors were in need of a bank's support were relatively few. One may attribute the lack of medium-scale projects in this period to the inadequacy of the banking system in the Shenzhen SEZ. According to published statistics, since 1982 the branch offices of the four Chinese banks in the Shenzhen SEZ have been more willing to support overseas investors with loans. In 1982, the Agricultural Bank of China agreed to lend a total of Rmb 200,000 to three Hong Kong investors in agriculture and fishery joint-venture projects. It also advanced as much as Rmb 3 million to the Xiangmihu Holiday Resort, also a joint venture with investors from Hong Kong. It is reported that the People's Construction Bank is prepared to support massive land development projects, especially those related to the 'seven linkages and one levelling'. The branch office of the People's Bank of China is said to be prepared to accept mortgages and hire-purchase of houses and consumer durables, and to advance loans and credits to ordinary citizens of the Shenzhen SEZ for private business and individual enterprises. International banking practices are also taking root in the zone as observed, for example, in the popularity of credit cards.

Between 1982 and mid-1984, the branch office of the People's Bank of China in the Shenzhen SEZ had advanced loans to 57 enterprises, including joint-venture and co-operative production projects as well as a few sole proprietorships. The loans were divided between foreign exchange (US$39 million) and Rmb (Rmb 92 million). From mid-1984, the branch office of the People's Bank of China in the Shenzhen SEZ is to be vested with the power to fix its own rate of interest for deposits taken, and loans advanced to enterprises, in the SEZ. As a result the banking system in the Shenzhen SEZ will be more responsive to changes in international money markets (*Wen Wei Po*, 7 June 1984). Furthermore, the banks will exercise a supervisory role over their clients. In the past, investment projects without the involvement of banks were carried out with little attention to the feasibility of the project. Normally a series of feasibility studies has to be undertaken before loans can be obtained from banks. Meanwhile, before granting the loan or acting as an underwriter, the bank also undertakes a thorough investigation of the feasibility of the project and the investor's ability to repay. Hence, repeated examinations and investigations of the investment project minimize the possibility of blind investment and eventually benefit all parties concerned. After obtaining loans from the bank, enterprises have to improve their system of accounting, which can only lead to healthier development of the enterprise. It is expected that the banking ordinance will soon be enacted, paving the way for a better banking environment for both local and overseas banking agencies.

A well-established banking and financial system with a complete set of banking ordinances will provide a much better investment environment for investors in the Shenzhen SEZ.

The Special Zone Currency

One issue which is hotly debated inside the Shenzhen SEZ government and in banking circles in the zone is whether there is a need to issue a special zone currency.

Under the present monetary system, Rmb is not a commonly accepted currency in the international foreign exchange market; this is a hindrance to capital flow and trading activities between the SEZ and the outside world. This limitation certainly weakens the attraction of Shenzhen to outside investors. The foreign exchange coupon, issued by the People's Bank of China, is a readily convertible currency elsewhere in China, but not outside China because it is not recognized by other countries. Neither Rmb nor the foreign exchange coupons can satisfy the financial needs of the Shenzhen SEZ, as is revealed by the large circulation and the popularity of Hong Kong dollars. At present, all three currencies circulate within Shenzhen, but the presence of the Hong Kong currency has caused some concern to the Chinese government because it has weakened the position of the Rmb in the SEZ. Furthermore, the Chinese will suffer great losses in the event of a devaluation of the Hong Kong dollar. It has, therefore, been suggested that the branch office of the People's Bank in the Shenzhen SEZ should be authorized to issue a special zone currency. At the same time, by collecting the large sums of Hong Kong dollars currently in circulation within the SEZ and depositing them in the banks of Hong Kong, the Shenzhen SEZ could earn a sizeable amount of money in the form of bank interest.

It is very obvious that a sound financial system is necessary for the development of the Shenzhen SEZ. A close relationship with the international foreign exchange market will allow capital to flow in and out of the zone more freely. The object of requiring the central banks (or their branch offices in the SEZ) to issue a readily convertible special zone currency is the linkage of the Shenzhen financial system with the international financial market, making it more convenient for investors. However, the maintenance of its value and the containment of fluctuation within a tolerable margin will definitely be as difficult as with the currencies of many countries. A set of special zone currency laws, special zone banking ordinances and regulations on special zone foreign exchange control will be necessary for the success of this currency. In addition, experienced personnel in the financial field must be recruited in order to ensure the proper and efficient operation of the system. Otherwise the special zone currency may suffer from serious fluctuations in the exchange rate. The problem of speculation in the special zone currency should also be heeded. A team of experienced and talented banking personnel will be needed to manipulate properly the limited reserve to stabilize the currency's exchange rate during speculative buying and selling. An unstable currency will definitely do more harm than good to the investment environment of the Shenzhen SEZ.

Preferential Treatment and Investment Incentives

One of the primary objectives of businessmen investing in the Shenzhen SEZ is to make a profit. The profit–capital ratio, the return period, and whether the money can be remitted out freely are their main concerns. In deciding on the amount of investment and in evaluating the financial feasibility of a project, investors have to compare the 'opportunity cost' of their investment. Under normal circumstances, an investment decision on a certain project is made only when its expected earnings are greater than those of other proposed projects. Apart from profit, the degree of risk involved is another prominent factor affecting investment decisions. Wherever risk is greater because of uncertainty, the profit margin should also be higher. Usually, a bank deposit is regarded as the safest investment, so that the interest rates of overseas banks can be taken as the minimum desirable rate of return for any investment programme in the Shenzhen SEZ. A longer return period usually means greater uncertainty and thus involves more risk, so that the total profit margin of these projects must be higher or else the Shenzhen SEZ will not be able to attract these investments. The estimation of risk and uncertainty is very subjective, being based mainly on the investor's own personal experience, the experience of other investors, the amount of information available and the existence of insurance schemes and official guarantees. At present, the Shenzhen SEZ is in an unfavourable position due to the insufficiency of information available to investors, the lack of a sound legal and financial system, the inadequate provision of infrastructure and, most significantly, the lack of enough successful precedents to support the investor's confidence. These clouds of uncertainty concerning the structure and the operation of the SEZ have created a fairly high risk factor: as a result the investor must anticipate a higher level of profit before he commits himself. Only with a gradual improvement in Shenzhen's administrative, legal and financial systems and when the general regulations of the zone are more thoroughly understood by outsiders can the risk factor be reduced. Investors may then consider as viable projects with lower profit margins and longer return periods.

The preferential terms offered in the SEZ help to raise the profit margin of investment. The provision of locally produced machinery and raw materials at export prices, and tax exemption on imported capital goods for production help to reduce the overall cost of production. Cheap land utility costs and low wage rates, especially in comparison with Hong Kong, will increase the gross profit of investors. Furthermore, the low profit tax rate at 15 per cent (as compared with 20–40 per cent for joint ventures in China outside the SEZs) gives the investor a better chance of recovering his capital quickly. With these preferential terms, investment conditions in the Shenzhen SEZ are, undoubtedly, somewhat more favourable than those of neighbouring Asian countries (Table 11.1). Nevertheless, whether these preferential terms are attractive and sufficient depends not only on the size of the reduction in labour wages or land utility costs but also on whether investing in Shenzhen can provide a higher profit margin, subject to the degree of risk involved, than investing in other parts of China, Hong Kong, or export processing zones in developing countries. If Shenzhen does provide a higher profit

Table 11.1 A Comparison of Investment Conditions in Industry in the Shenzhen SEZ, Hong Kong, Taiwan, South Korea and Singapore

	Land Costs (per sq ft in HK$)1980		Wages (per worker per month in HK$) 1980			Tax Holiday	Corporate Tax
	Rent per year	Purchase	Unskilled	Semi-skilled	Skilled		
Shenzhen SEZ							
Shekou	2–4	—	Average 750			3–5 years (longer for needed industries)	15% from 4th–6th year
SEZ proper	1–3[1]	—					
Hong Kong							
Taipo Ind. Est.	—	65.0[2,3]	975	1,432	1,862	Nil	16.5%[4]
Outside	—	200[3]					
Taiwan EPZ	0.72	1.01–6.26	586.7	—	1,398.86	5 years	22–25%
South Korea (free export zone)	0.015–0.02	5.75–18.70	28.74–128.60	54.60–208.33	86.90–229.70	5 years (50% reduction from 6th–8th year)	20% (excess profit up to 35%)
Singapore	0.17	1.02–8.36	762.80	1,186.33	1,970.54	5–10 years	40% royalties, fees 20–40%

Notes: 1. Reduction of 30–50% since January 1983 depending on location in the SEZ.
2. Raised to HK$92.50 per sq ft since July 1981.
3. Lump-sum payment for 15-year lease.
4. 18.5% since 1984.

Source: Economic Reporter (English monthly), August 1980.

margin and less risk, the investment environment of Shenzhen can be regarded as attractive and competitive; otherwise, the reverse is true. Or if the anticipated profit margin attained is able to compensate for the degree of risk involved, Shenzhen is still attractive. Otherwise, investors will adopt a wait-and-see strategy, or simply direct their investment to other places.

It is noteworthy that the attraction of the preferential terms offered in the Shenzhen SEZ may vary among different sectors of industry. For example, marginal industries in Hong Kong may find the Shenzhen SEZ very attractive because these industries no longer enjoy any locational advantage in Hong Kong and are due to be eliminated. Consequently, the attractiveness of the Shenzhen SEZ to these industries is very great and to them the risk factor of Shenzhen is tolerable. However, this does not apply to large-scale and high technology industries which can still make profits in Hong Kong and other less risky areas. It is, therefore, necessary to provide even more generous preferential terms for these industries if they are to be attracted to the Shenzhen SEZ. The reason that real-estate development accounted for about 40 per cent of the total intended investment in the Shenzhen SEZ before 1981 is that such investment has a short return period, a smaller risk factor and a relatively high profit margin. The same applies to projects in tourism.

In conclusion, preferential terms offered by the Shenzhen SEZ should not be evaluated separately and independently from the risk factor, although the former is easier to compare and to spell out whilst the latter is less tangible and more difficult to measure. The authorities should not occupy themselves solely with the provision of generous preferential terms but should also seek out ways to minimize risks and uncertainties.

The Tax System

Taxation is one of the major issues that are of direct concern to investors in the Shenzhen SEZ but in which no law or regulation has so far been enacted. Although in Chapter III of the Guangdong SEZ Regulations, reference is made to the rate of income tax to be levied on SEZ enterprises, no stipulations on profit or sales tax are mentioned. The interpretation of such a situation is that (a) the term 'income tax' is taken to include profit tax — in other words, income tax applied to enterprises is, in fact, profit tax; and (b) sales tax need not be specified as products from the SEZ are meant for export rather than for the domestic market. The contents of the Foreign Enterprise Income Tax Law (applicable to the whole of China) which was adopted at the fourteenth session of the Fifth National People's Congress on 13 December 1981 and came into effect on 1 January 1982 are, in fact, related to profit tax. It is stipulated that the taxable income of a foreign enterprise is the net income in a tax year after deduction of costs, expenses and losses in that year. An attempt will, therefore, be made here to analyse the income tax situation as applied to the SEZ.

Income/Profit Tax

Investment in the Shenzhen SEZ enjoys a more favourable tax rate than it does in Hong Kong or in other parts of China. Prior to the promulgation of the 'Regulations on SEZs in Guangdong Province' on 26 August 1980, the tax rate was not uniform throughout the Shenzhen SEZ. The corporate tax rate levied on foreign enterprises in Shenzhen was usually 15 per cent; but in the Shekou Industrial Zone, all enterprises qualified for a tax holiday of 3 to 5 years from the date of commissioning, and thereafter only a 10 per cent corporate tax would apply.

With the promulgation of the regulations in August 1980, the rate of income tax levied on enterprises was set at 15 per cent throughout the SEZ. But in the case of the Shekou Industrial Zone, enterprises could still qualify for a tax holiday of 3 to 5 years before paying the 15 per cent tax. Under exceptions to the above rules, income tax for certain enterprises can be either reduced or exempted: (a) for enterprises with investments of US$5 million or over; (b) for enterprises using advanced technology and having a long cycle of capital turnover; (c) for enterprises whose type of business does not yet exist in China; and (d) for all enterprises established within two years after the promulgation of the regulations.

Preferential treatment given to the above categories of enterprises includes a reduction of the tax rate by 20 to 50 per cent or exemption from tax for 1 to 3 years. These enterprises are also exempted from all local income tax. The only exception is the Shekou Industrial Zone where enterprises whose investment agreements were signed before the promulgation of the Guangdong SEZ Regulations will be charged according to the originally agreed tax rate, which was usually 10 per cent.

By comparison, according to the income tax law for foreign enterprises applied to other parts of China, the tax rate ranges from 20 per cent (on annual income of less than Rmb 250,000) to 40 per cent (on annual income of over Rmb 1 million). In addition, a local income tax of 10 per cent on the same taxable income will also be levied.

Income tax on foreign enterprises will be levied on an annual basis. After paying all the necessary taxes, overseas investors and workers in SEZ enterprises can remit their earnings out of China, provided that the special zone's foreign exchange control measures are not violated. Investors who choose to reinvest their profits in the zone for five years or more can apply for exemption from income tax on that part of the profit being reinvested.

Losses incurred by a foreign enterprise in a tax year may be carried over to the next year and made up with a matching amount drawn from that year's income. Should income in subsequent years be insufficient to make up for the said losses, the balance may be made up with further deductions against income year by year over a period not exceeding five years.

Import and Export Duties

All the necessary means of production including machinery, spare parts and accessories, raw materials, and transport tools, are exempted from import duties. Depending on the individual case, import duties for consumer goods can also be exempted or charged at a reduced rate. However, all the items have to be used or consumed within the SEZ; otherwise duties will be levied in accordance with the customs regulations of China.

Similarly, finished and semi-finished products manufactured by enterprises in the Shenzhen SEZ for overseas markets will be exempted from export duties; but if the products are for domestic sale, duties will have to be levied, again in accordance with customs regulations. In general, it is intended that products of the SEZ should be exported on to the international market. Domestic sales are allowed only with the prior approval of the Guangdong Provincial Administration of the SEZs.

Land Use and the Provision of Infrastructure

Land is an important factor of production but it is in limited supply in many places. Hong Kong's economic growth, for example, is to a certain extent restricted by a shortage of land. The designation of an extensive area across the border from Hong Kong as an SEZ is important in terms of land provision. The availability of large pieces of land not only for present development but also for future expansion is an attractive factor to many Hong Kong investors — particularly since the Shenzhen SEZ is to be developed into a comprehensive economic entity, with investment opportunities available for a wide range of activities including manufacturing, agriculture, tourism, commercial and real-estate development and quarrying. Extensive areas of flat land requiring little reclamation or levelling work are essential to the reduction of development costs and to expedite the progress of construction.

Land Provision

Shenzhen is much larger than either the other Chinese SEZs or export processing zones in other developing countries. The Shenzhen Municipality has a total area of 202,000 ha of which 32,750 ha have been designated as the SEZ. This figure may not mean much by itself; but if we compare it with other SEZs or export processing zones (Table 11.2), the difference immediately becomes very obvious. The export processing zones shown in Table 11.2 are among the largest now in operation in Asia, but the Shenzhen SEZ is more than one hundred times larger than most of them. Even by comparison with other SEZs in China, Shenzhen is still unusually large for such a zone.

The Shenzhen SEZ undoubtedly has abundant land resources. But how suitable is this land for large-scale urban and economic development? According to estimates made by the Shenzhen government, about one-third of the zone's total land area (that is to say, 11,000 ha) can be classified as capable of supporting sizeable development and construction programmes (Table 11.3). Of this, 9,800 ha have been defined for planning purposes, and this is still an extensive area compared with other SEZs and EPZs.

These usable land areas are by no means evenly distributed throughout the Shenzhen SEZ (Fig. 11.6). The northern and eastern sections are generally of rather hilly or rugged topography with only a few isolated coastal plains suitable for urban development. However, towards the west, there is an almost continuous stretch of flat and low-lying land extending from Shenzhen Town westwards through Shangbu, Futian and Shahe to Shekou and Nantou. Here, the soil is well-structured and land levelling is not a difficult task. There is great potential for large-scale urban development along this Shenzhen–Nantou corridor. Outside this area where concentrated development is possible, Shenzhen's land resources provide opportunities for a variety of other land uses; for example, the rolling or hilly regions are often endowed with great scenic beauty which favours the development of tourist or holiday resorts. Furthermore, the region is endowed with rich resources of building materials. Fine freshwater sand, high-quality granite, marble and limestone are all readily available.

The Economic Aspects of Land Development

Apart from physical conditions, the attractiveness of a piece of land for development also depends upon the cost of using the land, especially for undertakings which require much space. Although different economic activities will respond differently to variations in land rentals, cheap land utility costs and long lease periods are always attractive to investors. According to Article 16 of the Provisional Land Regulations for the Shenzhen SEZ, land utility charges will be collected on all land used by enterprises whether they are sole foreign investments or joint ventures with the Chinese. Rates will vary according to location and types of business (for details, see Chapter 7). These rates are effective from 1 January 1982 and will be adjusted once every three years. In order to provide even more attractive terms for the investor, these standard rates were reduced by about 40 per cent in mid-

Table 11.2 The Size of the SEZs and Selected EPZs

Shenzhen SEZ	32,750 ha
Zhuhai SEZ	1,516 ha
Xiamen SEZ	12,550 ha*
Shantou SEZ	5,260 ha*
Bataan (Philippines)	345 ha
Kandla (India)	384 ha
Katunayake (Sri Lanka)	202 ha
Bayan Lepas (Malaysia)	202 ha
Masan (South Korea)	175 ha

Note: *Proposed size, subject to confirmation (see Chapters 1 and 3).

Table 11.3 The Classification of Land in the Shenzhen SEZ

Land Types	Area (ha)		Area Suitable for Urban Development (ha)
Flat land	7,260	(22.2%)	7,260
Existing built-up area	1,740	(5.3%)	1,740
Rolling/undulating	5,730	(17.5%)	2,000
Low-lying	1,460	(4.4%)	
Hilly land	15,910	(48.6%)	
Water surface	650	(2.0%)	
Total	32,750	(100.0%)	11,000

1984 (*Wen Wei Po*, 22 June 1984). Payment of the charges can either be (a) in one lot in which case payment has to be made within two years, interest free; or (b) by yearly instalments with an interest rate of 8 per cent per annum. In the latter case, in the event of any adjustment in the land utility charges, the new rate always applies. It is perhaps important to note that these land utility charges do not apply to the Shekou Industrial Zone, which is managed by the China Merchants' Steam Navigation Co. Ltd., and a different set of terms applies there. The average annual land utility cost in Shekou is HK$2–4 per sq ft (HK$21.4–42.9 per sq m). Working on an exchange rate of HK$100 = Rmb 28, the average land utility cost in Shekou ranges from Rmb 6–12 per sq m per year which is generally cheaper than the rates in other parts of the Shenzhen SEZ. In Shekou, the rates will be adjusted once every five years.

In view of the fact that the infrastructure is still inadequate, measures

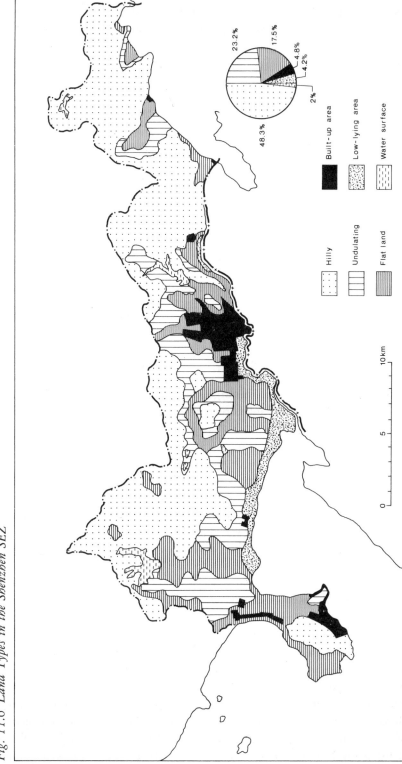

Fig. 11.6 Land Types in the Shenzhen SEZ

have been taken recently to improve the attractiveness of Shenzhen's land resources, especially in the more marginal areas. Among these measures is the introduction of a more flexible bill in connection with land utility charges (for details, see Chapter 7). Land in Shenzhen is divided into three categories according to location, accessibility and development potential. From October 1982 until 1985, land utility charges will be reduced by 30–50 per cent for these land categories, with the less attractive areas being given a greater reduction. Development projects in hitherto undeveloped areas such as hilly, undulating or low-lying (swampy) districts can be exempted from land utility charges for one to five years, depending on the nature of the project. Such an adjustment will certainly improve the competitiveness of Shenzhen's land resources, especially for large-scale and long-term development projects.

As discussed in Chapter 7, land development in the Shenzhen SEZ is under strict government control and all applications for the use of land must pass through the Shenzhen People's Government. The process of land development may seem long and cumbersome; but it is the intention of the Shenzhen authority to ensure that all land is developed in an appropriate manner and to protect the rights of the investors in the use of land that they have leased.

The Provision of Infrastructure

One of the implications of the large size of the Shenzhen SEZ is that the task of the provision of infrastructure is enormous. This is particularly evident when we consider that (a) prior to its designation as an SEZ the Shenzhen Municipality (originally Bao'an County) was an agricultural community with little urban development and was thus deficient in road communications and in the provision of various utilities and services; and (b) the usable or planned area of development is elongated in an east–west direction rather than being concentrated in a large compact district, making the provision of infrastructure yet more problematic.

Despite these difficulties, the provision of infrastructure is essential if large-scale economic development is to take place, and it has, in fact, been given top priority in the initial stage of the development of the Shenzhen SEZ. When Shekou was first developed in July 1979, basic construction was connected with the so-called 'five linkages and one levelling' which have largely been completed by now. These include: (a) a road link, mainly the construction of a 7.8-kilometre asphalt road joining Shekou with the Shenzhen–Guangzhou highway opened to traffic in January 1981; (b) a sea link, including the dredging of a 3,400-metre long and 5-metre deep sea lane and the construction of a 600-metre long pier capable of accommodating ships of 3,000–4,000 d.w.t.; (c) a water link, consisting of the construction of a 15-kilometre pipeline drawing on the Xili Reservoir and capable of transporting 20,000 tonnes of water per day; (d) an electricity link, including the supply of 1 million kW of electricity per year from the China Light and Power Company of Hong Kong to the Shenzhen network and the construction of local power stations; (e) a communication link, consisting of a microwave telephone service station constructed and open to use in early 1981, which provides 600 telephone lines and 60 microwave transmission lines; and (f) levelling work, which involves the levelling of hill slopes and the reclamation of coastal waters to provide more land for the construction of factories and other uses. It has been estimated that the total cost of infrastructure provision in Shekou has amounted to about HK$3 billion (fieldwork, 1982).

In the Shenzhen SEZ, infrastructural provision takes the form of 'seven linkages and one levelling' which include: (a) a road link; (b) a gas link; (c) an electricity link; (d) a water link; (e) a sewage system link; (f) a storm drainage system link; (g) a communication link; and (h) land levelling. Much attention is given to the construction of an efficient road network. On the other hand, Shenzhen is handicapped by the lack of a good harbour in spite of its coastal location. In the east, along Dapeng Bay and Daya Bay, there are stretches of deep water, but the rugged topography with steep slopes running into the sea means that there is little flat land for development. In the west, along Shenzhen Bay and the Zhujiang (Pearl River) Estuary, silting has prevented the formation of large deep-water channels. Development in the Chiwan area adjoining Shekou is now under way (the so-called 'small-scale five linkages and one levelling': part of the infrastructure facilities will be dependent on Shekou and thus only smaller-scale development is required at the present stage), but the piers for 5,000–10,000 d.w.t. ships are meant to serve as the rear service base of the South China Sea oilfields and can only benefit other developments of the Shenzhen SEZ to a limited extent.

According to conservative estimates by Chinese scholars, the cost of infrastructure provision for the 9,800 ha of land in the Shenzhen SEZ would amount to at least Rmb 36.7 billion (Chu, 1982). But up to now, it seems that infrastructure provision has not managed to keep pace with development needs. Experience from other export processing zones in Asia has already shown that the lack of a sufficient and well-established infrastructure is a major cause of failure. It is, therefore, essential that work on the provision of infrastructure should accelerate to prepare the way for the development that is anticipated. Furthermore, these services must be maintained at a high standard so that there will be no unnecessary inconvenience to enterprises.

Efforts have been made, firstly in Shekou and later in Bagualing (near Shangbu), to build a number of standard factory buildings supplied with the necessary utilities to induce small- to medium-scale industries to produce in Shenzhen. Investors are, thereby, released from the tasks of site formation and the installation of various public utilities and facilities. However, for enterprises in the Shenzhen SEZ which have been allotted land for development, the investors themselves are required to undertake the installation of public utilities according to the requirements of the municipal plan, including, for example, the installation of power lines, water supply lines, drainage works, sewage systems, gas lines, and telecommunications facilities. They assume responsibility for all costs incurred in connecting these to the external mains.

Labour and Labour Productivity

Administratively, matters concerning labour in the SEZ are handled by the Shenzhen Labour Services Company (which is under the Shenzhen SEZ Labour Department) whose terms of reference include assisting entrepreneurs in the recruitment and training of workers, and providing guidance for workers and entrepreneurs in drawing up the labour contract. According to the provisional regulations on labour and wages, labour contracts have to be concluded between the employers and the employees. The contract should specify the terms of employment, dismissal and resignation; the job specification; wages and rules for bonuses and penalties; working hours and holidays; labour insurance and welfare; labour protection; and labour discipline.

Once the recruitment of labour has been approved by the Labour Department, the entrepreneur can either do the recruitment himself or ask the Labour Services Company to introduce workers to him. But it is understood that some form of assessment is required to pick out the best people. After employment, the workers will undergo a probationary period of three to six months. If necessary, the enterprise can organize training courses for its workers to improve their skills. Termination of service can take several forms.

(a) *Resignation*: workers can submit their resignation giving reasons; if the reasons seem adequate then the resignation should be allowed. However, if the enterprise has provided the worker with special training for more than three months, then the worker cannot resign unless he has completed one year's service after training; otherwise he must compensate the enterprise for all the costs of his training.

(b) *Dismissal of redundant workers*: if changes in the line or technique of production result in there being an excess of labourers and it is not possible to retrain them or to assign them to other posts, the enterprise can terminate the service of these workers. Dismissed workers are entitled to one month's salary for every year of service. Workers whose service is less than one year shall be paid one month's basic salary. For probationary workers, the compensation is half a month's salary.

(c) *Disciplinary measures*: a worker who has violated regulations or caused damage to the enterprise may be subject to warning, the recording of his demerit, a reduction in salary or even expulsion according to the seriousness of his offence. All cases of dismissal have to be reported to the Shenzhen SEZ Labour Department. Workers, however, have the right of appeal to the management, the Labour Department and ultimately to the local People's Court.

The above regulations and procedures, however, are not applicable to expatriates or to workers recruited from Hong Kong and Macau. Their terms of service will be determined by the board of directors of the enterprise concerned and clearly specified in the contract.

Since early 1984, efforts have been made to simplify the labour recruitment procedure and the terms of employment. Instead of going through the official Labour Department, individual enterprises are now permitted to undertake the recruitment of workers themselves according to their own needs. Entrepreneurs are given the right to work out and sign contracts with their employees and to dismiss workers if they think it necessary. Employees, on the other hand, are also allowed to resign from their jobs and look for alternative employment. An increasing number of enterprises in Shenzhen have adopted this new labour system (*Wen Wei Po*, 11 June 1984).

Labour Costs and Productivity

Wage rates in the Shenzhen SEZ are generally higher than those in other parts of China, but the exact amount depends very much on the nature of the enterprise, the type of work and the level of skill required. There are, as discussed in Chapter 8, four categories of labour in most industries (probationary, contract, skilled and technical workers) and hence four different wage rates. But on average, the monthly wage rate for workers employed in foreign enterprises is about HK$750 which is much lower than that of Hong Kong. In addition to the basic wage, a bonus may be given to workers who have exceeded their production quotas.

It is generally agreed that depending on the proficiency of the workers an annual increment in remuneration of 5–15 per cent will be made. The wage rates cited above represent the amount to be paid by the entrepreneur. Of this, only 70 per cent goes to the workers as basic and floating wages, 5 per cent will be reserved for the employees' welfare fund and other benefits, and the remaining 25 per cent is used for workers' insurance and the various forms of subsidy that the state provides for the workers.

According to the provisional regulations on labour and wages in the Shenzhen SEZ, the enterprise is free to decide on the form and method of remuneration which does not need to be a fixed monthly salary. Payment can be made by hours or days, or according to piece-work. Various kinds of reward and bonus systems are allowed, and overtime pay is required for working hours in excess of those specified in the labour contract. Furthermore, workers are entitled to public holidays, home leave and special leave with pay according to the laws of the People's Republic of China.

Low labour costs alone, however, need not be an attractive locational factor. Of equal importance is labour productivity which depends on the education and technological capacity of the workers, their attitudes towards work, the absentee rate and the degree of resistance to new production and management methods. When Shenzhen was first established as an SEZ, inexperience of the new economic and production system, together with the generally low educational level of the workers, resulted in relatively low productivity, especially in comparison with neighbouring Hong Kong. Fortunately, improvements are gradually being made. The adoption of the piece-work and bonus system has provided incentives for the workers to increase their productivity. Furthermore, investors have been free to decide upon the system of management of the enterprise, the recruitment and dismissal of workers, and the implementation of work by contract and other forms of payment terms. However, it is still felt that more long-term training programmes need to be designed and implemented to further upgrade the level of labour productivity: these may be organized both by the Shenzhen government and by the individual investors.

Labour Supply

The large variety of activities to be developed in the Shenzhen SEZ together with the initial emphasis on developing labour-intensive industries (such as electronics and textiles) mean that the demand on labour will be great. Unlike many export processing zones in Asia, Shenzhen is not located on the fringe of a large metropolitan area where the labour supply is abundant. Despite the large size of the SEZ, in 1978 Shenzhen was only a small border town with a population of about 20,000. An insufficient supply of labour, together with the low educational level of local workers, means that highly skilled labourers will have to be recruited from other parts of China to meet the demands of the rapidly expanding economy. By 1980, the population of the Shenzhen SEZ had grown to almost 85,000 — mostly due to immigration from other parts of China rather than natural increase. Only about half of the total population, that is 41,000 people, form the working population, and of these 16,000 are engaged in agriculture, 9,000 in industry, whilst the rest are spread over a variety of occupations. As the economic base of Shenzhen is to be manufacturing industry, it is planned that most of the working population will be engaged in industrial production in the years to come. Table 11.4 shows the population and labour situation in 1980 as well as the projected figures until the end of this century. It can be expected that most of the increase will be accounted for by immigration.

Because of the large spatial extent of the Shenzhen SEZ, the distribution of population will be quite uneven. Chapters 7 and 8 have already summarized the distribution of population (potential workers) by districts as indicated in the Shenzhen SEZ master plan. The plan will provide potential investors with an approximate idea of the planned development in the various districts within the Shenzhen SEZ.

Table 11.4 Population and Labour Statistics of the Shenzhen SEZ

	1980	1985 (projected)	1990 (projected)	2000 (projected)
Total population	85,000	250,000	400,000	800,000
Working population	41,000	120,000	200,000	500,000
Industry	9,000	50,000	80,000	200,000
Agriculture	16,000	20,000	15,000	10,000

Since a large proportion of the labour supply is to be recruited from other parts of China, it is essential for the Shenzhen Labour Services Company and for individual enterprises to set appropriate standards for the selection of potential workers and to exercise control over the quality and quantity of labour inflow. At present, the labour force in the Shenzhen SEZ belongs to two broad categories. The first consists of construction workers, including those concerned with the provision of infrastructure. Basic construction work in the Shenzhen SEZ is carried out by various construction teams recruited from other parts of China. The number of workers in each team may vary between several dozen and several hundred. Most of these are temporary workers on contract for a particular construction job. At present, these temporary construction workers number about 80,000 in the Shenzhen SEZ. The other category of workers are those involved in various commercial and industrial activities and they form the permanent population of the SEZ. Recruitment of this group of workers has to be more selective, both in terms of skill and sex composition. At present, there is an insufficient supply of service personnel in the Shenzhen SEZ. Also, the number of women working in the zone is higher than the number of men: in 1980 the sex ratio was 93.5:100. With the economic expansion of the SEZ, the criteria for the recruitment of workers should be more rigorous.

Management Personnel

One of the major obstacles to the development of Shenzhen as an SEZ is the lack of well-trained professional management staff. Prior to the adoption of a more pragmatic and open economic policy and the promotion of the Four Modernizations, little attention was given to the importance of scientific management techniques. It was not until October 1978 that Deng Xiaoping, in an address to the Ninth National Congress of the Federation of Chinese Trade Unions, stressed that an overhaul of the management of agricultural and industrial enterprises was essential to the modernization of China. However, time is required for the training and education of such professionals and for the development of indigenous entrepreneurship. In the Shenzhen

SEZ, experienced management personnel can be recruited from other parts of China, but few of them have received formal training in modern management techniques. The application of outdated management methods to a modern enterprise can be a hindrance to development. In local enterprises, the usual system is a line organization emphasizing a rigid vertical style of management with little horizontal communication between departments. Furthermore, the management of the enterprise is usually in the hands of a few senior officers who act according to the directives of government authorities. Thus, the Shenzhen SEZ lacks a team of efficient and well-trained management staff capable of meeting the demands of the rapidly growing economy. As a result, a fairly high degree of dependence on foreign entrepreneurship and management personnel has become inevitable in the early stages of the zone's development. Many enterprises are now recruiting these professionals from Hong Kong and overseas. However, efforts have been made to train and educate the local staff, either by sending them abroad to attend formal courses in management or by training them on the job in modern enterprises in the SEZs. It is hoped that a pool of efficient, well-qualified and experienced management staff can be gradually built up to serve the needs of the Shenzhen SEZ.

Conclusion

In the past few years the Shenzhen authorities have worked hard at improving the investment environment of the SEZ. Obvious changes have been observed, for example, in the provision of basic facilities and infrastructure, the reorganization and streamlining of the administrative system, the enactment of SEZ regulations, the provision of financial services, the adjustment of land utility costs to improve the attractiveness of Shenzhen's land resources, the simplification of labour recruitment procedures and terms of employment, and the implementation of various training programmes for local staff and workers. All these measures are aimed at the provision of a firmer foundation for the rapid economic growth that is anticipated in Shenzhen and also at the promotion of greater confidence amongst potential investors who have, in the past, expressed some concern as to the efficiency of the Chinese government and the security of their investment in the SEZ. In spite of the many improvements that have been made, there are still issues that require further clarification and more decisive action by the Chinese government. Amongst these issues are the introduction of an SEZ currency (which will be tested in the Shenzhen SEZ in 1985); the stabilization of the governmental structure (following the announcement in 1984 of a further reorganization of Shenzhen's administrative system); the enactment of commercial laws; and the clarification of policies relating to the co-ordination of development among the various special zones in China. The Shenzhen SEZ has the resources (including a large spatial extent, a good geographical location and strong central government support) to become very prosperous. A favourable investment environment is essential to the full exploitation of Shenzhen's advantages and potential.

In this chapter, reference has been made to some of the key concerns that may affect the potential investor's decision to participate in the development programmes of the Shenzhen SEZ. The discussion of issues is by no means exhaustive. Other factors, such as political stability, the tariff and export quota system, and the availability of local capital, are also relevant in assessing an area's investment climate. However, it has been the intention of this chapter to focus on issues that are of more immediate concern and more directly related to the SEZ. These discussions will be useful not only to overseas investors but also to Chinese officials who are concerned with the planning and development of the zone.

PART IV: CONCLUSION

12. Modernization and the Lessons of the Special Economic Zones

DAVID K. Y. CHU AND KWAN-YIU WONG

IN the preface to this book, it was made clear that the primary objective of establishing special economic zones is to further the modernization of China. However, the word modernization may carry different meanings in different contexts. It is thus pertinent to discuss briefly what exactly the word modernization means, on the one hand to a social scientist trained in the West, and on the other hand to a Chinese official.

The Western Conception of Modernization

According to the *Oxford English Dictionary*, the word 'modern' has two areas of meaning relevant to our discussion: (a) of the present or recent times and (b) new and up-to-date. Modernity and modernization are the nouns of 'modern': modernity means being modern and modernization means the process of making something suitable for present-day needs and bringing it up to date. Whilst the definitions stated in the dictionary give perhaps the most concise and precise meanings of the three words, social scientists (both theorists and practitioners) would never be satisfied with just learning their dictionary meanings. Indeed, in simple terms, what most social scientists have striven for in the past few decades is to modernize their society and to understand the process of modernization. It is thus of interest and of importance to see how they interpret the three words in different contexts.

In contemporary Western social science literature, modernization as a process leading to a state of society which is 'modern' has at least three interpretations. First, modernization is conceived of as an attribute of time and an evolutionary change. Second, modernization is defined historically as the process of change in Western Europe from feudalism to the capitalist society. Third, modernization is seen as a programme or policy orientation of an élite in a new and developing nation or state (Nash, 1977, p. 17). However, the evolutionary approach suffers not only from tautological and arbitrary arguments, but also from being ethnocentric, abstract and unconvincing (Nash, 1977, pp. 17–18). Consequently, the dominant practice among Western social scientists today is to conceptualize modernization as a general process comprising 'both economic development and cultural change' (Moore, 1977, p. 33), with the latter referring to the wide anthropological sense embracing social structure as well as beliefs, values and norms. Notwithstanding the two emphases, most social scientists consider that economic development is central to the process of modernization and provides the best set of indicators to measure the performance of areal or ethnic units, because it stands

both as an autonomous goal distributively and collectively and as an essential means for implementing educational, political and even some recreational and expressive goals (Moore, 1977, p. 33).

On these premises Moore argued that the process of modernization is a process of rationalization, including

monetization and commercialization, technification of production and distribution, education, bureaucratization, demographic rationalization, and secularization (Moore, 1977, p. 35).

The interpretation of modernization given by Moore will lead to

increasing uniformity in most significant features of attitudes, values and actual structural behaviour in the world's societies (Moore, 1977, p. 31).

Moore's arguments could exemplify the school of thinking which holds that after modernization the various countries of the world will display a remarkable uniformity and the process of modernization will not vary from one country to another.

However, not all Western social scientists conceptualize modernization in the same way as Moore. For example, Hoselitz (1955) noted the historical and situational bases for differentiation in the patterns of economic growth. Geographers like Ginsberg (1957) and Mabogunje (1980) have repeatedly stated that both the course and destination of economic development may differ because of differences in resources, spatial organization and cultural norms. Moore, too, noted the diversity among nations in their progress towards rationalization, but he attributed such diversity to ignorance, error and other limits of rationality (Moore, 1977, p. 40). The strongest opposition to Moore's argument has been promoted by Nash. Although he in general agrees with the suggested relation between modernization and the application of a growing body of tested knowledge, a value system conducive to the search for new knowledge, mobility, more rewards channelled to higher performers and the presence of a critical mass of certain kinds of persons at the institutional centre of the modernizing society, he considers that both the form and the process of modernization could vary between different countries (Nash, 1977, p. 20). Indeed, he went so far as to suggest that

the current intellectual formulations of the process of modernization are drawing farther and farther away from the historical and processual facts in the transitional nations of Africa, Asia and Latin America (Nash, 1977, p. 16).

In his view, modernization as

an historical process and lived-in reality, is what is happening in those countries and regions attempting and aspiring to be modern in their own cultural idioms (Nash, 1977, p. 16).

In other words, unlike Hoselitz, Ginsberg and Mabogunje whose arguments differ from Moore's concerning the paths of economic development and growth but not with regard to modernization, Nash holds the divergent view that modernization could take different shapes and different paths in different contexts.

To sum up, there is no consensus among Western social scientists on the roads to modernization nor on the shapes of modernization. However, there is general agreement that modernization is a complex process which may embrace many phenomena such as economic development, political development, social development, cultural development and perhaps ecological and environmental improvement.

China's Conception of Modernization and the Chinese Road to Modernization

The Chinese interpretation of modernization can be illustrated by the statements made by Xue Muqiao in his book entitled *China's Socialist Economy* (1981). As he is the chief economic adviser to the Chinese government and the most prominent and influential economist in the Chinese political hierarchy, his book is the most authoritative on the subject.

He first states that the Chinese version of modernization is *socialist* modernization. He quotes from Marx and Engels that socialism must be based on large-scale *modern* production and from Lenin that

a large-scale machine industry capable of reorganizing agriculture is the only material base that is possible for socialism (Xue, 1981, p. 234).

The decision of the Third Plenary Session of the Eleventh Central Committee of the Chinese Communist Party, held in December 1978, to redirect the economy as of 1979 towards socialist modernization was attributed to the awareness that we [China] are now some twenty years behind the developed capitalist countries in science and technology and in industry, and forty or fifty years behind them in agriculture (Xue, 1981, p. 235).

Nowhere in his book does he mention national defence which is the fourth aspect of modernization (after agriculture, industry, and science and technology) as proposed in the Third and Fourth National People's Congresses by Zhou Enlai. Premier Zhou believed that the Four Modernizations might take China into the forefront of world affairs by the end of this century. According to Xue, the reasons for China's backwardness in agriculture, industry, and science and technology are: (a) China embarked on socialist construction from a very low level of productive forces; (b) errors were made in 1958 as a result of the lack of experience in socialist economic construction; and (c) serious damage was inflicted upon production and the economy during the decade of the Cultural Revolution. The objectives as well as the meaning of socialist modernization in China are thus to 'catch up with the advanced levels in capitalist countries', 'to prove the superiority of the socialist system to the people of China and the World' and 'to win ultimate victory over capitalism' (Xue, 1981, p. 235).

The indicator of modernization suggested thus far is the improvement of the people's standard of living. According to Deng Xiaoping, the target is set at US$800 per capita per year by the year 2000 (*Ming Pao*, 19 April 1984). The key to improving the people's living standard is the raising of labour productivity which in turn requires a speedy modernization of industry and agriculture. Xue further pointed out that

until we [China] base our industrial and agricultural production on advanced science and technology and raise labour productivity substantially in both fields, we shall not see any significant rise in the people's living standard, nor an end to the country's poverty and backwardness (Xue, 1981, p. 235).

The Central Committee of the Chinese Communist Party stated that China has to modernize in her own way in order to take into account her particular circumstances as a large country with a quarter of the world's population and a rigid economic management structure (Xue, 1981, p. 242). The deployment of redundant staff from overstaffed enterprises and of as many as 200 million redundant farmers from the agricultural sector will therefore create problems which have no precedent in the processes of modernization in other countries. A solution suggested by Xue is that

in China's socialist modernization, we should continue to develop large, medium-sized and small enterprises simultaneously and employ mechanized, semi-mechanized and manual means at the same time. To lay the basis for our scientific and technological advances,.it will be necessary to set up a number of enterprises using the world's latest technology . . . While purchasing advanced technology from abroad, we should consider whether to aim at the highest or at a relatively low degree of automation (Xue, 1981, p. 243).

He continues that 'though the level of automation is a bit low, it will still raise our labour productivity several times under improved management. This will enable us to accelerate modernization through self-reliance . . . Rising production and technical advances will enable China to raise the level of her modernization' (Xue, 1981, pp. 243–4).

Ma Hong, another senior economist in the Chinese government, suggested that China's road to modernization would lead to the following situation at the end of the century (Ma, 1983b, p. 19).

(a) The gross industrial and agricultural output value will quadruple over that of 1980 on the basis of improved economic results.

(b) The organization of production will become more rationalized and agriculture, light industry and heavy industry will grow proportionately.

(c) The gross national product and output of major industrial and agricultural products will take front rank in the world.

(d) The advanced technologies of the economically developed countries in the seventies or early eighties will be popularized in China.

(e) Some sophisticated Chinese technologies will be the most advanced in the world.

(f) The utility rate of resources and energy and the depth of processing will rise remarkably and the product mix of exports will change considerably.

(g) There will be a remarkable rise in people's cultural and educational levels.

(h) People will be comparatively well-off.

(i) There will be great improvements in the ecological environment.

(j) People will continue to have an increasing awareness of socialism and communism.

Based on these elaborations by Xue and Ma of China's planned course and conception of modernization, one can see that China's modernization does not comply with the first and second meanings of modernization in Western social science literature (as supplied by Nash), but it is very close to the third sense — a programme or policy orientation of an élite in a new and developing state. For China, modernization is a programme of correcting technological backwardness so that productivity and the people's living standard may be improved.

The Conjunction and Disjunction of the Western Conception with China's Road to Modernization

Although it appears that Western social scientists of today like Moore and Nash employ the word 'modernization' in a different sense from the Chinese usage, a closer analysis reveals that the two sides are not entirely at variance. Similarities exist in at least two aspects.

First, as Nash suggested, there may be different courses of modernization in different parts of the world. China's socialist modernization differs radically in concept from the paths of modernization followed in Western countries.

Second, China's proposals to modernize its economy differ very little from some of the elements in the process of rationalization proposed by Moore, namely, commercialization, technification of production and distribution, and education. To some extent, China's current policies are also close to Nash's thesis on the application of a growing body of tested knowledge, a value system conducive to the search for new knowledge, mobility and more rewards for higher performers. These are in fact fundamental preconditions for economic growth. In Chinese terminology, they are

objective economic laws and China must draw [its] blueprints for transforming the country in conformity with objective economic laws (Xue, 1981, p. 239).

The details of implementation of the economic laws vary because China must take account of its special 'conditions'.

However, the major difference between the two interpretations lies in the attitude to cultural change. To Western social scientists, cultural change is part and parcel of the process of modernization. In the plans for the Four Modernizations of China, cultural change has not been included. Although cultural changes are implicit in the Chinese adoption of new approaches and new policies, such as empiricism, a value system conducive to the search for new knowledge, mobility (both sectoral and spatial) and the bonus system, one must agree that these policies are largely self-generated and are derived from lessons learnt during the last three decades. Other cultural changes accompanying the intended importation of foreign technology, management policy, capital and perhaps the capitalist way of thinking are, on the other hand, foreign and not readily accepted as part of the Chinese process of modernization. At the extreme, the 'undesirable' cultural changes are considered as 'spiritual pollution' or 'ideological contamination', so that they become threats to socialism and communism. To the Chinese Communist Party and the Chinese government, these foreign importations and their undesirable consequences must be minimized, if not entirely eliminated. To ensure that the importation of foreign technology, management techniques and capital, and the implementation of those official reforms necessary to Chinese modernization cause the least possible damage to the country, these measures must be tested, experimented with and quarantined. The SEZs are China's laboratories for conducting these experiments.

The SEZs as a Model for Chinese Modernization

Although the SEZs were only initiated in 1979, they have captured nation-wide, if not world-wide, attention. In China itself, they have been heralded as a model with significant implications for the Four Modernizations:

The SEZs have created an enormous amount of material wealth. They are leaders of affluent areas and they provide new scientific technologies and advanced management experience to inland China (*People's Daily*, 29 March 1984).

Other places in China should therefore learn from the SEZs and support them. In other words, after five years of experimentation, many importations from foreign countries had successfully passed the required tests or had been modified to suit Chinese 'conditions'. Places outside the SEZs are then permitted to adopt some of the measures experimented with in the SEZs. The chapters in this volume attempt to describe and analyse the Chinese SEZs and various aspects of their development objectively and critically. In Chapter 1, the experiences of the Asian export processing zones are discussed: it is pointed out that the Chinese SEZs evolved from the same concept, and are necessary if China is to take advantage of the new international division of labour. In spite of their similarities, however, China's socialist background and the larger areal extent of the SEZs present challenges and opportunities which other export processing zones may not necessarily share.

The experiments conducted in the SEZs may help to solve many practical economic problems arising from the rigid and inefficient centralized economic system. However, the capitalistic flavour and reliance on foreign investment also render the SEZs liable to criticism as non-socialist and it is hard to justify them in ideological terms (Chapter 2). Practical results and endorsement by the Chinese leaders are employed as the most powerful answers to critics (Chapters 2 and 3). However, among the four SEZs, it is only the Shenzhen SEZ which is well endowed and which has attained remarkable progress in the last five years. The performances of the Zhuhai, Xiamen and Shantou SEZs have been less satisfactory (Chapter 3). Consequently, the Shenzhen SEZ has become the most publicized model of the four Chinese SEZs. It is against this background that subsequent chapters are devoted to analytical assessments on chosen issues concerning the Shenzhen SEZ.

Wong provides a thorough treatment of the trends and strategies of industrial development observed in the Shenzhen SEZ (Chapter 4). He points out that the Shenzhen government has repeatedly confirmed that the foundation of economic development in the SEZ should be manufacturing industries. However, to utilize the factors of industrial development fully, the Shenzhen SEZ authorities should consider an organic combination of capital- and labour-intensive industries as well as the integration of large, medium-size and small industrial enterprises. A modern industrial structure, as Wong explains, is not necessarily a conglomeration of large-scale factories, but rather an integration of small but modern enterprises with large firms. The former will be doing subcontracting work for the latter. On tourism, another mainstay of the present Shenzhen SEZ economy, Lee Fong points out that most of the tourism projects and operations in Shenzhen are monotonously devised, providing prototype recreation and competing for the same clients. She suggests that a modern tourist industry should stress diversity and that the Shenzhen government should consider its environment as a whole and allocate various activities and functions to different resorts, catering for people of different ages, groups of varying leisure interests and people travelling for varied purposes. In terms of agricultural modernization, Shenzhen should break away from its former principle of self-sufficiency and change to an export-oriented cropping system. Whether the production is in vegetables, flowers or animal husbandry, the criteria for any decision should be profit maximization and cost minimization per unit of effort. Indeed, agricultural development in Shenzhen as a whole seems to follow this trend closely but probably not fast enough, as observed in the chapter by Zheng, Wei and Chu. All these findings support the suggestion that the Shenzhen SEZ economy is now undergoing the process of rationalization, commercialization, technification of production and perhaps repetition and standardization which may sometimes be counter-productive and short-sighted, as in its tourist industry. In general, the Shenzhen SEZ economy has been acquiring a modern structure and assuming an organic composition.

The experience of other Asian countries reveals that poor planning and mismanagement always lead to the failure of export processing zones. In Yeh's chapter on the planning system and planning process of the Shenzhen zone, he outlines many issues that need to be solved. Among them, the uncertainty of the planning environment is the most insurmountable obstacle. The possibility of realization of the planning targets is subject to decisions made outside the SEZs, and thus beyond the direct control of the planners. Problems of population growth and transportation are studied by Chu. He indicates that as the Shenzhen SEZ is now building a city of close to a million residents (permanent and temporary) in two decades on an extremely poor urban foundation, problems such as insufficiency in road capacity, in housing and in other urban facilities are not unexpected. The most serious problem is perhaps in the inevitable social stratification within the Shenzhen SEZ community. Chu also indicates that such characteristics of secularization as a craving for more material comfort, rising expectations and a fondness for Hong Kong television programmes are now emerging. On the one hand, these characteristics could be regarded as the logical outcome of economic growth. On the other hand, however, they reveal that the social and cultural changes predicted by Western social scientists are indeed taking place in the rapidly developing semi-open economy of the Shenzhen SEZ.

The two chapters on the environment (Chapters 10 and 11) attempt to give an overview of Shenzhen from two different perspectives. Lam and Hsu examine the Shenzhen SEZ as a human habitat, forecasting the possible environmental changes in Shenzhen by the year 2000. They suggest that if the current environmental policy of the Shenzhen SEZ authority persists, the zone will remain a relatively habitable place for the 800,000 residents by the turn of the century. From a very different perspective, Wong and Chu study the existing investment environment of the Shenzhen SEZ. They agree that there have been remarkable improvements in terms of administrative structure, legal and financial systems, infrastructural provisions and development of human capital in the Shenzhen SEZ in the last five years. Indeed, the trend of improvement is likely to continue. This, undoubtedly, is the best assurance for future economic growth in Shenzhen.

The chapters substantiate the argument that Shenzhen has been undergoing a rapid process of modernization. As the largest and the most successful SEZ, Shenzhen is logically a model for the other three SEZs. Likewise, its experience will be equally useful to Hainan Island and to the 14 city-ports that are to be opened for massive foreign investment. Less publicized but even more widespread are several measures pioneered by the Shenzhen SEZ that are being taken up or promoted, with or without much modification, in other parts of China beyond the special zones. One of these is the tender system in construction works. In the past, contracts for construction work were awarded to local construction teams or companies irrespective of their cost-effectiveness. The Shenzhen SEZ was the first place in China to invite tenders from construction teams all over the country, and to award contracts to the most cost-effective construction team or company. Consequently, the zone has saved a lot of money on the construction of its infrastructure. The tender system developed by Shenzhen has now become standard practice in China.

The second measure that deserves mention is the introduction of contract labourers. Workers are hired on contract and will be dismissed for absenteeism and other faults. The breaking of the 'iron rice-bowl' has led to a remarkable increase in labour productivity and labour discipline. The system of contract labour has been seen as a panacea for many of the ills in the inefficient management of industry in other parts of China, and many new recruits will now be hired on contract terms.

The third measure, though still under trial in other Chinese cities, is the home-purchase scheme. In 1984, four inland Chinese cities were experimenting with home-purchase schemes for workers who are required to pay one-third of the price of the house whilst the remaining two-thirds is subsidized by the workers' employers. The scheme will be applied to another 66 Chinese cities in 1985 (*Ming Pao*, 8 April 1984). Although the home-purchase scheme in these cities is different from that of Shenzhen, in which workers have to pay the price in full, the rationale of treating housing as a commodity is the same. Accompanying the home-purchase scheme is the beginning of a new attitude that workers should receive less subsidy but higher wages (including bonuses). In the Shenzhen SEZ, this new attitude has been gradually accepted by both the public and the governmental agencies (fieldwork, 1983). Consequently, rental and other subsidies are declining in number, and those who work in Shekou but are not participating in the home-purchase scheme have to pay for their lodging with rental calculated on the basis of construction costs and depreciation (Li, *et al.*, 1982). The housing policy in other Chinese cities is now under review.

Apart from the home-purchase scheme, higher rentals and fewer housing subsidies are suggested as solutions for the current shortage of housing in China (*China Daily*, 1 June 1984).

Apart from these innovative measures, other practices in the Shenzhen SEZ are also regarded as good examples, but it is difficult to state whether they have influenced the decisions of the Chinese government in Beijing because similar successful practices are also found outside the SEZs. Among these practices are the separation of commercial functions from the state and government departments, the enactment of laws and increasing emphasis on the role of the legal system and the democratic election of managers of factories. Indeed, the Shenzhen SEZ is doing very well in these aspects in comparison with other parts of China.

To conclude, the programme of SEZs is only five years old. Within such a short period of time, these zones have been modernizing very quickly. Judging by the fact that many of their innovative measures are being adopted by other places outside the SEZs, it is fair to say that they have contributed to the process of the modernization of China. It is perhaps too early to give a definitive assessment on the exact extent of their contribution. Nevertheless, this volume has indicated many salient features of the modernization process which is noticeably not being confined to the narrow interpretation of modernization as defined by renowned Chinese economists and officials.

Bibliography

Angangco, O.R., and Jurado, E.P. (1982), 'The export processing zone as a strategy for national development: the Philippine case', paper presented at the Seminar on Development Planning in Asian Modernization, Hong Kong Baptist College, 12–17 November.

Baron, R.R.Y. (1975), 'Seasonality in Tourism, A Guide to the Analysis of Seasonality and Trends for Policy Making', *Technical Series*, No. 2 (London, The Economist Intelligence Unit).

Batsavage, R., and Davie, J.L. (1978), 'China's international trade and finance', in *Chinese Economy Post-Mao* (Washington, Joint Economic Committee, USA), pp. 707–41.

Blunden, W.R. (1971), *The Land-use/Transport System* (Oxford, Pergamon).

Cai Renqun (1981), 'A discussion on the choice of locations and some rational scale of development of special economic areas in China', *Tropical Geography*, No. 1, pp. 54–9 (in Chinese).

Cannon, T. (1983), 'Foreign investment and trade: origins of the modernization policy', in S. Feuchtwang and A. Hussain (eds.), *The Chinese Economic Reforms*, pp. 288–324.

Ceng Jianhei (1984), 'The birth of an important decision', *Liaowang*, No. 24, 11 June 1984; reprinted in *Wen Wei Po*, 12 June (in Chinese).

Ceng Muye and Luo Fuqun (1983), 'The developing tourist industry in the Guangdong Special Economic Zones', in Sun Ru (ed.), *The Progressing China's SEZs* (Guangdong, China Finance and Economics Publishing House), pp. 134–47 (in Chinese).

Chang, S.D. (1968), 'The distribution and occupation of overseas Chinese', *Geographical Review*, Vol. 58, pp. 89–107.

Chen Qiaozhi (1981), 'Export processing activities in the Shantou area', *Gangao Jingji*, No. 6, pp. 55–8 (in Chinese).

Chen Zhaobin and Chen Mingge (1981), 'The establishment of Xiamen SEZ and its prospects', *Gangao Jingji*, No. 6, pp. 49–53 (in Chinese).

China Merchants' Steam Navigation Co. Ltd. (1981), *Investor's Handbook* (revised edition), *China Merchants' Shekou Industrial Zone in Shenzhen Special Economic Zone* (Hong Kong).

Chinese SEZ Handbook (1984) (Shenzhen Municipality, Public Information Office, and Hong Kong, New Evening Post (in Chinese)).

Chu, D.K.Y. (1982), 'The cost of the four SEZs to China', *Economic Reporter*, May, pp. 18–20, and June, pp. 17–19.

———(1983), 'The recent reform of administrative structure and the investment environment of the Shenzhen SEZ', in D.K.Y. Chu (ed.), *The Largest Special Economic Zone of China — Shenzhen* (Hong Kong, Wide Angle Press), pp. 1–10 (in Chinese).

Chu, D.K.Y., Wong, K.Y., and Ng, Y.T. (1984), 'Shantou SEZ as the Shekou of East Guangdong', *Wide Angle*, No. 143, pp. 25–7 (in Chinese).

Corden, C. (1977), *Planned Cities: New Towns in Britain and America* (Beverly Hills, Sage).

Currie, J. (1979), 'Investment: The Growing Role of Export Processing Zones', *EIU Special Report*, No. 64 (London, The Economist Intelligence Unit).

Dernberger, R.F. (1977), 'Economic development and modernization in contemporary China', in F.J. Fleron (ed.), *Technology and Communist Culture* (New York, Praeger).

Eckstein, A. (1977), *China's Economic Revolution* (London, Cambridge University Press).

Export Processing Zones Administration, Taiwan (1981), *Fifteen Years in the Development of EPZs* (Republic of China).

———(1982a), *EPZ Statistics at a Glance*, March (Republic of China).

———(1982b), *Export Processing Zone Concentrates*, July (Republic of China).

Feuchtwang, S., and Hussain, A. (eds.) (1983), *The Chinese Economic Reforms* (Beckenham, Kent, Croom Helm).

Fitting, G. (1982), 'Export processing zones in Taiwan and the People's Republic of China', *Asian Survey*, Vol. 22, No. 8, pp. 732–44.

Fong, M.K.L. (1982), 'Shenzhen tourism — contradictions in location and development', *Wen Wei Po*, 10 and 13 July (in Chinese).

———(1983), 'Shenzhen tourism — fallacies in locational setting and development', in D.K.Y. Chu (ed), *The Largest Special Economic Zone of China — Shenzhen* (Hong Kong, Wide Angle Press), pp. 71–81 (in Chinese).

Foshan Revolutionary Committee (1976), *Zhujiang Delta Agricultural Record*, mimeograph (in Chinese).

Friedman, E. (1979), 'On Maoist conceptualization of the capitalist world system', *China Quarterly*, December, pp. 806–37.

Frobel, F., Heinrichs, J., and Kreye, O. (1980), *The New International Division of Labour*, translated by P. Burgess (London, Cambridge University Press).

Ginsberg, N. (1957), 'Natural resources and economic development', *Annals, Association of American Geographers*, Vol. 47, pp. 196–212.

Gonzaga, L. (1977), 'Philippine planners at work', *Far Eastern Economic Review*, 5 August, p. 39.

Gourevitch, P. (1978), 'The second image reversed: the international sources of domestic politics', *International Organization*, Vol. 32, No. 3, pp. 881–912.

Griffin, E. (1973), 'Testing the Von Thünen theory in Uruguay', *Geographical Review*, Vol. 63, No. 4, pp. 500–16.

Guangdong Law Society (1981), 'A few noteworthy problems concerning the signing of business contracts with foreign business corporations —

as viewed from the present situation of Shenzhen', *Xueshu Yanjiu*, No. 6, pp. 42–6 (in Chinese).

Guangdong Provincial Administration of Special Economic Zones (1982), *Regulations of PRC on Special Economic Zones in Guangdong Province* (Hong Kong, Wen Wei Po).

Hare, P. (1983), 'China's system of industrial economic planning', in S. Feuchtwang and A. Hussain (eds.), *The Chinese Economic Reforms*, pp. 185–223.

Hong Kong Government (1981a), *Annual Report* (Hong Kong, Government Printing Office).

———(1981b), *The 1981–82 Budget: Economic Background* (Hong Kong, Government Printer).

———(1982), *Estimates of Gross Domestic Product, 1966 to 1980* (Hong Kong, Census and Statistics Department).

Hong Kong Government Information Services (1982), *Hong Kong 1982 — A Review of 1981* (Hong Kong, Government Printer).

Hoselitz, B.F. (1955), 'Patterns of economic growth', *Canadian Journal of Economics and Political Science*, Vol. 21, pp. 416–31.

Huang Zanqiang (1983), 'The market prices at Shenzhen SEZ are basically stable', *Gangao Jingji*, No. 1, pp. 58–9 (in Chinese).

Kang Ye (1981), 'Survey on Shenzhen and Zhuhai SEZ', *Gangao Jingji*, No. 2, pp. 30–4 (in Chinese).

Keller, S. (1960), 'Social class in physical planning', *International Social Science Journal*, Vol. 18, pp. 494–512.

Kreider, L.E. (1975), 'Free port', *Encyclopaedia Americana*, pp. 43–4.

Lenin, V.I. (1921), 'The Third Congress of the Communist International', in *Lenin's Collected Works*, Vol. 3 (Moscow, 1964).

Li Huajie, Huang Hansun and Ye Yurong (1982), 'The rise and development of the Shekou Industrial District', *Xueshu Yanjiu*, No. 1, pp. 13–18 (in Chinese).

Li Xuanhan (1981), 'On establishing the arbitration system in the special economic zone', *Gangao Jingji*, No. 6, pp. 45–7 (in Chinese).

Liu Guanghua (1983), 'Environmental protection in the development of the special economic zone', *Huanjing (Environment)*, Vol. 49, pp. 2–3 (in Chinese).

Lovbraek, A. (1976), 'The Chinese model of development', *Journal of Peace Research*, Vol. 13, pp. 207–26.

Lu Liao (1981), 'The recent development of the Shenzhen SEZ', *Gangao Jingji*, No. 4, pp. 49–51 (in Chinese).

Ma Hong (1983a), *New Strategy for China's Economy* (Beijing, New World Press).

———(1983b), 'Prospects for modernization in China — an economic perspective', 20th Anniversary Lecture, The Chinese University of Hong Kong, 28 September, published in *Chinese University Bulletin*, Supp. 7, pp. 1–20 (in Chinese).

Mabogunje, A.L. (1980), *The Development Process, a Spatial Perspective* (London, Hutchinson).

Mao Zedong (1962), 'Talk at an enlarged Central Work Conference', in S. Schram (ed.) (1974), *Chairman Mao Talks to the People* (New York, Pantheon).

——(1977), *A Critique of Soviet Economy*, translated by M. Roberts (New York, Monthly Review Press).

Michelson, W. (1976), *Man and His Urban Environment: A Sociological Approach* (Reading, Mass, Addison-Wesley).

Miossec, J.M. (1977), 'Un Modèle de l'Espace Touristique', *L'Espace Geographique*, Vol. 6, No. 1, pp. 41–8.

Mitchell, R.B., and Rapkin, C. (1954), *Urban Traffic: a Function of Land Use* (New York, Columbia University Press).

Moore, W.E. (1977), 'Modernization as rationalization: processes and restraints', *Economic Development and Cultural Change*, Vol. 25, Supplement, pp. 29–42.

Morton, B., and Wu, S.S. (1975), 'The hydrology of the coastal waters of Hong Kong', *Hydrobiologia*, No. 54, pp. 141–4.

Mun, K.C., and Ho, S.C. (1979), 'Foreign investment in Hong Kong', in T.B. Lin, R.P.L. Lee and U. Simons (eds.), *Hong Kong, Economic, Social and Political Studies in Development* (New York, M.E. Sharpe, Inc.), pp. 275–96.

Nash, M. (1977), 'Modernization: cultural meanings — the widening gap between the intellectuals and the process', *Economic Development and Cultural Change*, Vol. 25, Supplement, pp. 16–28.

Ng, Y.T. (1983a), 'Planned population and labour introduction in Shenzhen', in D.K.Y. Chu (ed.), *The Largest Special Economic Zone of China — Shenzhen* (Hong Kong, Wide Angle Press), pp. 39–47 (in Chinese).

——(1983b), 'Living and welfare in Shenzhen', in D.K.Y. Chu (ed.), *The Largest Special Economic Zone of China — Shenzhen* (Hong Kong, Wide Angle Press), pp. 101–8 (in Chinese).

OECD (1980), *The Impact of Tourism on the Environment, General Report* (Organization for Economic Co–operation and Development).

Ople, L.V. (1974), 'Malaysia: Planning with purpose', *Insight*, May, pp. 47–56.

Peet, J.R. (1969), 'Spatial expansion of commercial agriculture in the Nineteenth Century', *Economic Geography*, Vol. 45, pp. 283–301.

Pollock, E.E. (1981), 'Free ports, free trade zones, export processing zones and economic development', in B.S. Hoyle and D.A. Pinder (eds.), *Cityport Industrialization and Regional Development, Spatial Analysis and Planning* (Oxford, Pergamon), pp. 37–45.

Rabbani, F.A. (ed.) (1980), *Economic and Social Impacts of Export Processing Zones in Asia* (Tokyo, Asian Productivity Organization).

Robinson, H. (1979), *A Geography of Tourism* (Plymouth, MacDonald and Evans).

Salita, D.C., and Juanico, M.B. (1983), 'Local impacts and vulnerabilities of industrial development in developing countries: the Philippine Industrial Estates', *Asian Geographer*, Vol. 2, No. 1, pp. 27–36.

Schaffer, F. (1970), *The New Town Story* (London, Paladin).

Shenzhen Special Economic Zone Development Company (1982), *Investment Guide for Shenzhen Special Economic Zone, Guangdong Province, People's Republic of China* (Hong Kong, Wen Wei Po).

_____(1983), *Introduction to Shenzhen SEZ Investment Environment and SEZ Development Company*.

Shenzhen Special Zone Daily (1982), *A Travel Guide to Shenzhen* (Shenzhen, Zhonghua and Commercial Press).

Sinclair, R. (1967), 'Von Thünen and urban sprawl', *Annals, Association of American Geographers*, Vol. 57, pp. 72–87.

Skinner, G.W. (1978), 'Vegetable supply and marketing in Chinese cities', *China Quarterly*, No. 76, pp. 733–93.

State Statistical Bureau (PRC) (1983), *Chinese Statistical Yearbook, 1983* (Hong Kong, Economic Information and Agency).

Stobaugh, R.B. (1969), 'How to analyze foreign investment climates', *Harvard Business Review*, September–October, pp. 100–8.

Sun Ru (1980), 'The concept and prospect of the special economic zones in Guangdong', paper presented at the Seminar on China's Economy, quoted in *Wen Wei Po*, 9 March, p. 18; translated in Joint Publications Research Service China Report (hereafter cited as JPRS), No. 75423, 2 April, p.46; also translated (in slightly different wording) and published in *Chinese Economic Studies*, Vol. 14, No. 1, pp. 68–78.

Teng Weizao (1982), 'Socialist modernization and the pattern of foreign trade', in Xu Dixin (ed.), *China's Search for Economic Growth* (Beijing, New World Press), pp. 167–92.

Thompson, W.R. (1965), *A Preface to Urban Economics* (Baltimore, Johns Hopkins Press).

United Nations Industrial Development Organization (UNIDO) (1978a), *The Effectiveness of Industrial Estates in Developing Countries* (New York, United Nations).

_____(1978b), *Guidelines for the Establishment of Industrial Estates in Developing Countries* (New York, United Nations).

Van, Byung Gil (1980), 'Economic and social impacts of the Masan Free Export Zone in the Republic of Korea', in F.A. Rabbani (ed.), *Economic and Social Impacts of Export Processing Zones in Asia* (Tokyo, Asian Productivity Organization), pp. 67–73.

Vittal, N. (ed.) (1977), *Export Processing Zones in Asia: Some Dimensions* (Tokyo, Asian Productivity Organization).

Von Thünen, J.H. (1826), *Der Isolierte Staat*, translated by C.M. Wartenberg and edited with an introduction by P. Hall (1966) (Oxford, Pergamon Press).

Wang Kweijeou (1980), 'Economic and social impact of export processing zones in the Republic of China', *Industry of Free China*, Vol. 54, No. 6, pp. 7–27.

Wang Linsheng and Chen Yujie (1982), *China's Foreign Economic Relations* (Beijing, People's Publishing Society) (in Chinese).

Wen Wei Po (Hong Kong) (1979), 'PRC's special zones and export processing zones abroad', *China's Export Commodities Fair*, special edition, No. 2, Autumn, pp. 36–7 (in Chinese).

_____(1982), *Investment Guide for Shenzhen Special Economic Zone* (Guangdong).

Wilbanks, T. (1980), *Location and Well-being, an Introduction to Economic Geography* (San Francisco, Harper and Row).

Wong, K.Y. (ed.) (1982), *Shenzhen Special Economic Zone: China's Experiment in Modernization* (Hong Kong, The Hong Kong Geographical Association).

Wong, K.Y., and Chu, D.K.Y. (1984), 'Export processing zones and special economic zones as generators of economic development: the Asian experience', *Geografiska Annaler*, Vol. 66(B), No. 1, pp. 1–16.

Wu, F.W.Y. (1981), 'From self-reliance to interdependence', *Modern China*, Vol. 7, No. 4, pp. 445–82.

Wu Yongming and Yi Zhaoqiu (1981), 'Problems of industrial allocation in Shenzhen and Zhuhai Special Zones', *Jingji Tequ Dili Wenji* (Guangzhou, Zhongshan University), Vol. 1 (in Chinese).

Wu Yufeng, Jing Ziyu and Liu Guoping (1981), *Tourism Economy* (Beijing, Beijing Publications) (in Chinese).

Xu Dice (1981), 'On the problems of choosing the location of Zhuhai Special Economic Area', *Tropical Geography*, No. 1, pp. 60–4 (in Chinese).

Xu Dixin (1981), 'China's special economic zones', *Beijing Review*, Vol. 50, 14 December.

Xue Muqiao (1981), *China's Socialist Economy* (Beijing, Foreign Languages Press).

Yang Anquan, Lin Xingqing and Lu Zengyong (1982), 'A preliminary study of the development and utilization of the tourist resources of Shenzhen', *Tropical Geography*, No. 3, p. 51–7 (in Chinese).

Yearbook of China's Special Economic Zones (1983), (Hong Kong, Yearbook of China's Special Economic Zones Publishing Company) (in Chinese).

Zhang Kedong (1981a), 'Recent passenger and freight flows of Shenzhen SEZ, projection and analysis', *Jingji Tequ Dili Wenji* (Guangzhou, Zhongshan University, Department of Geography), No.1, pp. 8–16 (in Chinese).

_____(1981b), 'A preliminary study of the port of Zhuhai', *Jingji Tequ Dili Wenji* (Guangzhou, Zhongshan University, Department of Geography), No.1, pp. 17–19 (in Chinese).

Zhang Zhizheng (1983), 'The leading role of market regulation under the direction of the State Plan', in *A Collection of Works on Economics —*

A Symposium on the Reform of Economic Structure and Economics of Special Economic Zones (Guangzhou, Zhongshan University, Economics Department), pp. 244–52 (in Chinese).

Zheng Deliang (1983), 'Looking at our special economic zones from the development of export processing zones in the world', in *A Collection of Works on Economics — A Symposium on the Reform of Economic Structure and Economics of Special Economic Zones* (Guangzhou, Zhongshan University, Economics Department), pp. 286–304 (in Chinese).

Zheng Tianxiang, Chen Heguang and Wei Qingquan (1981), 'Some population problems in the construction of the Shenzhen Special Zone', *Jingji Tequ Dili Wenji* (Guangzhou, Zhongshan University), Vol. 1, pp. 20–4 (in Chinese).

Zheng Tianxiang and Wei Qingquan (1983), 'Special economic zones of China', *Economic Geography*, Vol. 3, No. 4, pp. 248–53 (in Chinese).

Zou Erjun and Jiang Ping (1983), 'Introducing Xiamen SEZ', in *Yearbook of China's Special Economic Zones*, pp. 315–21 (in Chinese).

Periodicals and newspapers:

    Beijing Review, China
    Cheng Ming, Hong Kong
    China Daily, China
    China News Agency, China
    China Reconstructs, China
    Economic Daily, China
    Economic Reporter, Hong Kong
    Hongqi, China
    Ming Pao, Hong Kong
    Nanfang Daily, China
    People's Daily, China
    Shenzhen Special Zone Daily, China
    South China Morning Post, Hong Kong
    Ta Kung Pao, Hong Kong
    Wen Wei Po, Hong Kong
    Xinhua News Agency, China

Index

ACCESSIBILITY, 3, 63, 67, 70
Accumulation rate, 29
Administrative structure, 58, 60, 62, 76, 176–84; *see also* Shenzhen Municipal People's Government
Agricultural Bank, 189
Agriculture, 2, 7, 26, 29, 47, 51, 55, 57, 59, 78, 80–1, 89–107, 134, 160
Agronomic Institute, 114, 115, 147–9, 152, 156

BAGUALING, 61, 65–6, 70, 201
Baguio EPZ, 3
Bamboo Garden Hotel, 83
Bank of China, 185, 189
Banque de l'Indochine et de Suez, 189
Banque Nationale de Paris, 189
Bao'an County, 59, 97, 102–3, 131, 177–80
Bataan EPZ, 3, 6, 9, 12–13, 16, 18, 21, 198
Bayan Lepas EPZ, 6, 198
Bijia Shan Silver Lake, 84
Bizijiao, 86
Building materials, 61, 67, 71, 73–4
Building permits, 109, 120–1
Bureau for Material Allocation, 34–5

CENTRAL PLANNING REGION, SHENZHEN, 115–17, 141, 168
Chegongmiao, 65, 70, 113–15, 144, 147–9, 152–3, 156
China Merchants' Steam Navigation Co. Ltd. (CMSN), 35, 61, 65, 77, 108, 117, 120, 131, 137, 177
Chinese Communist Party, 210–11; Shenzhen Municipal Communist Party, 180–1
Chiwan, 43, 67, 73, 87, 115, 117, 134, 144, 147–9, 152, 156, 161, 172
Chung Koon Co., 187
City-ports, 37–9; Beihai, 54; Dalian, 54–5; Guangzhou, 35, 43, 46–7, 55, 80, 82, 89, 102, 134; Ningbo, 54; Qingdao, 54–5; Shanghai, 40–1, 55;

Tianjin, 40–1, 55; Wenzhou, 54; Zhanjiang, 87
Climate, 99, 161, 164–5, 168, 172; temperature inversion, 165, 168
Clothing, 16, 61, 67–8, 73–4; garments, 12, 13, 16
Collective industry, 67; rural, 68; urban, 68, 73
Commerce, 2, 57, 81; commercial development, 58, 78
Committee on Overseas Chinese Affairs of Guangdong Province, 65, 177
Communes, 26, 68, 88–9
Communication and transport, 3, 17, 34, 43, 46, 50, 58, 77, 81, 90, 102, 126, 140–58
Compensation trade, 7, 9, 10, 36, 68, 79
Competition, 21–2, 39, 83
Co-operative production, 7, 9, 36, 68
Customs-bonded factories (CBFs), 22–3
Customs-bonded warehouses (CBWs), 22–3

DAIMEISHA, 84, 115, 134, 144, 146–9, 152, 156, 168
Dalingxia, 153
Dapeng Bay (Mirs Bay), 113, 164, 170, 201
Daya Bay, 161, 165, 171–2, 201
Deng Xiaoping, 26, 27, 37, 51, 54, 205, 211
Diversification, 80, 103; of industries, 61, 69; of products, 61, 69, 73
Dongdu New Port, 50
Dongguan, 97, 151
Duties: import and export, 11, 15, 196; duty-free goods, 16, 23, 80

EAST LAKE HOTEL, 87
Eastern Planning Region, Shenzhen, 113–16, 141, 168
Economic development zones (EDZs), 37, 40, 54–6
Economic planning, 33–5; First Five Year Plan, 29; Fourth Five Year Plan, 29

Electricity supply and generation, 43, 47, 50, 116, 161, 165

Electronics industry, 11–12, 14, 33, 59–61, 65, 67, 69, 72, 74

Employment, 6–8, 12–13, 59, 71, 74, 78, 123, 211; unemployment, 13, 19, 21

Export processing zones (EPZs), 1–24, 36, 54–6, 74, 87

FINANCE: financial participation, 7, 9; financial system, 10, 57, 77–8; financial structure, 189–90

Food, processing industry, 61, 66, 73–4; products, 59

Foreign capital, 9–10, 25, 27, 32–3, 37–8, 42, 57

Foreign exchange, 6, 7, 76, 79, 86, 88; coupons, 191; earnings, 7, 8, 10–12, 55, 76, 78, 86, 107

Foreign investment, 7, 9–10, 14, 19–20, 33, 50, 55, 60, 67, 75–6, 78, 81, 123, 128; foreign investors, 2, 6, 10, 16, 18, 20, 22, 37, 79–80

Foreign trade, 30–3, 86

Foshan, 151

Free port, 2, 24

Free trade zone, 1, 2, 24, 36

Free zone, 22–4

Freight flows, 146, 151–2, 154

Friendship Restaurant, 30, 83

Fujian, 7, 35, 40–2, 50, 54–5

Futian, 65, 70, 77, 115–16, 134, 143–4, 146–9, 151–3, 156, 168, 170; Futian Development Project, 124–5, 127, 133

GARLOCK FURNITURE FACTORIES, 30

Gongbei, 47

Gu Mu, 37

Guangdong, 7, 35, 40–2, 54–5, 79, 82, 88, 96

Guangdong Bureau of Trade, 19

Guangdong Law Society, 187

Guangdong Provincial Administration of SEZs, 177

Guangdong Provincial People's Government, 176–7

Guangdong Provincial SEZ Development Company, 177

Guangming Farm, 30, 106, 177

Guangxi, 40–1

HAINAN ISLAND, 35, 54

Home-purchase scheme, 216

Hongkong and Shanghai Banking Corporation, 189

Hong Kong–Guangzhou Expressway, 124, 129, 153

Hong Kong–Shenzhen relationship, 7, 10, 16, 43, 61, 65, 67–8, 71, 79–80, 82–3, 88, 99, 102, 106, 113, 116, 127, 129, 151, 170, 174–5; border check-points, 116, 125–6, 151

Hopewell Group (HK), 133

Hospital, 138

Houhai, 65, 70, 115, 134, 144, 147–9, 152, 156–7

Housing, 8, 11, 17, 19, 58, 82, 97, 127, 136–7

Hu Yaobang, 37, 51, 54

Huiyang, 97, 151

Huli Industrial District, 50–1, 55

INDONESIA, 9, 11, 14, 41

Industry, heavy, 40–1, 59–61, 65; light, 41, 59–61, 65–8, 73–4; industrial allocation, 70–4; industrial development, 8, 46–7, 50–1, 54, 57–8, 89, 115, 117, 160, 162–3; industrial districts, 63–7, 70; industrial location, 61–7, 70; industrial management, 206; industrial organization, 67–8; industrial production/output, 11, 14, 29, 57–9, 75–7, 128; industrial structure, 59–61, 69, 71, 162–3; industrialization, 2, 3, 8, 69, 78

Inflation, 19, 20, 36

Infrastructure, 3, 6, 8, 11, 17–18, 22–3, 51, 55, 58, 63, 66, 69–70, 76, 77–8, 87, 112, 122, 200–2

Intermediate processing, 7, 9, 58, 68

International division of labour, 3, 24, 26, 28

Investment environment, 10, 23, 42, 59–60, 74, 176–207

Iri Free Export Zone, 3

JOINT VENTURES, 7, 9, 30, 33, 36–7, 42, 51, 55, 68, 83–4

KANDLA FREE TRADE ZONE, 3, 6, 11–12, 16–17, 20, 198

Kaohsiung EPZ, 3, 6, 9, 18

Katunayake Investment Promotion Zone, 6, 9, 11, 13–14, 198
Krebang EPZ, 3
Kuichong, 61, 161, 171, 177, 187

LABOUR: contract, 216; costs, 7, 21, 43, 69, 135 (*see also* Wages and income); dismissal, 202; female, 12, 13, 18–19; productivity, 75, 77–8, 102; supply, 3, 12–13, 47, 69, 72, 106, 134–5, 204–5; training, 13–14, 71, 77
Land: provision, 196–200; site preparation and capital costs, 125; transactions, 118–19
Land use: certificates, 109, 118–19, 120–1; charges, 7, 11, 22, 78, 118–20, 125, 198–200; pattern, 90, 96–7, 113, 115
Law, 10, 58, 76; Foreign Enterprise Income Tax Law, 194; Law of the People's Republic of China on Chinese–Foreign Joint Ventures, 188
Lease period and leasehold system, 7, 118–19
Legal Consultancy, 188
Legal system, 10, 57, 60, 76–8, 184–9
Li Xiannian, 37
Liang Xiang, 180
Liantang, 65, 115, 134, 144, 147–9, 152–3, 156, 157
Liu Shaoqi, 26–7
LMK Nam Sang Dyeing Factory, 187
Longgang, 61, 177
Longhu Industrial District, 47, 51, 55
Longhua, 61, 177
Luohu, 66–8, 70, 76, 80, 115–16, 127, 134, 143–4, 147–9, 152, 156, 177, 180, 183–4

MACAU, 31, 41, 46–7, 50
Mamiao wharf, 151
Mao Zedong, 25–8, 54, 60
Masan Free Export Zone, 3, 6, 9–12, 14–15, 17, 198
Mawan, 67, 161
Modernization, 6, 8, 16, 19, 27–9, 35, 37, 42, 71, 73, 107, 174, 205, 208–17

NAKASONE, YASUHIRO, 55
Nantou, 65, 115, 117, 131, 134, 143–4, 147–9, 152, 156–7, 177, 183–4
Nantze EPZ, 3, 6, 9, 18
Nanyang Commercial Bank, 189
Nuclear plant, 171

OPEN ECONOMIC POLICY, 8, 24, 68; open-door policy, 39, 42, 54–5
Overseas Chinese, 10, 41–2, 47, 50, 54
Overseas Chinese Enterprise Company, 65, 77, 120

PASSENGER FLOWS, 141–50
People's Bank of China, 189–90
People's Construction Bank, 189–90
People's Liberation Army, 132
Pepsi-Cola Bottling Plant, 87
Petroleum, 31, 51; petrochemical industry, 67, 73–4, 161; refinery, 50, 74; South China Sea oilfield and service base, 43, 67, 73, 87, 115, 117, 201
Pollution, 87; air, 165–9; charges, 119; control, 172–4; emission standard, 173; environmental standards, 173–4; waste heat, 171–2; water, 168–71
Population: 1982 census, 132; composition and characteristics, 89, 127, 141, 204–5; density, 115, 159; distribution, 140–2; growth, 89, 128, 131–4, 140, 204–5; immigration, 89, 132–5; target, 113, 115; temporary residents, 89, 132, 205
Port facilities, 16, 18, 23, 43, 46–7, 50–1, 55, 115, 117, 126, 151, 201
Preferential treatment and incentives, 1–3, 6–7, 10–11, 14–15, 21–3, 32, 46, 51, 54, 57, 62, 69, 135, 191–4
Price level, 136–7

QIANHAI BAY, 117
Qianshan, 47
Quarrying, 112, 116

REAL ESTATE, 2, 7, 12, 21, 51, 57–9, 77, 80–1
Recession, 8, 13, 20–1
Recreational facilities, 43, 46, 79, 87–8, 138
Regulations: Foreign Economic Contract Regulations for Shenzhen SEZ, 186;

Provisional Administration Regulations for Shenzhen SEZ, 186; Provisional Entry/Exit Regulations, 58, 122, 186; Provisional Labour and Wage Regulations, 58, 122, 186; Provisional Land Regulations, 58, 118, 122, 186, 197; Provisional Regulations for Business Registration, 58, 122, 186; Provisional Regulations on the Introduction of Technology, 186; Provisional Regulations for Plan Preparation and Approval, 110–11; Regulations on SEZs in Guangdong Province, 176, 184, 186, 195

Santa Cruz Electronics EPZ, 3, 9, 11, 13
Science-based industrial parks, 14, 21, 24; Hsinchu Science-based Industrial Park, 21
Second-line border fence, 82, 126, 129
Self-reliance, 25–8, 31–2, 54
Sewage treatment, 170–1
Shahe, 63, 65–7, 70, 77, 115, 117, 120, 134, 144, 147–9, 152–3, 156, 161, 174, 177
Shajiao, 161, 165, 174
Shangbu, 61, 65–7, 70, 76, 115–16, 134, 143–4, 146–9, 152, 156, 161, 168, 170, 183–4
Shannon International Airport, 2
Shantou SEZ, 6, 30, 35, 37–8, 47–51, 54–6, 198
Shatoujiao, 82, 115, 125, 134, 144, 147–9, 152, 156, 168, 171
Shekou Industrial Zone, 35, 43, 47, 60–3, 65–6, 70, 77, 84, 86, 108, 112, 115, 117, 120, 131, 134, 137, 144, 147–9, 152, 156, 161, 168, 172, 174, 177, 201
Shenzhen Bay (Deep Bay), 84, 112, 164, 170–1, 201
Shenzhen Bay Hotel, 87
Shenzhen Lawyers' Office, 188
Shenzhen Municipal People's Government, 109, 121, 132, 176–84, 200, 206–7; Architecture Department, 109, 120–1; Building Construction Company, 109, 121–2; Environmental Protection Office, 172, 185; Labour Department, 202–3; Office of External Affairs, 184–5; Planning Department, 109, 120–1, 124, 133;

Shenzhen District Property Company, 116; Shenzhen Labour Services Co., 126, 185, 202, 204–5; Shenzhen Municipality Tourism Company, 82; Shenzhen Overseas Economic and Technical Liaison Office, 180; Shenzhen SEZ Construction Company, 109–10, 120–1, 184–5; Shenzhen SEZ Development Company, 110, 118, 120–1, 184–5; Transport Department, 177
Shenzhen–Nantou Road, 66, 153
Shenzhen Office of the Chinese External Trade Arbitral Committee, 188
Shenzhen Reservoir, 43, 84, 87, 112–13, 115, 134, 144, 146–9, 152, 156, 184
Shenzhen River, 164, 170
Shenzhen SEZ Outline Master Plan, 76, 84, 108–17, 122, 124–8, 132–4, 159
Shenzhen SEZ Social and Economic Development Plan, 58, 77, 108
Shenzhen Town, 66–8, 80, 115–16, 127, 131, 134, 143–4, 147–9, 152, 156, 168, 184
Shenzhen University, 117, 137–8
Shiyanhu, 84
Shuibei, 65
Shuiwei, 157
Singapore, 2, 41, 50
Social problems, 18–20, 43, 47; social integration, 127–8; social stratification, 138–9
Sole proprietorship, 6, 7, 9, 42, 51, 68
Songgang, 61, 177
Special zone currency, 190–1, 206
Spiritual pollution (ideological contamination), 37, 55, 213
Standard factories, 8, 61, 65, 67, 70, 72, 201
Starling Inlet, 164, 171
State capitalism, 36–7
State Planning Commission, 33–4

Taichung EPZ, 6, 9
Takugin International (Asia) Ltd., 189
Tax, 7, 29, 192, 194–6
Technological transfer, 6–7, 13–14, 21, 78, 106
Tender system in construction work, 216
Textiles, 14, 31, 59, 61, 65, 67–8, 73–4
Topography, 99–101, 112, 161
Tourism, 2, 7, 12, 47, 50–1, 57–8,

77–89, 97, 112; tourist resorts, 55, 79, 84

URBAN PLANNING, 89; physical planning, 108–30, 172; planning environment, 123–5; planning standards, 127

WAGES AND INCOME, 11–13, 18–19, 29–30, 58, 72, 78, 83–4; 103, 135, 203
Wanzai, 47
Warehousing, 8, 47, 55
Waste disposal, 160
Wenjindu, 151, 168
Western Planning Region, Shenzhen, 115, 117, 141
Wu Nansheng, 34
Wushigu, 116

XIAMEN SEZ, 6–7, 30, 36–8, 50–6, 198
Xiangmihu, 84, 115, 134, 144, 147–9, 152, 156, 190
Xiaomeisha, 84, 86, 113, 115, 134, 144, 147–9, 152, 156, 158
Xichong, 84
Xili Reservoir, 43, 79, 82, 84, 115, 134, 138, 144, 146–9, 152, 156

YANTIAN, 115–16, 134, 144, 147–9, 152, 156, 183–4

ZHONGSHAN, 46, 88
Zhou Enlia, 27, 211
Zhuhai SEZ, 6, 30, 33, 35, 37, 43, 46–7, 50–1, 54–6, 198
Zhujiang (Pearl River), 99, 164, 201